Call me ELIYAHU

Tales told by an Elliott

Elliott Isenberg

Nobody's
Home Press

San Francisco

Cover and Graphics designed by Vinny Olimpio

Nobody's Home Press, LLC
nobodyshomepress@gmail.com

ISBN: 979-8-9904072-0-6

Praise for CALL ME ELIYAHU

I cannot help but have deep admiration for the way Elliott opens the *Introduction* to his book, **Call me Eliyahu:** *For all of us there comes a time in life's journey where we want to make sense of our present life in terms of our individual past and the past of humanity itself; for me that time is now.*

This is a commitment we would all do well to emulate. Elliott shares and examines the span of his own life and, when relevant, gives us engaging and remarkable stories of his close relatives. Elliott sets these life stories against first-hand accounts of the emerging 20th Century counter-culture—one of the most transformative periods in modern cultural history—and shows how it continues to shape our 21st Century.

Beginning with an exploration of what it means to be born into a Jewish family, he introduces us to his parents and older brother, Edward. The story of seven-year-old Edward's escape from Nazi Germany is truly outstanding, worthy of any work of literature or mainstream film. Elliott's hatred of the Nazis became an abiding (and understandable) preoccupation through his life, and one of the stories he sought to shed from his psyche (with *The Work* of Byron Katie) on his path to freedom.

Elliott's own life is infused with the questioning, rebelliousness and spirit that found its voice in the 1960s. These were the times when it was still realistic to hitchhike or backpack overland to India, and when Elliott arrived at the ashram of Neem Karoli Baba, his spiritual seeking began in earnest, defining the course of the rest of his life.

As well as his search for Truth—which plays like a background tanpura in an Indian raga—Elliott writes about remarkable events such as his near-death in the maelstrom of a Tsunami. His descriptions of visceral fear in this chapter kept me completely engaged.

Throughout his journey Elliott sought wise men and guides—from Ram Dass to Sunyata (Emmanuel Sorensen, the Danish mystic), and many, many others. He shows a courageous commitment to uncovering the true nature of Reality, and he often writes about himself with unsparing honesty.

Elliott also enjoys sharing the fruits of his seeking; the *Bibliography* and *Glossary* included in the book are a valuable and comprehensive guide to wisdom, especially the Eastern—Buddhist, Hindu, and also Taoist—approaches to understanding ourselves.

Call me Eliyahu is more than an autobiography; it is a living testament to a life fully engaged—with history, with culture, and with the deepest questions of human existence. Elliott invites us into his journey with candor and courage. I recommend this book wholeheartedly to anyone drawn to the counter-culture era, to spiritual seeking, or simply to readers who appreciate a life told with honesty and depth.

Julian Noyce
Founder *Non-Duality*
Press & *New Sarum Press*　·

In this captivating autobiography, Elliott recounts his long search to answer the timeless question, "Who am I?"

He shares with his readers the insights gained along his spiritual journey, illuminating the signposts that guided him step by step toward a truth at once elusive and illusory.

His gripping account of the tsunami ordeal in Chapter Six left me breathless.

Nachshon Lustig,
author of The Silent Lullaby
and One Way Ticket
(*both available in Hebrew only*)

A captivating and intriguing memoir. As Eliyahu's true-life stories are much better than fiction, this book immediately pulled me in and fully engaged me. His writing is always interesting and often thought-provoking. He connects with the reader through his warm and focused storytelling. I'm enjoying this book immensely and taking my time, going back to read some passages a second time to pick up additional nuances and messages.

If you are any kind of free spirit, a progressive thinker, someone who wants to effect positive change in the world, or perhaps a modern-day Hippie, I think you'll enjoy this book very much.

Charlie Kaz,
San Francisco, California

A memoir of fearless, truthful life born within a family scrubbed in the horrors of the Holocaust, nurtured through the ideals of socialism, catapulted with the flame of spiritual quest for enlightenment, rocketing throughout the world seeking peace and happiness for all beings not excluding oneself.

Deeply reflective, the book merrily capers exotic experiences towards the author's self-insight and progressive awakening, along the way it is aptly illustrated with poems and insights of diverse sages and saints of personal meaning to the author.

This is a book I found best read a few pages or less at a time, returned to, and then savored. It is honest and warm in its humanness. I liked the way the book explored the interrelationship of divine goodness and devilish evil, finding grace in foible and courage, ending with a key to authentic awakening.

I grok this romp to Peace.

Steve Ellis,
Felton, California

This book is dedicated to my brothers

Howard and Edward —

indeed, it was made possible

through their love and generosity.

CONTENTS

List of Photographs x

Chronology xii

Introduction xv

Part I: Before My Birth

1. How did my brother get a passport out of hell? 1

Part II: A Search for Understanding

2. Love is letting go of fear 31

3. Good minds like a think 77

4. A restless heart seeks a moment of rest 119

5. Can a noisy mind get a glimpse of THE GREAT SILENCE? .. 159

6. "TSUNAMI !!! Grab a coconut tree !!!" 174

Part III: A Quest for Innerstanding

7. Can a Dane create new words for the English language? ... 196

8. Can my mind unhook from its stories? 220

9. The wake-up call: waking up out of the dream of me 238

Epilogue 277

Bibliography 280

Glossary 290

In Defence of Logical Punctuation 312

Acknowledgments 314

Index of Names 334

Endnotes 341

LIST OF PHOTOGRAPHS

1. Elliott with his mother (1947)
2. Elliott with his brothers (1948)
3. The three brothers (1950)
4. The boy (1953)
5. Frieda and Morrie (1954)
6. Elliott in Hawaii (1977)
7. Barbara at Fort Jesus in Mombasa, Kenya (1970)
8. Elliott at Fort Jesus (1970)
9. Neem Karoli Baba (1973)
10. Ravi Khanna, Neem Karoli Baba, and Draupadi (1971)
11. Elliott arriving in San Francisco (1978)
12. Elliott in a Tai Chi class with Judyth O. Weaver (1980)
13. Elliott looking up (1980)
14. Morrie yawning at the very spot where he will be buried (1999)
15. Morrie visiting his own gravestone (2003)
16. Sunyata in Almora, India (1973)
17. Tibetan lama and artist Drugu Choegyal Rinpoche (1992)
18. Allyson and Alex Grey at *The Chapel of Sacred Mirrors* (CoSM) in New York City (2006)
19. Byron Katie (1997)
20. Adyashanti (2006)
21. Karl Renz (2007)

22. Ramana Maharshi (1940)
23. Nisargaddatta Maharaj (1975)
24. Ram Dass (2018)
25. The elephant is 3 days old (2019 in Thailand)
26. The tiger is—hopefully—tame (2019 in Thailand)
27. Elliott in a devotional moment (2021)
28. Taken on a morning walk in San Francisco (2022)
29. Steve Forrest (2023)
30. A laundromat in Warrenton, North Carolina (July of 1963)
31. Elliott is protesting at his graduation (June 1966)
32. A commune in Salisbury, Rhodesia (March of 1971)
33. My family (August of 2000)
34. The psychedelic commune called Millbrook (1966)
35. Elliott buying the last gun ever bought in San Francisco (2015)
36. Elliott while writing this book (September of 2023)

Poster One: As you thinketh . . .
Poster Two: F . . . E . . . A . . . R . . .
Poster Three: When the fear *arises* . . .

Page 332: Elliott's astrological chart
Page 333: Prasanna Seth's Portrait of Albert Einstein

CHRONOLOGY

September 1930—Morris Isenberg, father of Elliott, arrives in Berlin in an attempt to escape home-grown anti-Semitism in the quotas for medical schools in the USA

Spring 1933—Morrie meets Margaret, Edward's mother; Hitler comes to power in Germany

April 6th, 1935—Edward Leonard Isenberg is born

September 1935—Morrie leaves Berlin for the USA

July 1942—Edward arrives in St. Louis, Missouri

May 4th, 1944—Morrie marries Frieda Epstein in Denver, Colorado

December 7th, 1944—Elliott is conceived on the third anniversary of Pearl Harbor Day

April 30th, 1945—Hitler commits suicide

September 18th, 1945—Elliott Stephen Isenberg is born

October 15th, 1947—Howard Warren Isenberg is born

June 3rd, 1966—Elliott refuses his diploma at his graduation from Amherst College to protest the awarding of an honorary Master's Degree to Robert McNamara, an architect of the war in Vietnam

July 1966—Elliott is arrested in Grenada, Mississippi

April 1967—Elliott visits the Soviet Union with other students attending the London School of Economics (LSE)

June 1968—Elliott graduates from the LSE with a Master's Degree in Sociology

April 1970—Elliott meets Barbara Bau in the Nairobi Youth Hostel and they travel together for the next year

September 1970—Elliott climbs to the top of Mt. Kilimanjaro

February 1971—Barbara and Elliott consume a dose of LSD and have (almost) the same hallucination

March 1972—Elliott reads **Be Here Now** in a commune in Ann Arbor, Michigan and decides to go to India to meet Neem Karoli Baba

March 1973—Elliott meets Neem Karoli Baba

September 11th, 1973—Neem Karoli Baba leaves his body

December 1973—Elliott leaves India to return to his home in NYC

November 29th, 1975—Elliott is washed inland for 1/6th of a mile (250 meters) by a 20 foot wave that crashes into Halape campground in Volcanoes National Park on the Big Island of Hawaii

September 1978—Elliott begins his graduate work at the California Instiute of Asian Studies (CIAS); the same week he is given (in a dream) the name of Eliyahu by Neem Karoli Baba

July 1981—Ralph Metzner commands that Elliott write his doctoral dissertation on 'evil'; in the same month, Elliott meets Emmanuel Sørensen, a Danish mystic with the name Sunyata

June 1983—Elliott gets his PhD in Psychology from a graduate school re-named the California Institute of Integral Studies (CIIS); Sunyata attends his graduation ceremony

August 13th, 1984—Sunyata dies a few days after being hit by a car near his new home in Fairfax, California

August 1993—John Threlfall sees two slightly curved horns appear on the top of Elliott's head

October 2004—Elliott does the 10-day **School for the Work of**

Byron Katie and asks himself: "Who would I be without my story?"

October 9th, 2007—Elliott is taken to Mt. Shasta by Karl Renz and has "a moment of clarity" at a spring called "The Source" or "The Mouth of God"

February 2008—Elliott realizes that he deluded himself when he thought his "moment of clarity" was a Self-realization

September 18th, 2015—Elliott does a meditation about his 'bucket list' and a desire arises to write a memoir

August 2015 and every other August through 2018—Elliott attends a week of happenings in the Black Rock City desert of Nevada called **Burning Man**

2016—Elliott joins the *Ultimate Medicine Group* that meets every Saturday morning at Peet's Coffeehouse on Blossom Hill Road in Los Gatos where the participants are mutually dedicated to the wake-up call

October 15th, 2018—Elliott writes the first word of his memoir in Chiang Mai, Thailand

December 5th, 2023—Steve Forrest, the leader of Elliott's weekly Los Gatos *Ultimate Medicine Group*, leaves his body

April 2024—**Call me Eliyahu** is first published

INTRODUCTION

We dance round in a ring and suppose,
But the Secret sits in the middle and knows.

— Robert Frost, _The Secret Sits_

FOR ALL OF US THERE COMES A TIME IN LIFE'S journey where we want to make sense of our present life in terms of our individual past and the past of humanity itself; for me that time is now. I am taking deep—and sometimes brutal—honesty as my watchword in these pages as I owe this honesty to myself and to you, the reader.

Even though I was born the year the Holocaust came to its conclusion, the first chapter of this book describes how the Nazi government shaped the lives of my family. Called _How did my brother get a passport out of hell?_ this is the story of how my older brother, a 7-year-old boy, escaped from the clutches of the Nazi regime halfway through the Second World War. His escape came years after the last of the _Kindertransport_ Jewish children had reached a safe haven in England. My brother, Edward, may well have been the last Jew to leave Nazi Germany with a valid visa.

Call me Ishmael are the first three words of Herman Melville's novel _Moby Dick_. In this novel, Ishmael is the outcast and the exile who is the only one to survive after Ahab and the rest of the crew are drowned when the great white whale, Moby Dick, sinks the whaling vessel called the _Pequod_. In the Epilogue of _Moby Dick_, Ishmael quotes the Book of Job: _I alone have escaped to tell thee._ Like Ishmael, I have escaped more than one life-threatening moment to be able to tell you this story of my life.

Tales Told by an Elliott

I don't feel I need to say much about my subtitle *Tales Told by an Elliott*—except that it is taken from the Shakespearean verse that is second in fame only to Hamlet's "to be or not to be" soliloquy. Macbeth speaks these lines just after he has been informed that his wife, Lady Macbeth, has first gone mad and then died. Macbeth knows he has a lot of blood on his own hands and he may be realizing that he too is about to receive his own *karmuppance*:

> To-morrow, and to-morrow, and to-morrow,
> Creeps in this petty pace from day to day
> To the last syllable of recorded time,
> And all our yesterdays have lighted fools
> The way to dusty death.
> Out, out, brief candle!
> Life's but a walking shadow, a poor player
> That struts and frets his hour upon the stage
> And then is heard no more:
> It is a tale told by an idiot,
> Full of sound and fury,
> Signifying nothing.
> *Macbeth*, Act V, Scene 5, verses 19 - 28

Let me also say a few words about the name that appears in the title of this book. Eliyahu is the way the name Elijah is pronounced in its original Hebrew. Eliyahu was the name that I was given before I was born. My parents knew that they would get a boy and as is the Jewish custom, they named me after a relative who was no longer living. I once saw this name Eliyahu (in Hebrew) at my grandmother's grave, where inscribed on her gravestone was the name of her father (my great-grandfather) who never left Belarus. My mother told me that I was named after him. She put *Elliott* on my birth

xvi

certificate rather than either Eliyahu or Elijah, because when I got the name the Nazis had not yet been defeated. My Mother thought it was more prudent to give me to have an Anglo-Saxon name like Elliott just in case the Allies lost. This is my name in its original Hebrew form:

$$\text{אֵלִיָּהוּ}$$

Eliyahu means *Jehovah is God*, as the name derives from the elements אל (el) and יה (yah). Jehovah is יה (yah) and אל (el) refers to the Lord or that which rules. I take my name to mean '*Reality Rules*'.

As a child, I was told that Elijah did not have a physical death because he left the earth when a chariot of fire pulled by fiery horses lifted him up to heaven in a whirlwind (2 Kings 2:11). When I was so young that I still believed that I might meet Santa Claus or grow up to be Superman, I had this innocent childish fantasy:

At the moment of my death, there would suddenly appear above my deathbed a chariot of fire pulled by fiery horses. As I was disappearing in a luminous whirlwind, I could just barely be heard above the loud neighing of the fiery horses as I said my good-byes to all my friends.

At school, I was always called Elliott. But when I entered my graduate school called the California Institute of Asian Studies (CIAS), I began using the name *Eliyahu*. I preferred Eliyahu because when it is said aloud, it sounds harmonious to my ears—particularly the 'hooo'—like *Eliya-hoooo*.

After I picked the title to this book as *Call me Eliyahu*, I had this dream:

I go into a huge underground library and I find the section on Elijah. There is an entire shelf of huge dusty leather volumes and each volume has the name Elijah in a different fancy typographic script as the first word of a longer title that identifies a particular man who once lived long ago.

As I am looking at these volumes, I realize that right above me is a big round hole of an opening through which I can see a turquoise blue sky. This hole is *in* the library, but yet somehow not *of* the library. And peering down at me through this opening is an old friend who I have not seen in many years. My friend calls down and asks what I am doing down below.

I tell my friend that I am in the section of the library about Elijah and I am planning to write a book about one Elijah.

He inquires, "Which one?"

I answer, "This one. I am writing a memoir about my own life."

My friend guffaws as he is surprised by my answer. I laugh with him. I see that neither of us can argue with the reality that I really am an Elijah who can write a memoir about "one Elijah".

My friend moves on.

I awake.

This is my interpretation of the dream: I am in the underground, which means to me this book is an attempt to bring what is unconscious into consciousness. And the turquoise blue sky above is an awareness of a consciousness that has no boundaries. In the dream I am not completely captivated by the 'dusty leather volumes' chronicling the many Elijahs who have existed over the last 3000 years, but I am just adding the story of this one particular Elijah to the library of humankind.

The friend above is not a specific person, but I would like to suggest that it might be you, my reader.

1

How did my brother get a passport out of hell?

Why is Chapter 1 about my brother's escape from Germany? My seven-year-old brother Edward's journey across wartime Europe and the Atlantic ocean is so much more than the story of one small boy—it deserves a place in history. It is the story of little human miracles, one after another.

My Brother's Escape

I CONSIDER MYSELF A CHILD OF THE HOLOCAUST. I was conceived on the third anniversary of what President Franklin Delano Roosevelt called *a date which will live in infamy*—the Japanese attack on Pearl Harbor on December 7th 1941. On that anniversary of that infamous attack, my parents—who had been married for only seven months—made a toast to the seeming progress of the Allies against the combined might of the Nazi and Japanese war machines and then spent a cozy night in their bed on the US military base in Springfield, Missouri. My mother told me that she had a feeling that she became pregnant that night.

My Father Joins the Army

My father, Morrie Isenberg, had signed up to fight the Nazis the week after the Axis Powers—Japan, Germany, and Italy—had each declared war on the United States. To join the army, he had to resign from his residency in psychiatry at Mount Zion Hospital in San Francisco. As he handed in his resignation, the administrators of the hospital acknowledged that they well understood why a Jew might give up a career-enhancing position to be a simple soldier in the United States Armed Forces.

His First Post

My father (who for the rest of this chapter I will refer to as Morrie) said he expected to be sent to Europe because he informed the recruiter that he spoke German as fluently as most Germans. In 1935, Morrie had passed eight of the most difficult written medical exams, followed by an oral exam—all in German—at Friedrich Wilhelm University in Berlin. This confirmed him as a doctor with a medical degree (MD) recognized world-wide. He (foolishly) thought that the Army would think his knowledge of the German language might be useful in a war against Germany and that he would therefore be assigned to the European front. Instead, throughout the entire war, he was assigned to be an army doctor at induction centers on bases in St. Louis, Kansas City, Denver, and eventually Springfield, Missouri. His job was to carry out evaluations for the troops that were being drafted to fight in the Second World War. Morrie was told he had to work an 8-hour day and each hour he had to evaluate 60 potential troops to determine their mental fitness to be a soldier. Except in the rarest of exceptions, all of these potential army soldiers were not volunteering their service, but each had received a letter from the draft board that it was mandatory to report to an army base for induction.

Considering that he only had one minute to make his determination if a soldier was mentally fit, he drew up a test of three questions. Morrie would ask each man:

First: *"What year was the 'War of 1812'"?*
Then: *"What was the color of George Washington's white horse?"*
And lastly: *"Who is buried in Grant's tomb?"*

These were not trick questions—every recruit that said "1812", "white", and then "Grant" passed the mental health component of the admission test required to become a soldier in the US Army. Morrie said he was quite surprised that around 25% of recruits said that they did not know the answers or said that the questions were too difficult for them. Generally, Morrie rejected every recruit that did not answer two out of three correctly: "1812", "white", and then "Grant".

Now the story gets more complex: Morrie, being a doctor, was automatically given the rank of captain at the beginning of his army service, but his commanding officer (one rank up from him) was a man who had worked himself through the ranks to major. This major was watching Morrie and even came in one day to watch him carry out a mental health examination. He confronted Morrie and said that the 25% rate of rejections was much too high and that he perceived that many of these men were purposely giving the wrong answers so that they could escape their national duty.

Morrie did not agree. He maintained that a man who would malinger to escape service would not make a good soldier—however, the major pulled rank on a mere captain and countermanded Morrie's rejections.

Three months later, the major came back to Morrie with an apology—every single recruit that he had sent to the theater of war (where he had countermanded Morrie's rejection) was now back

3

in St. Louis with a disability—and the government was going to pay them life-time benefits for their particular disability. Some had bullet wounds in their toes—were they self-inflicted? Who can prove that a person has really shot himself in the toe during a fire fight when there are actual enemy soldiers shooting actual bullets? Others were depressed, and some had what we know today as PTSD—post-traumatic stress disorder. So Morrie continued his three-question mental health exam throughout the rest of the war.

A Telegram from the Secretary of State

In April 1942, after four months at the induction station in St. Louis, Morrie received a surprising telegram. It is not every day that one receives a message from the United States Secretary of State. The name on the telegram was Cordell Hull, who had been Secretary of State since President Roosevelt came into the Presidency in 1933. The telegram stated that the United States had closed its German Embassy after the Declaration of War on Germany on December 11th 1941—and among the documents taken back to Washington DC from the Embassy in Berlin was a signature of a 'Morris Isenberg, US citizen' saying that an infant with the first two names 'Edward Leonard' had been born as his son on April 6th, 1935.

The telegram went on to say that a treaty had just been signed with Joachim Ribbentrop—the Foreign Minister of Nazi Germany—permitting the dozen or so civilians caught in each country on the day of the Declaration of War to return to their country of origin—it then went on to ask two questions:

1. *Is this Edward Leonard Isenberg indeed your son?*

2. *Do you want him back?*

Morrie responded in the affirmative to both and heard nothing more until Edward appeared three months later at the St. Louis train station (after Morrie had been given warning by another telegram that Edward was to arrive the very next day).

Before telling the saga of Edward's journey, it is necessary to describe how a son of Morrie—biologically my half-brother—lived his first seven years in a Nazi State.

Morrie Isenberg: MD to be

Beginning in his 6th grade when a teacher had told him he might be able to become a doctor, Morrie had wanted to go to an American medical school. Being the valedictorian of his high school class in Boston, he was admitted into Harvard. From the beginning of his schooling at Harvard, he knew that there were strict quotas that restricted the entrance of Jewish students into medical schools. But due to economic constraints, he realized that he had to work 40 hours a week (in a bottling factory) to support himself while many of his fellow Jewish students could apply themselves to their studies full time. Morrie was also told that all students regardless of race or religion could be admitted to Friedrich Wilhelm University (*Friedrich-Wilhelms-Universität*—now, *Humboldt-Universität zu Berlin*). This was the most prestigious medical school in Germany and had a global reputation for being on the cutting edge of medicine. Morrie had also heard that the University was on the Unter den Linden, the best-known and grandest street in Berlin.

So from the beginning of his Harvard career, Morrie took a class in German each semester. At that time all admissions to Friedrich Wilhelm University were governed by a tradition left over from the Middle Ages. In this centuries old tradition, every-one was allowed to attend classes in the medical school if they had a college diploma and paid the tuition fee. Very few, though, were able to pass the tests at the end of their classes to get a degree.

Morrie goes to Berlin

When it became time to apply to medical schools, Morrie had only achieved a B average while many of the other Jewish students had an A average. As Morrie suspected, he was rejected by the most prestigious American medical schools because they had filled their Jewish quota with A students. So in the spring of 1930, he left America to go to the medical school in Berlin where everyone who had a college degree was accepted, since here was a university open to all without the limitation of a Jewish quota.

In the Berlin of 1930, he enjoyed the freedom of the Weimar Republic. Although Berlin of the early 1930's was a place of political and social unrest, it also had cheap cabarets, restaurants that served unlimited hot rolls, and what was most important to my father—a level of erudition about modern theories of the mind. In Berlin, Morrie was introduced to the psychoanalytical theories of Sigmund Freud and Carl Jung and he felt proud that he was able to read them easily in their original German. Although some of their writings had been published in English, most were still unpublished and he had never heard of them at Harvard.

Teaching English to Nazis

Morrie made his living in the Weimar Republic by teaching English. He would take anyone who answered his advertisement on the bulletin board in the Friedrich Wilhelm University Student Union. During the first years of his stay in the Weimar Republic, he noticed that he was getting more and more students who were members of the Nazi Party. He later learned that the local Party had put out a directive for all their members to learn English. These members were all middle-class students and quite polite. When my father would ask them why they joined the Nazi Party, the most common answer was that they thought the Nazi Party was the wave of the future and it would also be best for their career advancement. My father realized that most of his Nazi students either suspected—or possibly even were sure—that he was Jewish. My father did have blue eyes and blondish-brown hair, but many recognized the name *Isenberg* as a common Jewish surname.

Most of his Nazi students saw Jews as competitors. One told my father he did not go along with Adolf Hitler on 'the Jewish question' since he felt Germany need not be *Judenrein* (Jew-free), but rather the Jews should have a subservient role to make Germany great again. (When he said this, he looked to see if there was any reaction from Morrie, but my father would remain silent and stone-faced—like the iron mountain that is the English translation of the name Isenberg.)

A Nazi student teaches Morrie some (true) Jewish history

One Nazi student taught Morrie about Jewish history. He asked if he knew how Jews had gotten their last names—which were often German. When Morrie said he did not know, the young Nazi explained how the rulers of Prussia in the 18th century were finding it too difficult to tax the Jews because so many would have the same name—for instance, my Hebrew name is Eliyahu ben Moshe—Elijah son of Moses. Often the same village would have many people with the name Eliyahu ben Moshe—or, even if there was only one in a village, the next village would have another. This was too confusing for the (non-Jewish) tax collectors, so the rulers of Germany and Austria decreed that every Ashkenazi Jew had to get a permanent family surname, a name that they required to be German. According to Morrie's Nazi student, all Jews had to pick names from one of four categories: animals, occupations, inanimate objects, or place names. (When Morrie told me the story, he felt proud of his Nazi student who taught him about his own social and cultural history.) Here are some obvious examples that fit these four categories:

7

1. *Animals:*
   - Wolf = wolf
   - Baer = bear
   - Adler = eagle
   - Loeb (or Leyb) = lion

2. *Vocations:*
   - Garfinkel/Garfunkel = diamond dealer
   - Aptheker = druggist
   - Goldsmidt = goldsmith
   - Zucker/Zuckerman = sugar merchant
   - Koch = cook
   - Brenner = literally "a burner"; a distiller of alcohol
   - Bronfman = maker of distilled liquors

3. *Inanimate objects:*
   - Stein = stone
   - Margolin = pearl
   - Topf = pot
   - Rothschild = red shield (or coat as in a coat of arms)

4. *Place names:*
   - Berliner = someone who comes from Berlin
   - Frankel = someone who comes from the Franconia region of Germany
   - Frankfurter = someone who comes from Frankfurt
   - Isenberg = iron mountain (although 'iron' is more commonly 'eisen')

Morrie's Nazi student then finished his story with a zinger—he said that any Jews that refused to get a surname within the necessary two years would be given, and could not revoke, a name whose intent was degrading or even scatological. Here are some examples of names that were actually given to Jews (the Nazi told my father the last two with a particularly gleeful expression):

- Niemand = nobody
- Affengesicht = monkey-face
- Mausfall = mouse-trap
- Wanzreich = rich in bedbugs or the kingdom of bedbugs
- Goldwasser or Goldwater = urine
- Scheisse = shit
- Kot = excrement

Hitler comes to power

Life at the University changed dramatically within a week of Hitler gaining power in April 1933. All Jewish professors were dismissed from their jobs and Jewish students were no longer allowed to take the medical exams to become an MD. Morrie said he knew 43 Jewish students at Friedrich Wilhelm University at the beginning of 1933 and he was the only one left by the end of that year. Morrie did not look particularly Jewish, and when people asked him his religion, he would say in an authoritative tone: "Evangelische!" (which was Morrie's proper German translation of 'evangelical').

The book burning and what happened afterwards

But the academic freedom Morrie loved at Friedrich Wilhelm was soon swept away and even burned up. One of his Nazi students told him that there would be a book-burning (*ein buch brennt*) on the second Wednesday of May on Unter den Linden, near the Opera House, and at the end of the burning, Joseph Goebbels would be the main speaker (Morrie stayed away).

Among the books burned that day were all the writings that could be found of Sigmund Freud, who was viewed by the Nazis as a decadent Jew. As Sigmund Freud's books were burned on that Wednesday, a prepared statement of a special 'fire oath' was sworn against Freud's writings in which all the students said together what they were against in his writing and what they were for:

AGAINST: the soul-shredding over-valuation of sexual activity
FOR: the nobility of the human soul

Today there is a plaque on the Bebelplatz commemorating what happened on the 10th May in 1933. The plaque contains a quotation from the German poet Heinrich Heine (whose books were also burned that day) from his play *Almansor* referring to the burning of the *Koran* by the Spanish Inquisitors:

Dort wo man Bücher verbrennt, verbrennt man auch am Ende Menschen.

Where they have burned books, they will end in burning human beings.

However, Morrie was not so lucky on another day at the Unter den Linden. He heard of a big parade there, where he would be able to see Adolf Hitler in person. He learned that the medical school was to be closed for this celebration and all of the top Nazis were going to be at the parade in person. My father was curious, but also cautious and he stayed in the background. Looking at the Nazi leaders each happily standing up and waving to the crowd from their limousines, he was surprised that these leaders did not seem concerned for their own security. My father heard a group of nearby Storm Troopers enthusiastically singing *Die Fahne Hoch!* (*Raise High the Flag*) which was a song written by Horst Wessel, whom the Nazi Propaganda Minister Joseph Goebbels had turned into a Nazi martyr. My father said at the hospital where he was doing his medical internship that there was a room never to be used again for a patient—in this very room, Horst Wessel had died in 1930 from his wounds after (a not immediately successful) assassination by a Communist. While Wessel was still trying to recover from his wounds, Joseph Goebbels had visited Horst four times. My father said the room had become like a shrine, adorned with flowers, photos, and large black swastikas inside a white circle on a red background.

As Hitler's car became visible in the distance, everyone's arm went up in a salute and all shouted *Heil Hitler!* For some reason, my father had not figured out in advance that he might be conspicuous as the only one who would not be saluting. He tried to sneak into an alcove of an apartment building, but some young Nazi thugs figured out that he was there to avoid saluting and started beating him up. Luckily, my father was able to break away and run into the densely packed crowd where the thugs could not pursue him.

Margaret and Morrie

The next character in this story is Margaret, whom my father met on a Berlin park bench in the spring of 1933. He was 27 years old, she was 22, and my father felt an instant attraction. When he visited Margaret's apartment, he discovered that she was living with her mother, a kind, matronly woman who was excited that her daughter had brought home a man. As Hitler had become Chancellor of Germany just a month before, my father thought it necessary to tell both of them that he was Jewish. They both responded that they did not support the anti-Jewish propaganda that was the daily fare of German radio and newspapers. My father began to spend more and more time with Margaret and her mother and gradually gave up his old student quarters.

His relationship with Margaret inadvertently got my father into great trouble on the *Rosh HaShanah* (Jewish New Year) of 1934. In his four years of studies, my father had never missed even one class, but on this day, without my father even knowing that it was *Rosh HaShanah*, he and Margaret had spent the early morning making love. My father decided that it was too late to go to class and instead of going to the university, they went for what was meant to be a pleasant leisurely stroll on *Leipziger Straße*, a wide street that ran through the center of Berlin. My father was surprised to see that no one was entering the big department store named Tietz. He went to its front door and he saw a big sign that said: CLOSED FOR ROSH HASHANAH. Taking a short walk to *Leipziger Platz*, where there was another big Jewish-owned department store called *Wertheim's*, he found that it was also closed and had a similar sign on its front door. My father realized that his lack of knowledge about the Jewish holidays had led him to miss a day of classes on the first day of the Jewish New Year.

When my father appeared at Surgical Grand Rounds in the hospital the next day, the surgeon (a loyal Nazi) waited for everyone to become quiet and then dramatically pointed at my father and said in a derogatory tone: "Herr Isenberg, what is *your* religion?" My father realized the Professor knew he had missed classes on Rosh HaShanah. Besides the shock of realizing that the Nazi surgeon was more aware of the dates of the Jewish holidays than he was, he perceived that he was in a lot of trouble. My father meekly said: "My religion is Evangelische". And yet the wrath of the Professor did not abate and he exclaimed: "We don't want your kind in my class or any class in this Universität!" As my father scrambled to leave the room, a group of medical students wearing Swastikas glared at him. My father feared that they might grab him, pull down his pants, and expose him for being a circumcised Jew. He left the room before the Nazis could take any action. My father never returned to Surgical Rounds and was not seen again at either the hospital or any class.

The news now spread across the university that there was still one Jew left in the midst of Friedrich-Wilhelms-Universität and that my father was that Jew! Not to his surprise, he suddenly lost all the Nazi students who had been so interested in learning English.

A Medical Doctor at last

Although he was never to appear on the grounds of the medical school again, he signed up to take the eight rigorous exams necessary to get a medical degree. It seems that the bureaucracy of the university was such that the exam department never got word of the Nazi professor's suspicions. In the Spring of 1935, my father learned that he had passed all eight of the exams—and yet there was still one more obstacle. Not only did one have to pass the eight exams, but it was also necessary to write a thesis and defend it orally. Because the word had gotten out that my father might be Jewish, he could not find anyone to be his thesis advisor—until he found an old professor about to retire who told him that he wanted to learn more about the parasitic worms of the Nile River—and would my father do a thesis on that topic? My father agreed and passed his oral exams in April of 1935 and achieved a Medical Degree the next month.

Things only get worse

The brutality of the Nazi regime was by this time becoming more apparent. An English friend of my father's who was studying in the School of Law at Friedrich Wilhelm Universität told my father that he was attending court sessions on Friedenstraße. In front of the courthouse, he would see thugs in Nazi uniforms ask the accused coming to court to show them their papers, and before they could even get into the court room for their trial, these thugs would drag the accused into the basement of the court-house from which he could hear screams.

The Nazis wanted to prevent race disgrace (*Rassen-schande*) and blood disgrace (*Blut-schande*) where the German word *schande* is the equivalent of the English word for 'shame'. But the Nazis wanted to make what they called 'the polluting of Aryan blood' not only shameful, but also illegal. My father and Margaret were married earlier in 1935, but the passing of the Nuremberg Laws in September of that year had rendered their marriage null and void. All marriages between Aryans and Jews were instantaneously declared against the law by the unanimous vote of the Reichstag (the German Parliament)—and these same laws made it illegal for any Aryan to have sex with any Jew. The Nazis did not want anyone to be able to claim marriage as a 'pre-existing condition' that might legitimize sex between an Aryan and a Jew. My father had seen a color photo in a magazine of a young blue-eyed German Aryan woman with her head shaven being paraded by the SS with a placard around her neck reading: *I have given myself to a Jew.* My father recognized that by staying in Berlin he was not only endangering himself, but also putting Margaret in danger—swastikas had begun appearing regularly on Margaret's mail-box. The overture that had been played was cacophonous, and he knew what was coming—a discordant opera of cruelty and brutality.

Edward Leonard Isenberg: a new American Citizen

Meanwhile a blessing had come to my father in the form of a little baby boy—Edward Leonard Isenberg was born on April 6th 1935. On the week Edward was born, my father did something that possibly saved Edward's life and certainly changed it forever. My father made a trip to the US Embassy in Berlin and made an entry in their register to the effect that a boy had been born as the son of an American citizen (this is now called a *Consular Report of Birth Abroad*). When the Embassy staff looked at this register in early 1942 and tried to match my father's name with those enlisted in the US Armed Services, my father's name easily popped up because there was no 'E' before the 'I' (as is most prevalent) in the name Isenberg.

Morrie goes back to America

My father had his MD and now his main goals were to get out of Germany and find a way to protect his son. Edward's grandmother had lost her own son when she was a young woman, and she had the time to dedicate to the child's well-being. As Morrie only had $100 to his name at the time he was ready to leave Germany, there was no way he could support a son while traveling to America. He also still did not know if he could find work in the United States with a German medical degree. He left for America in September of 1935, leaving Edward in the care of Margaret and her mother, Edward's grandmother.

My father had lived in Berlin from September 1930 to September 1935. At the mid-point of his stay, in March 1933, the German Parliament passed the Enabling Act, officially entitled the 'Law to Remedy the Distress of People and Reich,' which enabled Hitler to enact laws without the consent of the Reichstag. In the event that Hitler was ever to declare a national emergency, he by himself could then enact laws that were not allowed by the German Constitution.

World War II in Berlin

World War II started in 1939 and Margaret's mother died of liver cancer in 1940. Because Margaret had been assigned to work a 60-hour week in a munitions factory, she could no longer take care of Edward and placed him in a Quaker orphanage on the outskirts of Berlin. Margaret did not abandon Edward and would bring him home for the weekend several times a month. After 1940, Edward remembers some of those weekends as "terrifying"—he would be scared beyond any fear he had ever known trying to cover his ears to block out the deafening sound of the Allied bombs when he and his mother took refuge in the public air raid shelter in their apartment building. And after the weekend in what he experienced as "hell", he would go back to his orphanage for the weekdays, only to discover the sounds of bombing would continue, as a fuel storage tank less than a mile away from his orphanage was a target for destruction.

Life in the all-boys orphanage was not pleasant. Edward's mother had told him that he was half-Jewish and now she sent him to a school where part of the curriculum was to be bombarded with all that was 'wrong' with the Jewish people. His teachers taught that the goal of the Regime was to make all of Germany *Judenrein*—meaning Jew-free. Each morning, all the orphans had to do a *Heil Hitler* salute to the photograph of *der Führer* that was in the front of the room while they sang the first stanza of *Das Lied der Deutschen* (*The Song of the Germans*) that included these words:

Deutschland, Deutschland über alles,
Über alles in der Welt,
Wenn es stets zu Schutz und Trutze
Brüderlich zusammenhält.
Deutschland, Deutschland über alles,
Über alles in der Welt!

Germany, Germany above all
Above everything in the world
When, always, for protection and defense
Brothers stand together.
Germany, Germany above all
Above all in the world.

In their free time, the children at the orphanage would play war games in which they would pretend to fight British soldiers.

Edward's Journey

One morning at the begining of July 1942, the Swiss Ambassador to Germany appeared at Margaret's house on a Sunday—he was chauffeured in a big black limousine with a Swiss flag flying from the front of his car. Margaret remembered him as extremely "soft-spoken" and "meticulously dressed". The Ambassador explained to Margaret that he had the visas in his possession to let her son Edward leave Germany to be with his father in St. Louis, Missouri. He explained that the child's father was now there as a captain in the American Army. He said that he could not take Edward without her signing a Statement of Release to be given to the Quaker orphanage where Edward was living. After she signed, he made her understand that only one train a day left Berlin for Paris—every afternoon at exactly 3pm. The Ambassador said he had arranged for Edward to be on that train the very same day and he asked Margaret to be there.

The Ambassador now went directly to the orphanage—where the big limousine with a Swiss flag pulling into the driveway created a commotion among the students. Soon the orphanage director called Edward into his office and told him that his father had requested that he come to America and that his Mother had given her consent. The Director told Edward that he had 30 minutes to gather all his possessions. All the other kids were jealous that Edward was the one chosen to leave this oppressive institution and they barely said good-bye to him.

When Edward and the Swiss Ambassador arrived at the Berlin train station, Margaret was awaiting and she immediately embraced Edward and started crying. The Swiss Ambassador explained that he had procured five visas and each was placed on a separate piece of string that could be hung around Edward's neck. On the top one was the name of Joachim Ribbentrop, the Foreign Minister of Nazi Germany, and beneath it were cards with the visas and signatures of the Foreign Ministers of Vichy France, fascist Spain, and fascist Portugal—and lastly, there was the signature of Cordell Hull, the US Secretary of State. Along with the five visas, there was a sixth placard that contained the address of my father at a St. Louis Army Base. The Swiss Ambassador explained to Edward and Margaret that he was giving Edward no money—as everyone knew there were thieves on the trains who would steal money even from little children. He said that Edward would not need a ticket as he had called up the train station the day before informing them of their unusual passenger and that the visas would serve as his ticket. When the three of them entered the big train compartment, the Swiss Ambassador explained to all those in the train-car that Edward had no money or food, and he asked whoever might have a little extra food to take care of him.

A train leaves Berlin

Then the train whistle blew, Margaret started crying more loudly and gave Edward a final big hug, and she and the Swiss Ambassador scrambled off the train. Moments after the train left the station, several people befriended Edward and gave him food and comfort. When they asked Edward where his parents were, he would explain (in German) that his mother was in Berlin and his father in America, and he was making this journey to meet his father for the first time.

Edward noticed as they were going across Germany that all the civilians were leaving the train, and by the time they reached the French border at midnight, the only other passengers were members of the German armed forces. The border guards had been warned to look out for Jews who might be trying to escape Germany with forged documents, and they studied the five visas around Edward's neck very carefully indeed. They decided that they could not be sure they were authentic as they had never before seen the signature of their own Foreign Minister, Joachim Ribbentrop. It was now illegal for any Jew to leave Germany except as a prisoner on the way to a concentration camp. Rather than get in trouble for letting a Jew out of the country, the border guards decided to take Edward off the train and call the German Foreign Office on Monday morning. Whoever answered the phone the next morning at the German Foreign Office knew about Edward's case and verified that Joachim Ribbentrop had signed a treaty letting a few foreign civilians out of the country and that it was indeed Joachim Ribbentrop's signature on Edward Isenberg's exit visa.

Edward was given permission to board the next day's train—and there was one more setback before he got through Vichy France. As the train was approaching Paris, Allied bombers knocked out the tracks up ahead as part of their strategy to disrupt the pro-Nazi government's infrastructure. But the tracks were soon fixed and the train sped onward through Paris, and then fascist Spain and fascist Portugal. My brother got off the train in Lisbon and was taken to the Port of Lisbon to await the next boat to America. Edward was lucky in that it was less than a week before a ship arrived that was heading to America. Everyone knew that German submarines were torpedoing American ships—so the regular fare had been greatly reduced from its pre-war high, but Edward paid no fare at all—whoever was in charge of collecting tickets aboard that ship accepted the five visas of the 7- year old boy as the price of admission.

Edward was befriended on the ship by a non-Jewish German family—a mother, a father, and their two little girls—who were trying to escape the war in Europe. Edward noticed that the parents fed the best food to their two children and gave him more of the bread and fewer of the delicacies. After the ship arrived safely in New York City, the German family was turned back by custom officials and forced to return on the same boat; they were told that since the American government was afraid of German spies, no refugee from Nazi Germany would be let into America without a visa that bore the actual signature of the US Secretary of State.

Travelers Aid offers a helping hand

Edward's USA visa bore the actual signature of the US Secretary of State, so Edward was let into America. The customs officials saw the placard with my father's address at the army base in St. Louis and they gave Edward into the care of Travelers Aid, an international voluntary organization that even today offers 'a helping hand along the way'. The Travelers Aid volunteers sent a telegram to the address on his sixth placard saying that Edward had arrived safely in America and would be coming from NYC and pulling into the main train station of St. Louis on the next afternoon. Just in case my father was not there to receive Edward, these volunteers found someone to accompany Edward on his journey to St. Louis.

The man that Travelers Aid found to accompany Edward was an African American sergeant who was being transferred to an Army base in San Francisco. He had lived in Germany for several years and spoke fluent German, which was crucial for Edward as he did not yet speak one word of English. Travelers Aid instructed the sergeant not to let Edward off the train in St. Louis if his father was not there to pick him up. If that were the case, he was to get off the train with Edward and find out from the Army base about where his father might be. The sergeant was a good-humored companion, who fed Edward a big meal at Grand Central Station.

"That could be your father"

When my father received the telegram from Travelers Aid, this was the first time he learned that his son was alive since a letter from Margaret that had come the previous December right before there had been the Declaration of War with Germany. When the train pulled into the station at St. Louis, it was the middle of the afternoon and the only person standing on the platform was my father, wearing the uniform of a US Army captain. The sergeant pointed to the man in the Army uniform and said: "Das könnte dein Vater sein." (*That could be your father.*)

So Edward saw my father for the first time since he was five months old, went up to him hesitantly on the train platform, and said (in flawless German): "My father, I presume?" (*Mein Vater, nehme ich an?*).

After the shock of recognition and Edward's realization that my father spoke German as well as he did, my father asked if he had come with anyone. Edward pointed up to the train window and there was the face of a smiling man in a sergeant's uniform, who must have been delighted that their journey had such a happy ending. Edward told my father that the man in the window spoke German and my father walked up to the train window—and through the window they held hands—and my father said this phrase three times: "Vielen Dank! Vielen Dank! Vielen Dank!" (*Many Thanks! Many Thanks! Many Thanks!*)

As he finished expressing his sincere gratitude, the whistle blew, the train moved on, and my father was left with a hurt and wounded human package.

Making a home away from hell

There was joy in the reunion and yet Edward still experienced the shame that he was at fault for being a Jew. Edward was so hungry that he would often eat another meal after finishing his first. He refused to speak another word of German, and yet he still had a German accent so the children of the other soldiers in his Army school would call him a German or a Kraut, and they would try to bully him (as they would like to bully any enemy). Edward learned how to defend himself—and how to fight.

When Edward would awaken during the night with frightening dreams about his previous life in Germany, my father would assure him that he was now safe in America. My father had Edward circumcised, which was not a pleasant experience for a seven-year-old. Edward took out all his aggressions on his new dog who he named 'Tarzie', but then he was traumatized again when Tarzie ran out into the street and was killed by a car. Edward did well at the army school and within a year, he was speaking excellent English with only the slightest trace of a German accent.

Divorcing Margaret

Morrie did not want to go back to Germany and Margaret did not want to come to America. This made it easy for Morrie to get a divorce by mutual consent. Morrie started dating other women as he wanted to be married again.

Frieda

Edward had yet another shock when Morrie met Frieda, his future wife and my mother. Edward did not like being put out of my father's bed, although he was already nine years old. The irony is that my father only met my mother because of Edward.

There was only one other Jewish boy on the Army base—his name was Larry, and he was the eldest son of Mae and Harry Friedman. Mae was Frieda Epstein's best friend from 2nd grade in their Bronx elementary school, and she was on the base because her husband was a doctor of internal medicine for the officers. When Mae heard from Larry that there was another Jewish boy in his class who had managed to escape from Nazi Germany, she began her match-making plans. Frieda was coming in March to visit Denver from her Bronx home in New York City.

Frieda's life had its challenges, as she was an elementary school teacher commuting every day to work at a school in Harlem where the students were all African Americans (known as 'Negroes' in those days). My mother realized that the life circumstances of her students were often extremely difficult; there were issues around hunger, poor sanitation, and absentee parents. The whole elementary school was to be closed for a two-week Easter break beginning the last week of March in 1944, and my mother decided to visit her good friend Mae by taking a train to the Army Base where Mae was living in Denver.

Mae set up a match-making plan. She would invite Morrie to dinner the night after Frieda arrived. The outcome was so much better than Mae's most grandiose dreams; Morrie immediately fell in love with Frieda. Frieda was now a 33-year old woman during a time when society considered it quite probable that at her age women who were unmarried were doomed to become 'old maids'. In addition to her age, Frieda would not have been considered good wife material—she was a committed card-carrying member of the Communist Party, and she was not going to consider marrying anyone who was not a 'leftist'. When my father asked her out for a date on the evening after they met, she figured out she would ask my father one question to see if this relationship had the potential to be a marriage. The question my mother asked was: "Do you believe in the Unions?" My father had gauged the drift of my mother's politics, and he knew he was being tested, so he said: "Frieda, I so much believe in the unions." With those words, their future marriage was cemented and the way was cleared for the birth of first Elliott (myself), then Howard.

There was one last obstacle—my mother had to get permission from her father for the marriage to take place. When her vacation was over, she went back to the Bronx with a picture of Morrie and Edward. The obstacle in the way of gaining her father's permission to marry Morrie was his previous marriage and the son of that marriage. Any divorce in those days was what in Yiddish was considered a *schande*—a shame or disgrace—and to have a son living with you from a *goyische* (not of the Jewish faith) German woman was even less socially acceptable in the Jewish community. But my mother's father realized the danger of Frieda becoming an old maid—she was not only a Communist but also quite shy—so Frieda got her permission.

My mother resigned her position at her school, gathered the few possessions that would fit on a train, and was back in Denver by the first week of May. My parents had a small civil wedding in the city hall of Denver, Colorado on Thursday, May 4th 1944—only Mae and Harry Friedman and Edward were present. My parents were in love and they lived in a motel near the army base.

Saved by the bomb

In late 1944, my father was moved to the Army base in Springfield,

Missouri. He was given orders in the first week of May—the week that Germany surrendered—to report for duty at the front in Japan on 1st September. Everyone knew that there was a high mortality rate for doctors serving on this front since the Japanese would bomb more fixed structures and the most visible structure in a camp of soldiers was often the makeshift hospital. My father was ready to go—even though by September 1st his wife would be more than eight months pregnant. But then the atom bombs were dropped on Hiroshima and Nagasaki—and my father's orders to go to Japan were cancelled the week after the Japanese surrender. The Army said that my father was now needed to give mental health exams to all the troops returning from both the Western and Eastern Fronts.

My father had the same 60 seconds to examine each returning soldier and he decided to ask them the same three questions:

First: "What year was the 'War of 1812'"?
Then: "What was the color of George Washington's white horse?"
And lastly: "Who is buried in Grant's tomb?"

This time he got a 100% success rate—the troops just wanted to go home, and they probably thought: *Why is this idiot asking me such stupid questions?*

I was born on September 18th 1945 in an army hospital in Springfield, Missouri and my first home was in a motel that sat facing U.S. Route 66, the paved highway that John Steinbeck called 'the Mother Road' of North America. After two months in Springfield, my mother left for New York City with Edward and me. Morrie was left to finish off his Army service until the holiday season in December of 1945. Edward and I shared a room together in my mother's parents' home in the Bronx borough of NYC for two years, and then Howard joined our little family in 1947.

The story now becomes less eventful and more 'normal'—there was hardly any drama or trauma as my parents moved from the Bronx, to Long Beach (in Nassau County on Long Island), to Rego Park (in Queens county of NYC), and eventually to the house we all lived in for 49 years in Forest Hills (also in Queens).

A letter from Margaret

I would like to conclude this story of Edward's escape from Nazi Germany by talking about Edward's relationship with his mother, Margaret. Even though Margaret lived in Germany until she was in her late 80s, the last time Margaret and Edward ever saw each other was in that Berlin train with the Swiss Ambassador standing by. My father re-established contact with Margaret after the war and Margaret told him that she had been praying for Edward throughout the war, not knowing for over three years whether or not he had ever arrived safely in America. My father kept the agreement (which he made in Berlin) to send her money each month—as long as she did not get married. Over the decades, Margaret lived with other men, but never married them, and eventually had another son and then a daughter—half-siblings to Edward.

My father and Margaret corresponded every month. Each month when my father received the letter from Margaret acknowledging the receipt of the monthly payment, she would include a paragraph about how she longed to communicate with her son first-born son Edward. Meanwhile, Edward was speaking English without a trace of German accent and wanted to forget everything about his German experience. Edward believed that Margaret had abandoned him to the Quaker orphanage when the going had gotten rough. Edward once told me that he thinks of his mother as 'Laodicean'. As I never heard this word before, I looked up 'Laodicean' in the dictionary and found that the word comes from the Christian Bible where it is used to refer to a person who is 'indifferent' or 'half-hearted'; the Bible says:

And unto the angel of the church of the Laodiceans write;
[. . .]

I know thy works, that thou art neither cold nor hot: I would thou wert cold or hot.

So then because thou art lukewarm, and neither cold nor hot, I will spue thee out of my mouth.

—*Book of Revelation 3:14-16* (King James Version)

My father could be quite consistent and persistent in his demands and every month he would tell Edward that Margaret wanted to write him a letter and he would ask Edward if he would relent and receive just one letter from his mother. Finally, nine years after the war ended when Edward was 19 years old, Edward said he would receive a letter. The letter arrived the next month (in 1954) addressed on the outside of the envelope to *Mein Sohn Edward*—and my father gave Edward the sealed envelope. My father later told me that he made a big mistake in not opening the sealed letter first, as he knew Margaret could be demanding. The letter expressed little affection towards Edward, but set out a list of Edward's obligations to his half-brother and half-sister whom he had never met: not only did she want Edward to establish relations with them, but she indicated that each of them might want to come to the USA. Edward showed the letter to my father, and even my father could not believe what Margaret must have been thinking when in her first contact with her first-born son in over a decade she expressed no affection but merely outlined Edward's obligations. Edward refused to ever receive another letter from his mother. My father continued to send Margaret the monthly checks until one month when Margaret was in her late 80s (in the late 1990s), the check was returned with the message that Margaret had died that month.

According to my study of the historical records, seven-year-old Edward was the last Jew ever legally to leave Nazi Germany.

My Informants for this Story of Edward's Escape

As I was born more than three years after my older brother made the escape described in this chapter, I am indebted to three informants: my father, my older brother, and Margaret.

Margaret, my father's first wife and Edward's mother, is the only one of the three whom I never met, but my father told me what she had said. My older brother Edward is now a grandfather and a retired doctor at the age of 89. Edward said he did not want to be interviewed for this book because it would bring up memories of the years in Germany that he would rather forget. Even though Edward made his escape from Germany over eight decades ago, my perception is that the scars are still too fresh. However, he did tell me this one story about what happened when he first arrived in America:

> *Dad took me from St. Louis to Boston in order that I could meet Aunt Rosie and Uncle Nathan. At one point, I asked first Uncle Nathan and then Aunt Rosie what their religion was and when they each said: "Jewish", I exclaimed to them in a loud voice: "That's terrible!!!" I still believed the propaganda propounded in my Quaker Orphanage that the Jews were an infestation of 'cockroaches' and 'vermin'.*

When I asked Edward why he did not believe that his own father was also 'terrible', he answered: "Dad was my father and my sole support and I did not judge him." He said he told me this story to show how effectively he had been brainwashed by Nazi propaganda.

Interviewing Morrie

When my father was 97 years and three months old, I was alone with him for two weeks in the home where I grew up. My mother had died two years before and my father's memory was even sharper than when he was younger. Looking back on his life, he told me he had no complaints and no regrets and he was ready (and more than willing) to meet his Maker. I gave up my usual visits to the museums of NYC to be with him, and we would sit around the table after dinner and I would question my father intensely about the details of his life as a child in Boston, at Harvard College, in the Weimar Republic, then in Nazi Germany, and all he knew about Edward's grand escape. My father would often show great emotion as he recalled the joys and sorrows of his life—he broke out into sobs when he recalled the day as a seven-year-old that he found out that his mother had been committed to a mental hospital. It was during these evening discussions (more than two decades ago) that I had the first glimpse that I might one day write up this story.

As a collector, I thought it might be a great boon for my future book if I could publish photos of the six placards—five visas and one address—prepared for Edward by the Swiss Ambasador to the Third Reich that was Edward's passport out of hell. I asked my father whether he still might have them—and he told me that he had a distinct memory of throwing them into the waste-basket in St. Louis before moving on to the Army base in Kansas City. I intuited what he had thought: *The package is delivered—no need to save the wrapping!*

Thanks to good people in challenging times

If we guesstimate how many people must have helped Edward in his grand escape, it had to be dozens. Crucial was Margaret signing a *Statement of Release* to free her only child to go on an unknown and dangerous journey to America. Then there were the train conductors and border guards that spoke five different languages—and each (after an interrogation) let a seven-year-old boy pass without any money or any ticket. And the people on the various trains kept Edward well fed. And there were the people who ran a ship who let him cross the Atlantic without paying a penny (although they gave him no food). And then there was the German family (who were refused admission to America) who fed Edward during the 10-day trans-Atlantic crossing. And maybe most important was the Swiss Ambassador to the Third Reich who had his Embassy staff spend several months procuring the five visas that would be Edward's passport from hell. My father told me he never made an attempt to thank the Swiss Ambassador for his efforts—the only communication legally permissible from America to the Third Reich was through American bombers dropping their 'messages' on German cities. Since all this happened eight decades ago, this diligent Ambassador cannot be alive any longer—so let me give my heartfelt thanks to the Swiss Ambassador's spirit and his fellow citizens who may be reading this. The Swiss Ambassador's kindly intervention made it possible for me to be born—it was through Edward that my parents met.

It was because everyone in Europe realized that the world was at war and these were extraordinarily stressful (and cruel and brutal) times that they supported a child's escape. No matter how much trauma a little seven-year-old child might endure in Berlin today, there would be no chance of them being given five visas and all the (free) assistance to make their way from Berlin to America. It was the very brutality and cruelty of the Second World War—along with everyone's realization that there was murder afoot—that brought out the kindness of people to a seven-year-old child who was still so vulnerable.

For me, this story is both horror-full and wonder-full. What is dramatically expressed is both the terror and the joy of the human condition. This leads me to a place of surrender and acceptance—in *life*, I see that we cannot get the positive without the negative. I would like therefore to conclude this chapter with a symbol that implies that if we can be *awake* to every mental state—including those that are terrifying and those that are horrifying—we can experience a whole that is greater than the sum of its parts. In symbolic-form, *Life* to me is like the dynamic movement between the interconnected opposites of the white and black in this yin-yang symbol:

2

Love is letting go of fear

"Why are you traveling?"
"So I may return to where I am."

— Dante Alighieri, *Purgatorio II*, 90–92 [1]

We don't stop playing because we grow old—
We grow old because we stop playing.

—This quote has often been wrongly attributed to such people
as: Benjamin Franklin, Mark Twain & George Bernard Shaw [2]

In this chapter, you will find that I learned lessons from a
maternal hippopotamus, a dung beetle, and Timothy Leary.

I WAS THE SUBJECT OF AN EXPERIMENT THAT lasted until my third birthday. My father was an accomplished psychiatrist who had been assigned the task at the American Institute of Psychoanalysis (AIP) in New York City (known informally as the Karen Horney Clinic) to give a series of twelve lectures on the writings of Sigmund Freud. Part of the reason my father was given this assignment was that he spoke fluent German and could give a running commentary on the subtler meaning of Freud's concepts in their original German. The first three lectures covered Freud's three main stages of psychosocial development: oral, anal, and genital. According to Freud's model, it is in the middle 'anal' stage (when the child is between the ages of 18 months and three years old) that the rules of society begin to inhibit his or her innate playfulness.

According to Freud, while the child just wants to play with their feces (which is the first thing that the child makes), society represses this natural desire and the result is often what we understand as an 'anal-retentive' personality. Such a personality hates messes, is obsessively tidy and punctual, and is often obedient to the rules of society.

My father felt that this theory appeared to be true and he persuaded my mother to collaborate in an experiment with the goal of making me more playful and spontaneous. He had my mother save my little baby doo-doo in a metal potty and every day when he came home, the first thing he would see is my little baby turds and he would always say the same thing: "Oh, how wonderful! Oh, how beautiful!" My older brother Edward told me that my little baby turds once fell out of my diaper when I was little more than two years old and I pointed at them and exclaimed: "Oh, how wonderful! Oh, how beautiful!" My parents had not told him about their experiment so he thought it really weird that a baby who was not yet three years old would say these words with such certainty.

My parents knew that this experiment was not socially acceptable so they kept it a secret from their fellow professionals and only told me about what they had done when I was in college.

This experiment was not tried on either of my two brothers, and I often hear comments about how differently they turned out from me. Both brothers became doctors, well respected in their professions–the older in vocational medicine and the younger as a pediatrician–and they did not deviate from my parents' expectations of what was considered socially responsible. They also had less of the rebel inside and followed career tracks to achieve what is known in our society as 'security'.

My father had a woman analyst named Kilpatrick who prophesied before any of his children had even entered college that all three of his boys would be doctors. My two brothers both went to medical school and by the time my younger brother had become a doctor, I had started planning travels that would take me around Africa.

After getting a degree in England at the London School of Economics, I travelled for six years in Africa, Europe, and Asia. During this time, my father lamented my life choices; he wished that I would stop traveling and to do what he believed would 'fulfill my potential'. Particularly when I was in India, I would regularly receive letters from him that would say he was to blame for my 'irresponsibility'. From thousands of miles away, he would write to berate me, saying that his experiment had failed–if only he hadn't told me that my shit was wonderful, then I would see that traveling endlessly without paying any attention to my societal responsibilites was a 'shitty' path. Both of my parents' position toward my travels could be summed up by a famous American yippie named Abbie Hoffman:

The Jewish position on abortion is that the fetus is only alive . . .
. . . after it finishes graduate school.

Safety LAST

From an early age I did not have the kind of fear responses experienced by others to circumstances considered to be 'dangerous'. My mother said I would often go to the edge of the subway platforms in a way that would create discomfort for her. I seemed to have strong bones and a hardy body and when I fell I rarely got hurt or even bruised. It seems to me that this apparent fearlessness is at least partly the result of my father's experiment, although a psychic told me that it was because I was born in the Year of the Wood Rooster.

Facing the fear . . . and doing it anyway

Later, when I was in a graduate program in psychology, I took a class that included an approach to typing people called the Enneagram. In this system of typing personalities, there are nine 'enneatypes' of ego-fixations and the goal is to find your enneatype and then to do work to free yourself from your particular ego-fixation. My enneatype is what is called the Six–the type where the fixation is on fear. There are two types of Sixes–'phobic' and 'counterphobic'. Although most Sixes are 'phobic'–meaning that they would (as might be expected) move away from that which they feared, I discovered that I was a *counter-phobic Six*–meaning that whenever I feared anything, I wanted to do it.[3] If I succeeded, I momentarily proved to myself that I am not *really* fearful. In this process, what most excited me was to go to the very edge–but not over the edge. I have always hated pain–even tiny amounts of pain–and I certainly do not want to be subjected to the type of pain that would be my fate if I ever failed in my risk-taking. As I am writing this, I do not yet fully understand this contradiction in my personality: if I so much hate pain, why was I consistently and constantly drawn to the edge? I now see one payoff of this risk-taking behavior was that I could tell myself the story that I was brave and courageous, thereby blocking my awareness of how

34

much fear there really was inside me. In recent years, I have thus come to see that real bravery requires vulnerability–so, I was really lying to myself when I manipulated the meaning of courage to fake fearlessness.

I have a good sense of whom I can trust and also I am usually good at calculating risks and it is these two skills that have contributed to keeping me alive and healthy. But as 'edges' are sometimes amorphous and incalculable, there have been more than a few times in this story of my life in which I have come very close to being in harm's way.

The story begins:

I will now follow a (mostly) chronological account of some of the emotional highlights of my first two and a half decades. In choosing what to tell about my life, I have picked incidents where there has been a significant opportunity for me to learn–particularly at those times when I found myself in life-threatening situations either through 'fault'–or 'no-fault'–of my own. I also want to describe an experience of how a synchronicity that occurred during my first LSD trip rattled the cages of my materialist worldview.

I considered myself a really 'normal' boy growing up in a Jewish neighborhood called Forest Hills in Queens. I had close friends and received good grades and my entire social group was academically motivated. We all walked to school even at the age of six or 7, and no one ever got abducted or harmed in any way. None of us ever considered not going to college–and amazing as it may now seem, I do not believe any of my high school classmates ever took any form of what is known as a 'drug' before we went away to college.

I was devoted to my mother. I felt loved by her and I felt she would always protect me. I was a momma's boy in that I would just try to do what gained love, appreciation, and approval from others and particularly from my mother. Only when the usual late teenage rebelliousness surfaced did I move into conflict with my mother—I then began to resent her certainty that she knew what was best for me. My father was supportive, but he was not an emotional man, and he was away from home most of the time working in Manhattan as a psychiatrist.

The Pee Wee Story

I have a glimpse of my child-like fantasies because of the good memory of my younger brother Howard. He remembers the PeeWee stories that I would tell several times a week for the years when I was around 7 years old and Howard was around 5. We two boys shared a bedroom, but my Mother could sometimes hear us from the living room and would shout: "Are you still talking? Go to sleep! NOW!!!" At that point we wouldn't go to sleep, but I would just begin to whisper much more softly. Each time I would have PeeWee—a newborn baby—confront a seemingly powerful adult and in the ensuing conflict, PeeWee would always win. Howard's favorite PeeWee story told the tale of how when PeeWee was born, he would realize that he had a small penis and that the doctor had a big penis. He would then bop the doctor on the head, pull down the doctor's pants and take the doctor's big penis for himself, and give the doctor his very tiny penis. Howard never tired of hearing this particular tale.

Growing Up Jewish

At an early age I was told how the Nazis had murdered the European side of both my mother's and father's families. This was a common experience among the inhabitants of Forest Hills since the neighborhood where I lived was mostly Jewish. I once went to a friend's home and I saw numbers from a Nazi concentration camp tattooed on his father's lower left arm and even though I knew the answer, I asked him: "What are those numbers?" He suddenly stood up, looking terrified, and yelled in an angry voice: "**Never** ask me that question again!"

I feel that I unconsciously imbibed the generalized fear in my neighborhood that one day there could be another persecution of the Jews. Although I was proud to be a Jew, I feared that one day my religion might cost me my life.

My mother's response to the horrors of the 1930's with the ascendency of fascism in Italy, Spain, and Portugal and of Nazism in Germany was to become a card-carrying member of the American Communist Party (I now perceive her dogmatic faith in Marxism was her way of finding comfort and order in a world that had gone beserk.) Although my brothers and I knew about her loyalty to this secular religion, we were under strict orders never to tell anyone outside our inner household. I once came across my mother's Communist Party card and I was surprised it did not have her name on it. When I asked her why she didn't put her own name on the card, she responded that teachers were not allowed to be members of the Communist Party and she wanted to be a public school teacher. At that time of the Cold War in the 1950s, a teacher could only get a job after he or she had signed a loyalty oath that said that they were not now nor had they ever been a member of the American Communist Party.

One special day for me each year was the *Passover Seder*. Even though my mother remained a card-carrying member of the Communist Party, she would insist that we leave the door wide open that one night (in the middle of New York City) because the Prophet Elijah might come. We would place an extra glass of super-sweet kosher Manischewitz Concord grape wine in the middle of the table for Elijah. As he never did come, my mother said that since my Hebrew name was also Elijah, I could drink this big glass of wine. This meant I would get a tiny bit tipsy once each year—I did look forward to Passover every spring!

Addendum from the Future—Alan Wilson Watts

When a decade after I had left my Forest Hills home (at this time I was living in a commune in Ann Arbor, Michigan), Alan Watts came to a Passover Seder presented by my commune. He was in town giving lectures on Eastern religions for the Philosophy Department of the University of Michigan—and I had invited him to come to our home for the ceremonial meal after he had finished with his evening lecture. Not only did he arrive right on time, but he sung the Passover prayers in perfect Hebrew. When the ceremony was over, he picked up the glass of wine that had been set aside for Elijah and before drinking the holy elixir down to the bottom exclaimed: "I am God—I have the right to drink this wine prepared for Elijah!"

The Joke that Kept On Giving

When I was 11 years old, I saw a big fat book in a huge Manhattan bookstore with the title: *10,000 Jokes*. I told my mother that I wanted it. When she questioned me whether I would actually read it, I promised her that I would read every joke. Just before my *Bar Mitzvah*—this rite of passage happens when a Jewish boy is 13—I finished the last joke and excitedly told my mother. She barely gave me a nod and I realized that I had done this task for myself and not for her. Now over six decades later, I only remember one joke—it was in the section of made-up rhyming epitaphs:

> Here *lies the body of William Jay,*
> *Who died defending his right of way.*
> *He was right—dead right—as he sped along,*
> *But he's just as dead as if he'd been wrong.*[4]

There indeed would be many times in my life when I benefitted from not defending my 'right of way'.

Getting into Amherst College

I was accepted into the prestigious Amherst College because I knew the answer to a certain question that my English teacher posed to the class while we were studying Shakespeare's *Julius Caesar.* He pointed out these two lines in the play:

> *Brutus: Peace! Count the clock.*
> *Cassius: The clock hath stricken three.*
>
> (*Julius Caesar,* act II, scene i: lines 193-194)[5]

He asked the class whether we noticed that anything was strange about these two lines and as no one answered, he went on to say that the Romans way of telling time was to use sundials and not clocks and that the first mechanical clock that could strike each of the hours was invented in Europe around 1300 A.D. He went on: "What is the correct word for the error in this phrase, *the clock hath stricken three?"*

I was the only one in the class who raised my hand and I gave the correct answer: "anachronism". The teacher was impressed and said: "Yes, you got the right word. See me after class." And when I went up to the front of the room after the bell rang, he said: "I am the guidance counselor for Forest Hills High School and I also have an agreement with my *alma mater* Amherst College that I can get one student in each year—do you want to go there?"

I am present at the making of history: civil rights in the 1960s

And go to that prestigious institution I did. During my freshman year at Amherst, I read these words of Martin Luther King's when he was imprisoned in the Birmingham Jail:

> *Let justice roll down like waters and righteousness like a mighty stream.*[6]

39

Inspired by this image of the mighty waters of justice rushing to an ocean, I signed up to do work for social justice in the South with the American Friends Service Committee (AFSC), the social action wing of the Quakers (the Religious Society of Friends). In Warrenton, North Carolina our group of 18 volunteers found there that most of the population who were then called 'colored' had been denied the right to vote by the minority who then called themselves 'white'. Everything in the town was segregated. During the entire summer, we had almost no contact with the white people, while the colored people greeted us with enthusiasm.

The March on Washington

At the end of the summer (28th of August 1963), I had the privilege of being among half a million people in the famous March on Washington. After listening to Bob Dylan and Joan Baez sing together, I heard Peter, Paul and Mary sing Bob Dylan's song *Blowin' in the Wind*. When Martin Luther King gave his *I have a dream* speech, I heard him say: "We will not be satisfied until justice rolls down like waters, and righteousness like a mighty stream". I remember thinking that the end of the speech was quite different from its beginning. In the paper the next day, I learned that Mahalia Jackson had exclaimed to Martin as he was going up to the stage: "Tell us your dream!"—and once he had finished reading what had been previously prepared, MLK delivered extemporaneously and spontaneously the entire famous "I have a dream" part of the speech.

Radical!

During my college years, I became the first President of the Amherst College chapter of the radical student group, *Students for a Democratic Society* (SDS). Although people on the left were a minority on the campus, we regularly held demonstrations against the war in Vietnam.

Refusing My College Diploma

Just two days before I was scheduled to graduate from Amherst College, it was announced that the Trustees of the college were going to honor Robert Strange McNamara, the then US Secretary of Defense, by presenting him during the graduation ceremony with an honorary Master's Degree. Considering that McNamara was known as the architect of the war in Vietnam, in my mind it was as if a war criminal was about to get respect and honor at my class's graduation. Even though we had all said our good-byes for the college year, we asked our anti-war comrades from other colleges: Smith, Mt. Holyoke, and UMass to join us in holding picket signs at the graduation. All four SDS chapters of the Pioneer Valley were excited about participating in this demonstration. Many of us graduates met the night before and we had discussions about how we were going to express our disapproval of who Amherst College had chosen to honor, and we all agreed we would wear white armbands over our black gowns. The more militant of us agreed to walk out together when McNamara's name was announced. And during the graduation, what I did actually surprised even myself. When I went up to walk across the stage to accept my diploma, I saw McNamara sitting in the front row and I asked myself this question: *Do I really want this diploma?* and I suddenly noticed that I was bending my head down and gently floating right past the President without having picked up my hard-earned diploma. Then a few minutes later when Robert McNamara's name was announced, 19 of us graduates flawlessly executed our walk-out—all wearing the white arm bands. The next day I found the photo of me walking out on the front page of The New York Times—and the article correctly reported that I was the only graduate to refuse my diploma. (After it was all over, I found that I had actually been awarded my Bachelor's Degree the day before my graduation—and all that I had really done by my protest was to refuse a piece of paper that stated that I had already been awarded the Degree.)

Addendum from the Future—Robert Strange McNamara

Many decades after the graduation walk-out, I met a lower classman who was an usher at my graduation. He met Robert McNamara going up on a ski-lift in Colorado, and once he said that he was from Amherst, the discussion moved to McNamara's relationship to that graduation day. McNamara told my fellow Amherst graduate that as he saw white arm-bands on the black gowns of the *summa cum laude* graduates, he first got the idea that this war in Vietnam might be an error. He said this led him to commission *The Pentagon Papers*, and for those of you who know the history of the Vietnam War, you will remember that it was Daniel Ellsberg's illegal publication of those top-secret 7,000 pages of *The Pentagon Papers* in 1971 that enraged President Nixon. As President Nixon resigned after it was revealed that he had some thugs burglarize the office of Daniel Ellsberg's psychiatrist in what became known as the *Watergate Scandal*, this tiny protest in a small New England College may have inadvertently changed the course of history.

Going South

Energized by this fight for justice, I wanted to spend that summer participating in the struggle for civil rights in the Deep South. I ended up having my most scary civil rights experience in Grenada, a town of around 8,000 people in the cotton-growing area of Mississippi with the reputation of being a segregationist stronghold. Grenada came into the news in July of 1966. Just the month before, James Meredith—the first black man to ever enroll in the University of Mississippi—had tried to march from Memphis, Tennessee to Jackson, Mississippi—a distance of around 200 miles (320 kilometers)—and had been shot (and thankfully not killed) during the second day of his demonstration. After that shooting, many of the civil rights groups had organized a Meredith March

Against Fear between the cities of Memphis and Jackson. When that march had gone directly through Grenada, a struggle ensued between the segregationist whites and the freedom-fighting blacks. Stories about demonstrations and arrests in Grenada were now consistently in the national news.

A Hitchhiker's Guide to the Deep South

My way of traveling in Mississippi was to hitchhike—and I had the hitchhikers uniform of clean clothes, short hair, and a beardless face. I would listen to the stories of whoever picked me up, and most were white men who expressed their views about the superiority of the white race.

In particular, I remember one middle aged white man who told me his theory about race relations in the south: "Good niggers do not want to have anything to do with these so-called civil rights workers. There are good niggers and there are sorry niggers. And there are more good niggers than sorry niggers. That 'coon' is making our niggers uppity—and those uppity niggers will soon become sorry niggers. Who is going to kill that . . . coon first?" And I realized that in his rhetorical question, the '. . . coon' that he was referring to was not a 'raccoon' but was Martin Luther King (MLK). When this man's car happened to park near a civil rights march of black people in downtown Grenada, I grabbed my tiny backpack and when he (correctly) intuited that I was about to join the demonstration, he looked both hurt and surprised. After being sure my door opened, I put my feet on solid ground while looking at him and said: "I appreciate the ride . . . and, sorry, I just happen to be on the other side."

The demonstration was being led by a stocky black man who looked like a minister and I walked up to him indicating that I wanted to join his march. After telling him my name, I asked him his name. He looked me straight in the eye and responded confidently: "I am Hosea Williams, unbought and unbossed." I knew that I had found the right place–Hosea Williams was second in command to MLK in the Southern Christian Leadership Conference (SCLC) and he had been one of the civil rights leaders attacked by police the year before on the bridge in Selma, Alabama in what came to be known as *Bloody Sunday*. I felt it was noble to join such a march, and a minute later a young black girl handed me a placard that said: "The Truth shall set us Free". I proudly walked behind Hosea Williams and the other demonstrators. I was among 35 blacks and one other white person. Except for Hosea Williams, all of us were teenagers or in our early twenties (I would be 21 years old that September).

But our march had barely started when this huge specimen of a man–his belt barely held in his big pot belly–got in front of the demonstrators and said: "I am Rufus Suggs Ingram and I am the Sheriff here. STOP!!!" I knew he was large and in charge. As we were all being dutifully non-violent, we did as we were told and came to an abrupt halt. We just stood there in front of him for a few minutes and then the same sheriff told us to all sit down on the sidewalk. I noticed the moment that we all sat down, Hosea Willliams disappeared–later I realized he must have known what was coming.

In the Deep South and in Deeper Doo-doo

After sitting for just a few minutes, the Sheriff pulled up with a police van and a school bus and proclaimed that we were all under arrest for having 'obstructed the sidewalk'. I wanted to point out to him that he had just told us to sit down on that very sidewalk, but he did not seem to be open for a discussion. We were quickly surrounded by the rest of the (white) police force and we two whites were put in our own separate van and the 35 blacks were put on the school bus. And then after we were all driven to the Grenada City Jail, the girls were separated from the boys, the two white boys were put in a big cell and the two dozen black boys were squeezed next to us in a tiny cubicle. In the next room, I heard the police talking about "nigger-lovers" and as I heard that word, it came home to me now (after all the excitement of the arrest had died down) that I might *really* be in trouble.

In response to my rising fear, I invented a Constitutional Right–which it turns out I do not have. I kept repeating to my prison guard: "I have a Constitutional Right to call my mother." I later learned that I do not have such a right to call my mother, but I only have the right to call a lawyer. Anyway, I was so persistent that the guard let me call my mother and I was quite happy when she picked up the telephone. I said: "Mother, I have good news and then I have some bad news. The good news is that I know where I am–Grenada, Mississippi. (And I pronounced it really slowly and even spelled the place letter by letter G-R-E-N-A-D-A). The bad news is that I am in jail and my jailers are calling me a 'nigger-lover' . . . ". Maybe the guard heard me and he screamed: "Your Constitutional right is now up–GET OFF that phone."

I went back to my cell and I was just contemplating that here I was in a jail in the middle of Mississippi and I might have this time gotten myself into a *real* mess. I realized that it was my desire to disobey social rules–and not my principles–that might be getting myself killed. Still lost in more than a little self-pity, I heard a police siren and then a moment later a professional-looking gentleman with a suit called me to my prison bars and he said that he was the Federal Civil Rights Attorney situated in Jackson, Mississippi. He told me that he had been sent there by Robert Kennedy–who was then a Senator from New York State. He told me that someone's mother had called the secretary at Robert Kennedy's office saying that she was a resident of Queens, New York and that her son was in jail in Grenada. He had used his siren to do a trip that would usually take two hours in only one hour. He handed me his lawyer's card with these exact words: "You are now on the map. Your life is no longer in danger. Good luck." By my New York accent, I think he had figured out that it was my mother who had made the telephone call. Leaving me, he went over to the cell with the black prisoners and delivered the same message.

This all happened on a Monday afternoon, and I was in jail until Thursday morning. I knew this was a bit excessive for having just 'obstructed a sidewalk'—I realized that I was just a pawn in the game of the white segregationists. Anyway, they did serve us three meals a day—and my prison-mate and I found a few coins at the bottom of one of his pockets so we played a game of who could throw the coin closest to the wall of our prison cell.

On Thursday morning, my small backpack was returned to me and I was told that I was going to court. The girls joined us again and 37 of us were in the courtroom. It turns out that we had a lawyer from the SCLC and he did all the talking for us. A court reporter read the charge that we had "obstructed the sidewalk on the main street of Grenada". My lawyer said all of us pleaded not guilty—and the judge said the date of our trial would be in two weeks and set the bail at $25 per person and the SCLC lawyer agreed to pay the entire $925 bail to the court.

As I was released, I realized that I had less than no desire to appear at the Grenada courtroom for my trial. I was more than willing to take whatever were the consequences of not doing my civic duty. I wanted to become a bail-jumper with every fiber of my being. I hitchhiked out of Mississippi and two weeks later ended up in San Francisco where I became a witness to the opening scenes of the Summer of Love in Haight-Ashbury. Getting really really stoned for the first time in my life, I was so grateful for being out of Mississippi and I did have this thought: *Life is but a dream.*

A school trip to communist Russia—by invitation from the Kremlin

After Amherst, I went to the London School of Economics (LSE) to get a Master's Degree in Sociology. My real interest was through studying social change to discover tools that might make a better world.

My most sobering experience came during a two-week trip to the Soviet Union that included the cities of Leningrad, Moscow, and Kiev. I did this trip with 70 other LSE students as a guest of the main Soviet Intourist organization—since some Soviet students had come as guests to the LSE the year before, the LSE had been given a return invitation by the Soviet government.

When we arrived in Russia in April 1967, there were no Western tourists. I quickly realized that the freedoms that I had become used to in the West—like freedom of the press or freedom of speech—did not exist in the USSR.

Confronting Authority in a Totalitarian State

I was interested in Leon Trotsky—the first commander of the Red Army after the Bolshevik Revolution—who had a falling out with Joseph Stalin and had been assassinated in Mexico City on Stalin's orders. In Moscow I visited the Lenin Library (now the Russian State Library) with a member of our tour who was fluent in Russian. There was no mention of Trotsky in the card catalog so we went to the special room where only foreigners or high officials of the Communist Party were allowed. We looked in all the English language encyclopedias and found only pages that had been torn out where there should have been an entry for Trotsky. Later that same day, our group of 70 LSE students was invited to meet the intellectuals at the university. One of the Soviet professors gave a brilliant speech showing that the American President Abraham Lincoln had really served the interests of an aspiring capitalist class in defeating the feudalism of the Southern Confederacy—and he ended his talk with these words: "Although Westerners may not want to face the historical truth of the class struggle, we in the Soviet Union remain committed to examining all the facts." In the question-and-answer period, I stood up to thank the speaker for giving me a new perspective on Abraham Lincoln and then told my experience at the Lenin Library earlier that day and asked why if the researchers of the Soviets were so "committed to examining all the facts" did they have to eliminate even the mention of Leon Trotsky from the Lenin Library? The speaker looked stunned and turned to his fellow academics for help (where none was forthcoming) and he meekly responded: "Leon Trotsky was not important in the Bolshevik Revolution."

Was I an Army Deserter?

When at the LSE, I participated in a movement called *The Resistance*. We were all young draft age American students who believed the war in Vietnam was both stupid and immoral. Even though we were legally required to carry our draft-cards on our person, in 1967 a dozen of us Americans at various English universities handed in our draft-cards at the US Embassy in London. I got an immediate response from my Draft Boards as they told me to report for induction in NYC into the US Army. When I did not show up, my Draft Board inducted me and issued a Summons for my arrest as a deserter from the US Army.

A fellow protester who handed in his draft-card the same day brought his case to the Supreme Court. The Court ruled that his real offense was not carrying his draft-card and that his Draft Board had acted improperly by drafting him and then classifying him as a deserter. The case against me was dropped. Again I lucked out—no punishment was meted out for my protest.

My worldview turned on its head by Weber

The writer who most changed the way I thought about the world during my years at the LSE was the German sociologist, Max Weber. Max Weber showed that ideas can be a powerful engine for social change. Considering that throughout the few thousand years of human history there had been many times that great riches had been accumulated, his question was why did capitalism first have its birth in Europe in the 17th century? In his book *The Protestant Ethic and the Spirit of Capitalism,* Weber put forward the thesis that the work ethic in Protestantism–where the goal was to save rather than to spend–had created the necessary mindset for the birth of capitalism. When Protestants espoused the idea that salvation would come from 'a calling' to work hard, they did not realize that they were laying the foundation for a new capitalist economic order. Before the birth of capitalism, many merchant groups had raised capital, but they had spent the money ostentatiously–so they had not saved the money necessary to fund a capitalist means of production. With the ethic that 'a penny saved is a penny earned'– and that penny saved would surely get you into heaven–capitalism had its beginning. The way I understood Max Weber is that he had turned Karl Marx on his head–and showed that the cultural norms of a society–what Marxists would call the 'superstructure'– could create a new means of economic production.

Africa: from social researcher to adventurer

My dream of fighting for social justice led me to pick the topic of *'ujaama* villages' for my Master's thesis at the LSE. *Ujaama* villages were an alternative form of socialism for the modern world that were being tried out in the countryside of Tanzania–from what I read, they seemed much kinder than all the existing socialisms. After I graduated from LSE, I decided I wanted to go to Africa to see for myself how these *ujamaa* villages worked. If I liked what I saw, I thought I would consider living in Africa and doing a PhD on the social organization found in *ujaama* villages.

In Africa, the way I thought about myself gradually changed from being an academically-minded social researcher to becoming an adventurer who wanted to explore parts of Africa rarely visited by tourists. I entered Africa in December of 1969 and left in August of 1971–so all together it took me 20 months to visit 20 countries (21 countries if I include my three week stay in Eritrea which at that time was still not a separate country from Ethiopia). To pay for the journey, I chose to take all $10,000.00 of my Bar Mitzvah money out of the NYC bank where it was in the name of both my mother and me and deposit all of it in a London bank where it was only under my name.

To get to Tanzania from where I was living in London, I took a train across Europe, a boat across the Mediterranean, and eventually travelled overland through Egypt, Sudan, Eritrea, Ethiopia, and then entered Kenya from the north.

Meeting Barbara

I met Barbara in Nairobi, the capital of Kenya, and we soon became lovers. This was a great event for me as we found we were attracted to each other and also compatible. I was excited that I had found a companion with whom I could be vulnerable and share my deepest feelings. Barbara had arrived in Nairobi with her best friend Bonnie. Bonnie was a New Yorker (from Manhattan) and Barbara had grown up in New Jersey—right across the Hudson River from Bonnie. Together they had bopped around the capitals of Europe for two months, and then they had decided to buy a Volkswagen Bug to see how far south they could get into Africa.

They had lots of adventures, but the trip became *really* dangerous when they were stopped in the north of what was then Ethiopia by a group of guerrillas in military uniform—the leader asked them to get out of the car. As they quickly saw that they were surrounded by armed soldiers, they obeyed. After a search of the car which revealed only camping gear, they were questioned on the reason they were in Eritrea. When they said they were just two girls trying to have an adventure in Africa, the head honcho of the group told them that they had been stopped by the armed wing of the Eritrean Liberation Front, and they were now free to proceed—and he actually apologized for having scared them.

They had arrived in Nairobi with their car in good enough shape to sell (and even make a good profit). We all met in the Nairobi Youth Hostel, but as Bonnie wanted to go to the Seychelles and eventually to India and Barbara wanted to stay in Africa, I became Barbara's new traveling companion.

Kenya

I was getting lonely traveling by myself in Africa, and I was so grateful to have Barbara as my companion. Barbara and I chose to celebrate our meeting by traveling up the coast of Kenya from Mombasa through Malindi and all the way to the small island of Lamu. In Malindi, we had an experience that was upsetting to both of us. Sitting at the table where we were both eating, we met a young American from West Virginia named Justin Adams who told us (I remember well his exact words): "I'm tired of hunting 'coon (meaning raccoon) in the hills near my home—I am heading to the Congo to sign up as a mercenary where I can get practice shooting at human targets." I could see he was all revved up to do exactly what he described. I felt so awkward even listening to him describing his murderous intentions that I jokingly blurted out: "Hah? So what you're really saying is that you want to have the experience of hunting humans?" Rather than responding, he just got up from his seat and never said another word. When Barbara and I went back to our common room, we discovered that Justin had taken all of Barbara's jewelry including a valuable golden necklace and Justin was nowhere to be found.

Uganda

Barbara and I really liked each other, but after Kenya we wanted to go in different directions for a while. While Barbara went to Tanzania, I wanted to go towards Uganda—so we agreed to go our separate ways and meet again in Dar Es Salaam, the capital of Tanzania. In Uganda, I spent a day at the magnificent Murchison

Falls, and then I hitchhiked a long ride with some tourists who were going south to Queen Elizabeth National Park. The people who had picked me up took me to see the tree-climbing lions in that National Park–I was told that the lions liked to hang out in trees because it is cooler than on the ground, but it seemed to me that they also liked the view. My ride was moving on and they just dropped me off at the Wilderness Camp of Queen Elizabeth National Park. Since I explained to the man in charge of the lodge that I was not the usual sort of tourist but really a hitch-hiker, he put me up in the much simpler African quarters–and I benefited by getting a much cheaper price. I woke up in my sleeping bag feeling great the next morning–a blue sky and refreshing air–and I soon discovered that I was the only tourist in the entire lodge. What to do?

A Hippie Meets a Hippo

I saw right below the lodge that there was a river at the base of a very steep hill. I had been told that there were animals all around the lodge, but being excited by the possibility of seeing an animal that was genuinely wild, I decided to take a leisurely walk down the hill to the river. I had a *Praktica* camera–and before going out, I carefully put on the telephoto lens–just assuming any animals that I might see would be far in the distance. When I got down to the river, I saw trees, grasses, and bushes growing near the bank. When I parted the last bush, I was surprised to see less than six feet away a mother hippopotamus with an adorably cute new-born baby. I became completely focused on getting what I thought would be a great photo–and I confess that I had the false assumption that because hippos were vegetarians, they were as peace-loving as another species who had almost the same name: *hippies*. Both the mother and child hippo seemed quite as laid-back as any hippie. I took my *Praktica* up to my eye to take a photo and all that I got in my camera view-finder was the eye of the mother hippo. As I had in my mind's eye a perfect photo of mother and child together, I was busy changing from my telephoto lens to my standard lens when out of the corner of my eye I saw the mother hippo began to snort steam from her nostrils. Looking up from changing my lens, I said to myself: *Shucks! That steam would have made a fantastic photo!* But then her mouth opened and out came the roar of a bellowing bullfrog on steroids that had been super-amplified over a loud-speaker. As I turned around to run, I got a glimpse of a mouth that was open 180 degrees. I never knew that a hippo's teeth were *that* long. Now she was charging me! Already running away, I could feel the hippo's hot breath on the back of my neck. I never ran so fast in my life. As I sped away, I started to cry: "HELP! HELP!" When a few seconds later I quickly turned around, I could see the mother hippo still charging. Below on the river there were two Africans in a small boat who had heard my cries and were staring at the scene of the hippo chasing me up the hill.

But how could they 'help' me? It seemed that only a bolt of lightning from the sky could have slowed down that charging two-ton hippo. To run faster, I threw off my camera. Eventually I looked behind, and to my relief, the hippo had stopped running. After staring me down from 20 feet away, she slowly ambled back into the river. I cautiously retrieved my camera, but I never again went back to that river.

Up in the lodge, I learned that my assumption that 'hippos' were the 'hippies' of the animal kingdom was an abysmal error. Not only are many people killed by hippos each year, but hippos are the mammal in Africa (and also in the world) that kill the most humans. And mother hippos are most fiercely aggressive right after they have their babies. There is a saying in Africa that the most perilous place on the continent is between a hippo mother and her baby calf. Clearly, I had not evaluated this situation correctly. What I thought might become my best photo of mother and child was in actuality a life-threatening predicament.

One of the Africans at the lodge told me that just the week before on a path right near the Lodge a man who rode his bike at night (even though he had been warned never to ride his bike at night without a light) had in the dark hit a hippo who had come up from the water to rest on the path and the hippo had opened her mouth—and taken off his entire arm down to the socket. I was correct that hippos are vegetarians, so this hippo was not interested in eating an arm—it just happened that as the man tumbled off his bike that his arm was in the wrong place at the wrong time.

I told this story of the hippo chasing me to a friend of mine who was a mathematician. He had read that hippos can run much faster than humans on flat land—so he wrote an article for his college math journal called: *When does the hippo get the boy?* In the article, he invented an equation that predicted whether the boy survived or not, dependent on the weight of the boy, the weight of the hippo, and—most importantly—the angle of the hill that the boy would run up to escape the hippo. One necessary corollary of his equation was that as the angle of the hill increased and the land was less and less flat, the weight of the hippo compared to the weight of the boy would give the hippo less and less chance of ever catching the boy. I realized on looking at the equation that I might not have survived if the hill that I had run up to get away from the hippo had not been quite so steep.

Tanzania

After Uganda, I traveled through Rwanda and Burundi and I entered Tanzania near the Gombe Reserve where Jane Goodall had been studying chimpanzees. Even in 1970, I knew that Jane's research had revolutionized our understanding of primates by such discoveries that chimps did make primitive tools—and would also occasionally eat meat. When I got to her camp, I found Jane was away traveling, but I did spend time with her researchers. And then the chimp-mother Flo arrived with her baby, Flint. Flo impolitely grabbed a banana from me and then consumed it with a fully open mouth (in a way that my own mother would not have approved)—and then Flint showed me how effortlesly he could climb a palm tree.

A question that I could not answer

Not far from the Gombe Reserve, I spent a night in an African village. The adults spoke no English, but I was lucky their teenage son wanted to practice his English. The son told me that he was going to sleep each night with a question in his mind—and because he had just learned I was from America, he thought that possibly I could answer his question. He continued: "I have heard that there are big buildings in America and that some are many storeys high." Pointing at his mud-hut with a thatched straw roof, he continued: "If you build a second storey, why wouldn't you fall through the floor?" As he was asking his question, I had a vision of the skyscrapers of New York City and I realized that I was a long way from home. I mumbled an answer about "bricks" and "steel", but I could see from his expression that these words were unfamiliar to him and I had failed to answer his question.

Climbing Mount Kilimanjaro

Eventually I hitchhiked my way through Tanzania to where I could see the majestic square-top of Mount Kilimanjaro. I had read that this was not only Africa's highest mountain, but also the highest free-standing mountain in the world (at 19,341 feet or 5,895 meters). Being 25 years old and feeling able, I knew that the top was where I wanted to go. During my first day of climbing, I was lucky to meet two guides and eighteen other hikers starting that same September day. It took four full days of hiking to get to the very top. One of the guides told me not to drink or eat anything for the last two days—he explained that if I followed his instructions, the nausea that always comes at the top (due to oxygen deprivation) would rapidly disappear. As the guide predicted, I did throw up when I got onto the glacier about one hour from the top where the scree came to an end (a place known as Gilman's Point), and because I did not have any food in my stomach for the last two days, the nausea (thankfully) went away quickly.

Of the 19 adventurers who began the climb, only six of us made it to Uhuru Peak, the name given to the very top of the mountain. From Uhuru Peak–known as 'Everyman's Everest'–I had the most expansive view of my life. In one direction at the center of the mountain was the white, deep, glacial, snow-covered caldera and in the other direction were the green grassy plains of Africa. And then I saw near me on this top of Uhuru Peak that there was a flame inside a closed box and nearby was a book to write a few words after one reached the top.

To my amazement, the last name in the book before mine was Justin Adams–the man who had stolen Barbara's necklaces in the Malindi hotel several months before. Because he had dated his entry, I realized that he had descended from the mountain just days before I began my ascent.

At the still point . . .

Coming down the mountain to where there were trees again, a traveler going up the mountain handed me a joint–and when I sat down, although the leaves of the trees were moving, I saw everything as absolutely still and not moving at all (for a long time). Writing about this, I realize I do not know how to put into words the total contradiction of actually seeing for at least a full minute *no movement*, but yet knowing with my mind that there had to be movement. The best I can do to describe the paradoxical experience of this moment is to quote these words from T.S. Eliot's *Four Quartets:* [7]

> *At the still point of the turning world.[. . .]*
> *[. . .] at the still point, there the dance is.*

[. . .] Except for that point, the still point,
there would be no dance,
and there is only the dance.

Mozambique

When I arrived in Dar Es Salaam (Tanzania), I got a letter from
Barbara saying that she was already in South Africa. I wrote to
her and suggested that we meet in Lourenço Marques (now called
Maputo), the capital of Mozambique. She agreed to meet me there.
After we celebrated our good fortune in meeting again, we decided
to travel the length of Mozambique by hitchhiking–our goal was to
just head north as far as we could go (which was near the border of
Tanzania). All our rides were either from Portuguese merchants or
the Portuguese Army–Mozambique was in the midst of a civil war
and never did a driver come by (going in either direction) without
stopping and inquiring about what we were doing on the road. No
one who stopped could believe that we were hitchhiking in the middle of a civil war–and if they were going in the same direction, they
then looked to see if they could find room to give us a ride. I should
mention that although we were on the main road of the country,
only about two cars and/or trucks passed by each day.

Picked Up by the Military

After a particularly long wait for a ride, Barbara and I were picked
up by a military platoon who were on their way to battle against
the African guerrillas who had organized to fight Portuguese
colonial rule. We rode on the back of a truck with a dozen young
Portuguese soldiers. I learned that we were the first foreigners who
they had ever picked up hitchhiking and they wanted to adopt us
as novelties and mascots—we were their 'Americanos'.

One of them had a Polaroid camera and proudly showed us one
of his photos. The photo showed five wooden stakes and on the
top of each stake was the head of an African man. The moment

Barbara saw the photo, she grimaced and looked away as fast as humanly possible. I had the opposite reaction and studied the photo quite closely. I could see that the heads were not cut off with a guillotine, but the raggedness of the necks indicated that the cutting was likely done by a machete.

Studying the photo, I let in emotionally the barbarousness of war. I was astounded how this smiling young Portuguese man could be so proud of his photo. I got that humans are capable of unfathomable cruelty once they believe the story that their enemy is 'evil'.

The Zambezi washes away a bridge

Little did we know that it was the rainy season in Mozambique, and we were soon stuck for three days on the Zambezi River just north of the town of Vila Fontes (now called Caia). When we arrived at the Zambezi, we found there was no longer a bridge on the main route to the north–the raging waters had washed it away. Barbara and I hired a boatman to take us in a canoe to the other side of the river. The Portuguese merchant with whom we were then hitchhiking a ride thought his truck might be too heavy for the small ferry that was supposed to come in a few days and he got the bright idea to hire the same canoe to tow some of his merchandise of heavy clay tiles across the river before the ferry came–we all watched as his merchandise (along with the canoe) sank slowly– but very steadily–into the river. The boatman jumped out of his canoe and swam to the shore, and we waited another three days until waters of the river became calm and a ferry arrived to take his truck across the river.

While Barbara and I waited on the north shore of the Zambezi for the truck driver to resume our hitchhiking, we lived in a hut where a six inch (15 centimeters) spider of the tarantula species lived right above our heads in the bed; somehow we both admired the spider and neither of us were ever scared or felt a need to make the spider move away.

What a dung beetle taught me

I did however have a fright when I had to leave the hut to take a dump. The Portuguese merchant explained to me that we were near a National Park inhabited by leopards and when the leopards were hungry, they would jump on the backs of people while they were taking a dump—so he told me to look carefully at the trees as I was squatting.

There was a break in the clouds and I figured it was time to do my ablutions. While dutifully following his directions, I heard a sudden noise and I looked up into the trees, but then I realized the noise was coming from the ground, and instead of seeing a leopard, I saw a huge dung beetle—she was at least three inches long (8 centimeters). I had just taken a dump—and the dung beetle made a bee-line (or was it a dung beetle-line?) toward the biggest turd and grabbed the solid oblong object with her huge pincers and then spent the next half-hour moving the turd so it was under a nearby bush and then burying herself under the earth with the turd—at the end of the half hour, all that was visible was a little mound of dirt that was absolutely still.

I went back to the hut and explained to my African host what had just happened. He told me that dung beetles were all around his hut and that it would be about a week before the dung beetle emerged from its pile of dirt—and often it would now be a mommy followed by a few newly-born cute little baby dung beetles. For the very first time in Africa, I felt envy. No, it was not envy of another person—I felt 'dung beetle envy'. Here I had been travelling around Africa for over a year and although I had learned much and had many adventures, I had never found peace—and now I realized this dung beetle was finding peace with my own shit. The thought arose in me: *When I am finally willing to live with my shit as comfortably as this dung beetle, only then will I find peace of mind.*

I realized that I had seen dung beetles once before in my

African travels—they had been all around the temples I had visited in the town of Luxor. However, in Egypt the dung beetles were not living creatures, but they were depicted as hieroglyphs in the tombs and also free-standing statues—the famous scarab beetles. What is called a 'scarab' in English is none other than a dung beetle. In Ancient Egypt, the scarab was the main symbol for transformation, rebirth, resurrection, and immortality. (Many years later in a museum I saw a beautiful scarab amulet that had been discovered inside King Tutankhamun's tomb.)

The Democratic Republic of Rhodesia

Once we left the enchanted Ibo Island, we travelled across Mozambique through Malawi and then over to what was then called the 'Democratic Republic of Rhodesia'. 'Democratic Republic' was as much of a misnomer as a name could be—it was neither a republic nor was it democratic. A small colonial minority of white people controlled the country and unlike East Africa, the Africans were intimidated and disenfranchised. The Africans in the streets did not look white people in the eyes (or say hello) when white people passed them in the streets. In East Africa, I had been impressed by how accepting the African people were and their kindness and their hospitality—and none of this was apparent in Rhodesia (now called Zimbabwe).

Barbara and I ended up staying with a community of white artists in Salisbury (now Harare). They considered themselves outcasts in their own country as they did not follow the racist ideology of their government. Martin, one of the artists, had an amazing talent of being able to imitate the sound of any bird by whistling in different octaves, pitches, and rhythms. Surrounding the commune where we lived with Martin was a forest, and Barbara and I would take walks with Martin and listen to his amazingly accurate replication of the call of each of the different species of bird. We felt so privileged to be the witness to a conference of the birds.

On an April weekday before the Easter of 1971, Martin showed us an envelope that he had gotten from a friend in England–inside the envelope was a blotter with ten tabs of LSD. Martin said that he really liked us and wanted to give each of us one of the tabs.

Neither Barbara nor I had ever taken LSD before. To understand what happened next, I would like to digress from the story of my African journey to give the story of my relationship to this substance called LSD.

'Turn on, tune in, drop out'

Although I had heard of LSD (acid), the first person who I ever met who had actually taken this substance was Timothy Leary. I met him when he gave a talk at Amherst College during my senior year. At this point, Leary was both famous and infamous–he was famous as a prophet for psychedelics and he was infamous as being the Harvard Professor who had been fired for sharing his LSD with his students. During his fascinating talk, Doctor Leary repeated these six words with growing emphasis: *Turn on, tune in, drop out.*

I will try to give the gist of what he said on that mild spring evening in the March of 1966. Leary told us all to *turn on* to LSD. He said that the scientific evidence showed that LSD was not harmful nor toxic and also non-addictive. He repeated several times that it was his assessment that acid was not a drug like alcohol, nicotine, heroin, or cocaine, because it was not useful for changing one's mood or escaping reality, but rather it was a tool, like a microscope or a telescope. He even predicted that as essential as the microscope was to biology and the telescope to astronomy, so would LSD prove to be for exploring the human psyche and consciousness itself. Once a person took this mind-expanding chemical, they would then be able to *tune in* to the sacramental nature of reality by worshipping the ancient wisdom stored in the trillions of cells of her or his own body.

Alas, there was a need for caution and he admitted that LSD

could be scary to the inexperienced user because they might become aware of not only the heavenly beings who reside in each of us, but also the internal ferocious demons. Thus he gave the directive to take the chemical among people we loved where we could turn off the busyness of our minds in a harmonious setting (meaning place) in which we could adopt a 'set' (meaning attitude) of gratitude and devotion. Finally, with the new wisdom gained from our inward journey, the result would be that we might be able to acquire the detachment to *drop out* of all the dramas in our life that were fake, phony, or the result of ignorance—including in his opinion America's war of cruelty and brutality against the Vietnamese people.

His last point was that if enough people around the globe turned on to LSD, then humanity as a species might be able to let go of its wars that were killing far more people than LSD ever could potentially harm or kill.

During the question-and-answer period after the lecture, he clarified that he was not suggesting that anyone should "drop out" of college or the work-force—he acknowledged that such an action might threaten that individual's survival—but what he was suggesting is that we use our LSD trip to discover a way to "drop out" of the inauthentic and manipulative game-playing that characterized so many social roles so that we could each in our own way become a more authentic human being. He agreed that LSD could cause accidents, casualties, and even deaths. He argued that the reason that LSD was dangerous is that it could be used in ways that were careless or stupid or even cruel, but his point was that this was no reason to ban a useful tool. Guns can be used violently and cars can be driven recklessly, so recognizing this, society has set up licensing guidelines about who is permitted to use guns or cars. Timothy Leary insisted it was our duty as the human species to become become psychonautic explorers of what he called *inner space.* For those who had bad trips, we could honor such explorers and adventurers who might have sacrificed their sanity—or even their life—but this was no reason for humanity to avoid its own duty to explore *inner space* with the same intensity and intelligence that we are putting into our explorations of outer space.

I could see that this would be a hard sell to the American public. How many mothers would want to risk the sanity of their own child because of a duty of the human species to explore *inner space*? My thought was what came out of Polonius' mouth when he overheard Hamlet: "Though this be madness, yet there is method in it."

I went up to the podium where Dr. Leary was surrounded by people who had attended the talk. I looked carefully because I could not quite believe my eyes: yes, Timothy Leary was handing out tabs of LSD to people in the audience who were requesting it. (At this time, it was still legal.) Realizing that if I so wanted, I might take LSD the very next day made me quite afraid—I did not know what ferocious inner demons might be unleashed and spring forth from deep in my unconscious. After the crowd had thinned out, I went up to Doctor Leary and said that I wanted his business card. He took a gold metal business card holder out of the inside of his jacket pocket and I saw it said on the outside the words: 'Turn on, Tune in, Drop out'. The card that he handed me from the inside of the folder had his name and the address of a residence in Poughkeepsie, New York called Millbrook.

I called the number on his card the next week. When, to my surprise, Dr. Leary answered the telephone, I told him I was interested in learning more about LSD. He said that he was giving a workshop the weekend after next—the cost was $75. Lucky for me, it was the week end before Easter and as college classes were out, I could come to his address in Poughkeepsie on the way home to my parents in New York City. I told him I would definitely come and he told me to be at the Poughkeepsie Greyhound Bus Station at 6 PM on the Friday that was to be the April Fool's Day of 1966.

I arrived at the bus station in Poughkeepsie in a driving rain on that Friday evening of April 1st. A young woman figured out that I was part of the course and handed me a typewritten card that read: 'SILENCE . . . until Saturday morning.' I remember the windshield wiper going back and forth as I sat in the back seat with the other course participants–none of us spoke even one word. Eventually we arrived at a three-storey house with many windows and I was ushered upstairs into my own private room that was painted in all the colors of the rainbow in a swirl and a whirl of psychedelic patterns and designs. I wondered what I was getting into . . . and I slept well.

The next morning I was told by the same friendly woman that had picked me up at the bus station that Timothy Leary would not be here this weekend as he had been called away to NYC and his younger sidekick, Richard Alpert, would be leading the course. My initial reaction was disappointment–I had barely heard of Richard Alpert (who is now the teacher named Ram Dass) and I assumed I would be missing the big honcho. Nevertheless, I soon discovered Richard was a good group leader and he gave each of the five participants attending the course a chance to say what brought us here. I found out that I was the youngest in the group and that none of us had ever taken LSD. The others already had professions in the dramatic or the healing arts and wanted to know what would happen if they ever took LSD.

When the participants were through sharing our personal histories, Richard Alpert talked honestly about his own life and told us that his motive in doing psychedelics was to find a way to end his own suffering. He felt that to further this desired outcome, he wanted to find a way to go deep into uncharted 'mystical' territories to systematize and program the psychedelic experience to eventually draw a 'mystical' map of this terrain. I could sense his excitement as he ventured forth on such an adventure. He confessed that he was at the stage of his life where he was still unable to stay in this 'mystical' state when he was not under the influence of LSD. Even though he could regularly take LSD and find for several hours, or even a full day, what he called his 'true nature', he found that when the trip came to an end he would have the same old hang-ups and neuroses and seemed to be just as caught up in his ego games as before the LSD journey. What he wanted now was to find a way to embody the LSD experience when he was not tripping. He said that he was currently making plans to go to India to see if he could find there a spiritual path that would allow him to abide in the state that he had glimpsed during his LSD experiences.

The staff at Millbrook were quite supportive and I ate the first dinner of my life that was called 'vegetarian'. On Saturday night, all the participants did free-form dancing to new age music with the white light of a flickering stroboscope. I was grateful that there was never any attempt to offer me LSD—I knew that I was not ready. When the course concluded on Sunday morning with a silent walk in the forest surrounding the estate, I did have the thought: *I really do not know what is the meaning of this word 'mystical', but some day I do want to try LSD. . . .*

Tangled Up in Lavender

Now to continue with my African journey—it was now five full years since I had met Timothy Leary and here I was with Barbara in the middle of Rhodesia. And I knew it was time to have my first experience—yes, now was the moment to take LSD. Barbara and I had spent many days together getting stoned on the marijuana that was available in every African market, but we both knew that LSD would be something different. We went to the main park of Salisbury where we went off the main pathways and chose to sit beneath a flamboyantly red flame tree (Royal Poinciana). It appeared that we were the only white people in the park—and the local African people that we saw were keeping a respectful distance and leaving us very much to ourselves.

A Mystical Experience

We consumed the LSD around noon and about a half-hour later I told Barbara that this was not really very different than getting stoned. She agreed with me and we just gave each other a look and a shrug to say that this experiment had been a big bust. Just a second after those words were out of my mouth, I had the first hallucination of my life. At this time, I considered myself a materialist and still did not know for myself what the word 'mystical' meant.

Sharing a vision

And suddenly . . .

I was on a rocky hill with my arms nailed into a crucifix and I looked down and my feet were nailed together by one big nail on the same wooden cross and I looked in front of me and there was a Roman soldier with a lance and he slowly came up to me and pierced me with his lance on my left chest in the area of my heart—I felt the pain of the wound in my chest area and was startled into my normal waking reality.

In total, my guess is that this visual image lasted for about three seconds. The hallucination seemed much more real than the reality around me—being on the crucifix, I had felt no grief nor fear but merely awareness of my predicament—I was but a witness until I woke up with the physical pain of the lance penetrating my chest.

I turned to Barbara and said, "Barbara, I have just had the most amazing three seconds of my life . . . " And before I could say another word, she said, "Elliott, I have also had an amazing experience—I was just Mary Magdelene watching Jesus get crucified".

I remained speechless for more than a moment—how was what Barbara said even possible? I knew that I had not told her anything about my hallucination—and here we were part of the same dream.

Like Hamlet, I now knew for sure that there was more in heaven and earth than was dreamt of in my philosophy.

Barbara and I had a long talk after our LSD journey—for both of us it was the most startling synchronicity of our lives. We had never even once mentioned Jesus during our months together and there was no way to explain how we both had the same image at once—one that was so foreign to both of our conscious minds.

You go your way, I'll go mine

During our post-LSD integration talk, Barbara and I agreed to go in different directions—she said she now wanted to go to India to study yoga and I told her that I had enough of being abroad as it was now over four years since I left America (over three years in London and now more than a year in Africa) and what I really wanted was to see my parents and brothers and also to see how America had changed.

Travelling Home

After Barbara and I parted, I planned to get a visa to go through South Africa (where I had a traveling companion patiently waiting for me in Capetown), and then get a cheap flight home to London from Capetown. But my plan was to be frustrated—I was refused entrance into South Africa by the South African Consular official stationed in Rhodesia, who asked me about my attitudes on race and when I said I believed that all races were created equal, he stamped on my visa application in dark red ink the big word 'REJECTED'.

Now the cheapest way for me to get back to America was to head north by taking a barge down the Congo River and then to hitchhike across the Sahara Desert to Europe. To prepare for the journey up the Congo River, I went to the biggest bookstore in Lusaka—the capital of Zambia—and found a copy of Joseph Conrad's *Heart of Darkness*[8]. In this book Conrad says the Congo

River resembles 'an immense snake uncoiled, with its head in the sea, its body at rest curving afar over a vast country, and its tail lost in the depths of the land'. I started my travels in the depths of the land and slowly travelled on a huge barge that had hundreds of passengers to the capital of the Congo (the capital had recently changed its name from Leopoldville to Kinshasa). I had plenty of time to read as the barge was only going at 3 miles per hour. *Heart of Darkness* described the cruelties of Belgian colonialism in the 19th century. The murderous racist trader Kurtz adds to a pamphlet that he is writing that justifies imperialism this handwritten exhortation: "Exterminate all the brutes!" Kurtz's home is surrounded by the cut-off heads of Africans each on its own stake. Right before dying, Kurtz weakly whispers the words: "The horror! The horror!" This resonated with what I felt was the same 'horror' that was happening every day during the then ongoing war in Vietnam. I wondered if humankind was ever going to be capable of moving beyond the 'heart of darkness'.

Crossing the Sahara Desert

I did finally hitchhike my way out of Africa right through the Congo and then eventually through the Sahara Desert. After riding the barges down the Congo River for two weeks, I was in Central African Republic, Chad, Cameroon, then passed through Kano in the north of Nigeria, and I ended up in Agadez (in the middle of Niger) waiting for a ride to take me north. I was told that a ride would come, but it might take a few weeks. Meanwhile, I lived at the house of a young Frenchman who was doing volunteer work for Le Service Volontaire International (SVI), the French version of the Peace Corps. There were no fruits or vegetables anywhere to be found, and the only meal in the one restaurant of Agadez was a soup made with the meat of 'old' camels–'young' camels were too precious to ever be sent to the butcher. At each meal I spent a long time chewing the meat that had been boiled for hours in a (failed) attempt at a soup.

After two weeks in Agadez, a truck came that was going the full 560 miles (900 kilometers) straight north to the town of Tamanrasset (in the south of Algeria). I was piled onto the top of a huge truck along with about 20 other travelers and lots of goats and chickens—I was the only foreigner. The whole truck was surrounded by water inside goatskin waterbags, but I was told I was only allowed to drink a few gulps at a time and only three times a day. When I asked why I could not drink more, I was told that it was necessary for this truck to "live like a camel"—meaning that camels will store water for difficult times. Because there was always the possibility of the truck breaking down in the middle of the Sahara, it might be another week or two until the next truck might see us to even know that we had ever been stranded in the desert.

The driver told me (in French) that as we were traveling in June, the radiator was in danger of blowing up during the middle of the day—so we would stop the truck each day for six hours. I was curious how high the temperature would get—when the truck stopped at 11 AM, I saw that it was 115 degrees Fahrenheit (46 degrees Celsius). Around 3 PM, it got up to 140 degrees Fahrenheit (60 degrees Celsius). Yes, although it was hot, it surprised me that it did not feel unhealthy—it was like being in a continuous dry sauna.

Although everyone else on the truck tried to sleep under the truck during each of these daily stops, I decided I wanted to explore the desert to find out if I could find anything alive. After my driver promised "by *Allah*" to make sure I was on the truck before he left, he gave me several gulps of water from the goatskin and I was amazed at how the evaporation made the water seem quite cool. I walked out to the middle of the Sahara Desert to see what I would find. I turned up many a rock and even dug under the sand, but I could not find any sign of life in hours of walking. Because I was curious to get a figure about how much it rained there, I eventually looked it up (when later that summer I went to visit the British Museum in London), and I read a statistic saying that there was 1/100th of an inch (1/4 of a mm) of rainfall per year in that part of Niger–and I figured out that would be the equivalent (for each year) of one big fat juicy dewdrop.

When we reached the oasis of Tamanrasset in the south of Algeria, there was a celebratory mood. We could finally drink as much water as we wanted and there was an abundance of fresh figs, sweet dates, and many other fruits. I watched how the main well of the town was lit up both all day and then all night–the caravans of camels would arrive in an orderly fashion to pull up to the well and each camel would in turn get their fill of water.

In Algiers, I was told by another traveller that there were many thieves around and that I should watch my belongings carefully. But I could not resist taking a swim in the heat of day in the Mediterranean. After having crossed the Sahara in even greater heat, the Mediterranean looked just too inviting. I was staying with a family in an inexpensive communal rooming house and none of us had individual rooms with locks–so I could see my belongings were highly vulnerable. While changing into my bathing suit in an empty room, I hid my money and passport separately in two huge thick books high up on a big bookshelf. After what was for me a highly enjoyable swim, I came back to my room and all my possessions were scattered over the room–but nothing had been taken–my camera had been stolen in Kenya long ago and the valuables that the thief wanted were safely tucked away in those in the books where I had hidden them.

My last destination in Africa was to be Marrakech. Hitchhiking again, my ride dropped me off in the middle of Fez (Morocco) at 2am in the morning. I had no idea where any hotel might be–all the signs I saw in that part of town were in Arabic without a word of English–so I decided to sleep in the middle of a big park. Because I had already been warned about the high level of thievery in North

Africa, I carefully put my money and passport in a money pouch suspended bandolier-like on a cross-body strap that went over my right shoulder and across my left breast—it was securely lodged beneath my T-shirt right up against my skin. After putting all my possessions in my backpack, I tightly tied the backpack to my person with a heavy cloth cord. I then crawled into my sleeping bag and went right to sleep.

I Am Robbed

At 5am I woke up to see the eyes of a young Arab boy—we were face to face just a few inches apart. Before I could see any more of him than his eyes, I saw a knife flash in front of me—this young boy was not interested in harming me, but with one forceful stroke and without injuring me, he cut the heavy cloth strap that tied my backpack to my arm. He grabbed the backpack firmly with both his arms and held it against his chest and started running away from me. The day was just dawning—so I could easily see his silhouette and thought I might be able to out-run him. I was only 25 years old and in good shape—but I quickly realized that I had a problem—I was barefoot and he had shoes. I had to watch him as he rapidly left the park and crossed a street and he soon disappeared among the busy streets of Fez as the city was just waking up.

An Excursion to Another Time in which I Was Willing to Give Up My Own Life

As I was chasing this thief in Fez, no thought ever entered my mind that if I caught up with him that he had a very sharp knife and all I had on was my underpants—and I had no weapon.

Twenty-five years later in San Francisco, I still seemed to have as little caution when I was confronted with a thief. For many years I had told myself that if I was ever to be confronted by any robber, I would just automatically give to him whatever he might want because what was really important was to protect myself

71

from injury or death. And now here is what happened:

I was walking home in what is considered a very safe neighborhood after a long and satisfying day of being a therapist. I noticed a young African American teenager standing on the corner against the wall of a house and I gave him my usual greeting—a friendly "Hello". He responded by sticking out a concealed object from under his jacket and saying to me in a throaty voice: "This is a gun—Hand over your wallet." I immediately thought of a slip for $80 in my wallet—I had just been to a bookstore to trade in some old books. The store gave me that slip so that I could buy used books from them at a later date and I remembered asking the book salesperson what would happen if I lost the slip and he curtly replied: "You lose your money." As I stood there—in danger of death—I said to myself that I would rather die than hand over my wallet (and lose my potential books). Then I started to wonder whether or not this would be an appropriate time to die: I realized that my parents were in their late 80's and that I had no wife and no children and I concluded quite confidently: "Yes, today's a good day to die." (I had just heard a Klingon in TV's *Star Trek: The Next Generation* say those exact words: "Today's a good day to die.") Now that I was ready to accept my own death at that very moment, I became quite still and entered into a meditative state. I saw that this young robber was still standing there in front of me with what might have been a gun pushing out from his jacket and I began carefully studying his face in case I had to identify him in a police line-up. (I can still see his face so clearly imprinted on my mind's eye that even now I could identify him in this never-to-be line-up.) As I stared fearlessly and calmly at his face, it seemed as though we were frozen together for a forever moment. His face was as impassive as mine but I knew that he must eventually realize that it would be he who must make the next move. Unbelievably, more than a minute passed until it dawned on him that nothing was going to happen and that he was just going to be standing there forever—foolishly—with a sharp object pointing out of his jacket.

Now he was no longer impassive and his expression changed to angry surprise. He pushed the concealed object out even further —still under the same jacket—and said:

"This REALLY is a gun. Give me your wallet—NOW."

I do not know where these words came from, but I responded: "I am just a poor student and I don't have a wallet. If you want, you can shoot me in the back." And I turned around and briskly walked away.

A few seconds later, I saw a meter man driving a small cart and I ran up to him in his little cart shouting: "Right there on that corner a thief tried to rob me. If you let me jump into your cart, we can catch a thief." He apologetically explained to me that he might lose his job if he would ever let anyone ride in his cart, but he said he would meet me at the corner of the attempted robbery.

On that corner, I explained to the meter man what had happened and he told me that just the day before he had met a man with a gash on his head where "a young black punk" had threatened that man with the identical words and then when the man had attempted to hand him his wallet, the victim had been hit on the head with the handle of a real gun and that the thief had run away with his wallet. He said thieves are now hitting people over the head with the purpose of fogging their memory so that they cannot remember their face clearly in a line-up. The meter man told me that he himself always carries an extra empty wallet on his person and that if he is ever to be confronted by a thief, he is planning to throw this extra empty wallet on the ground and drive away. We ended our dialogue by him telling me: "I never thought of telling a thief that he could shoot you in the back. What you did seems to me to be quite a clever strategy."

After Being Robbed, I am Robed

Now our excursion back into the future has ended and we are returning to the park in the center of Fez with me standing next to my sleeping bag in my underpants with my passport and American Express Traveler's Cheques in the money-pouch slung across my chest. And my shoes were next to my sleeping bag.

I realized that I was all right and that I still had possession of what was most valuable. So I wrapped the sleeping bag around my waist as if it were a towel after taking a shower and entered Fez where no one seemed to think I looked at all strange and I quickly found a tailor. The tailor was quite friendly and gave up all his other work to pay attention to my obvious need—he measured me in every direction and then he showed me many colors of light-weight cotton cloth and I chose a cloth that was a bright green.

I spent the next hour watching the tailor as he carefully sewed what for me was to become my perfect *djellaba*. For those of you who might not be familiar with Moroccan clothing, a *djellaba* is a long, loose-fitting unisex outer robe that goes down to the ankles and always includes a qob (pronounced 'cob')—this is a large baggy hood that comes to a point in the back.

Seeing how I looked a little strange even to myself in my new *djellaba*—which was now my only outer garment—I took a public bus to Marrakech. There I had two of the best weeks of my life. The local market was full of snake-charmers, fortune-tellers, belly-dancers, and even a group of whirling dervishes. I lived in a cheap hotel and I met an English chap named Jake (who had just crossed the Sahara with his motorcycle). We would often have mint tea together and just wander through the market.

A Serendipitous Meeting

My African story ends with a coincidence. After I left Africa via Casablanca, I travelled through Spain and in the very north I went into the Altamira Cave to see the famous palaeolithic cave paintings. After going underground through a series of twists and turns, I arrived at the chamber with paintings depicting a herd of bison. I could see that the artist exploited the natural contours in the cave walls to make these animals three-dimensional. I particularly admired one bison that had been made about 16,000 years ago and I wondered: *What art made in our time will still be admired 16,000 years from now?*

Leaving the cool cave, I started hitchhiking in my green *djellaba* in the hot sun and who should I see coming up on his motorcycle but Jake–this same Englishman who I knew from Marrakech. We hugged each other and I asked him where he was going and he said "London"–which was my destination too. He saw my look of expectancy and he knew that I wanted to come with him and he said: "I would just love to take you, but I'm sorry that I only have room for you and not for any of your belongings." I said: "Remember what I told you in our rooming-house–the story of how my back-pack was stolen in Fez–this is all I have!"–and I pointed to a shoulder purse that contained little more than a toothbrush and a tube of toothpaste. Jake said: "Hop on, mate!!!"

Later I realized that Jake must have remembered that my belongings had been stolen, and that he was just teasing me when said he could not take my belongings–he just thought that was a great line and he already knew I had no possessions. But it was true that if I had not had my big backpack stolen in Fez, there would have not been room for it along with me on a rather packed motorcycle.

A Gift From the Gods

We proceeded to spend two pleasant days traveling through the wine country of France–and just occasionally stopping at a local grocer for a simple lunch of bread and cheese and wine–and we would tease each other about the different national traits of the Americans and the English. While having this really good time, I kept thinking how none of this would ever have happened if my backpack had not been stolen. As we sailed across the English Channel (there was no Channel Tunnel then), I felt that at least for that moment I had not only what I needed, but also all that I ever wanted—the eternal presence of the present moment.

While writing this chapter, I was aware that all of the events described occurred over 54 years ago. My subjective experience is that all of this happened but a moment ago. From this 'god's eye' point of view, I added an extra verse (made up by me) to add to a popular 19th century American nursery rhyme:

Row, row, row your boat
Gently down the stream
Merrily, merrily, merrily, merrily
Life is but a dream

Walk, walk, walk your feet
Gently toward the stream
If you see a hippopotamus,
Don't forget to scream!

3

Good minds like a think . . .

I had been sincerely involved in worthy causes, such as the Civil Rights Movement. When I look back to recall my motivation, I find that although I was working for world peace, I had no inner peace. Despite my idealism, I had always been a materialist, but now I began to open my thinking and my heart to the non-material aspects of my life's journey. Looking back on this three month overland journey from London to New Delhi, my current perception is not that I entered upon the spiritual path, but that the spiritual path entered me.

THERE IS A PROVERB THAT SAYS:

Great minds think alike–
Fools seldom differ.

I find this proverb interesting because it points out a difference in the way I may evaluate the way others may reach the same conclusion as myself–the saying suggests that people who agree with me may not necessarily be great thinkers, but may merely share my own foolish misconceptions. If you do agree with the worldview presented in this chapter, I will leave it up to you, dear reader, to choose whether we are great minds or merely fellow fools.

My own experience of myself is that I only started in any serious way to think for myself after my materialist worldview was challenged. I laid out the foundation for a new thought pattern that was more spiritual during my one year of travel in Asia–from 27 to 28 years old. As a child, I had adopted the Communist ideology of my mother–which was a Marxist version of dialectical materialism. The general theory of the original dialectic (which is not in any way "materialistic") came from the German philosopher, Georg Wilhelm Friedrich Hegel, who posited a continuous unfolding of Absolute Reason by a mechanism that could be described as triadic:

THESIS–ANTI-THESIS–SYN-THESIS
AFFIRMATION–NEGATION– INTEGRATION

The theory that I learned at my mother's knee was that there was a greedy destructive capitalist ruling class (thesis) and our work was to fight for the advent of socialism (anti-thesis) and then humanity might have a chance for a communist future which was to be governed by this principle (syn-thesis):

> *From each according to his or her ability:*
> *To each according to his or her need.*[9]

My translation was: *Give what you can: Take what you need.* I saw the real purpose of this set of intentions was to build or create more value than one might consume or destroy–presumably the abilities would eventually be greater than the needs.

My mother's favorite proverb when she talked about the coming revolution was: *You've got to crack a few eggs to make an omelet.* She also liked this quote from Lenin: *If you chop down a forest, splinters will fly.* I took these sayings to mean that sometimes there must be violence if we are to move forward in this dialectic from thesis to anti-thesis, from capitalism to socialism. After many years of actively participating in movements for social change and studying where many revolutions have gone astray, I now see the only viable strategy for social change is non-violent. Whenever revolutionaries want to crack open eggs by executing members of their own society, I see such violence as inevitably leading to them getting egg all over their own faces—and if they have beards, onto their beards also.

Before I entered India, I had lost my belief that there could be a successful socialist (or communist) revolution during my lifetime. I still saw it as a noble, but never-winning, battle to create a vibrant non-violent counter-culture that would fight sexism, racism, consumerism, and all those vested interests that were obstacles to the progress of humanity.

Kingdom or Queendom?

In India I was introduced to a new way of thinking that no longer made social change in the material *king-dom* the primary goal of life—in its place, there gradually arose in my mind a spiritual *queen-dom* that placed its primary focus on self-knowledge and self-realization. As suggested in the term queen-dom, there was also a movement away from a belief in a male authority (whether it be God or Buddha) who demands that we obey rules and commandments, to an experience of female goddesses and *dakinis* who gently persuade us to discover our own true nature.

The fundamental idea was that there was always an infinite amount of light coming our way, no matter how much pain there might be at any particular moment. Thus, if any individual could just accept and even surrender to that pain, eventually it would pass, and that individual would (both inevitably and unpredictably) begin to glimpse that he or she was not an individual, but just an apparently separate wave on a truly limitless expanse of an ocean of consciousness. As this individual would be drawn closer and closer to his or her inherent essence and natural state, it would be seen that the true self was, is, and will always be the same full solid emptiness as this unchanging awareness.

Already the Ocean

By the time I left India, it was an axiom of my thinking that once I cleanse the dust (and sometimes mud) off my doors of perception, I would see my completeness as the ocean and not my separation as a wave. It would surely take work, the self-disciplines of meditation and yoga, to break my identification with what appeared to be a separate body-mind mechanism, but success was assured. As I learned not to focus on traumas related to the past or fears about the future, there would be an eventual realization that—exactly as I am in the here and now—my true nature was already whole and complete. What a present to be present for the pre-sent presence of Being my true Self.

What followed from this axiom is a corollary, or supplementary conclusion, that the term 'spiritual suffering' is a contradiction in term symbols. Once we no longer see ourselves as a wave affected by other waves, or affected by 'the slings and arrows of outrageous fortune', there is a new way of taking responsibility for whatever may befall us. There will always be pain, but the end of suffering is in sight, and whatever suffering does occur is not glorified, idealized, or romanticized. The idea here is that although pain is inevitable, suffering is optional; only when pain is resisted does there begin suffering. This notion is presented succinctly by Byron Katie who has promulgated this saying: "When you argue with reality, you suffer—but only 100% of the time."

From my present vantage point, I see this 'spiritual' point of view (anti-thesis) as a response to the 'materialist' point of view taught to me by my mother (thesis). I am still searching for some synthesis that recognizes our spiritual nature, but does not bypass the importance of engagement with society as a noble response to alleviate the suffering that still exists on this material plane. I like the way William Ernest Henley takes responsibility for his own fate in his poem *Invictus*:

> [...] *I thank whatever gods may be*
> *For my unconquerable soul.*
> [...] *Under the bludgeonings of chance*
> *My head is bloody, but unbowed.*

> [...] *It matters not how strait the gate,*
> *How charged with punishments the scroll,*
> *I am the master of my fate,*
> *I am the captain of my soul.*[10]

Travelling on

In March of 1973, I was plunged into this spiritual point of view at the ashram of Neem Karoli Baba in Vrindavan, India. Before I describe in the next chapter what happened at Neem Karoli Baba's ashram, I want to take this chapter to tell how I made the choice to go to India. I also want to describe some of my adventures through six Asian countries along the overland route that I took from Istanbul, through Pakistan and to the Indian city of Amritsar, which is 15 miles (25 km) past the border between Pakistan and India.

I was motivated to go to India by reading a book by Ram Dass (formerly Richard Alpert) called *Be Here Now*.[11] I read this book at a commune in Ann Arbor in Michigan, where in good 1960s style (in 1971) there was a sweat lodge in the backyard, people were doing yoga in the front room, and the freezer always had a good supply of LSD, in large white sugar cubes, for whatever guests might appear that day—and they always did appear.

The record player (yes, this was before CDs and way before the Internet) would often be playing music—someone's favorite song was Neil Young's *Heart of Gold*:

I want to live I want to give
I've been a miner for a heart of gold
[. . .] And I'm getting old
Keeps me searching for a heart of gold
[. . .] And I've crossed the ocean for a heart of gold [12]

When I heard the last line, the thought came to me that I would be willing to cross the ocean for 'a heart of gold'.

In March of 1972, someone had come to the commune and brought us a crisp and newly printed copy of the first edition of *Be Here Now*–the pages still made a loud crackling sound at the opening of a new page. I remember several of us trying to read it at the same time and I had to fold pages to keep my place in the book. The day I finished the book, the thought appeared in my mind:

I want to go to India to meet Neem Karoli Baba. Yes, even if Neem Karoli Baba is far away, I would be willing to cross an ocean to find a heart of gold.

And almost to the day one year later, I was at his ashram in Vrindavan, India.

What follows now is a story about what I saw along the overland route to India in 1973. It is obvious (to my thinking) that any such story is selecting a very few moments from myriads–billions, trillions, quadrillions, or even more than quintillions–of actual moments. The fact that all during my travels in the Muslim world from Istanbul to Lahore, I never saw a woman driving a car or working in a store has been left out–except that I am revealing it now.

Every story is highly selective, and I realize that I have selected these moments with a filter. So, what is the filter? My perspective is twofold. Firstly, I am looking at the moment when I discovered that my philosophical materialism was at best a too narrow lens through which to view reality. Secondly, just for my enjoyment (and, I hope, yours too) I want to tell a story that is both true and good. Modern journalism often focuses on 'bad news', while on this journey I learned much, which at least for me is 'good news'.

Overland to India
Searching for a heart of gold

My adventure began in London where a friend gave me a place to stay for a few months. I had been introduced to hatha yoga during my stay in Ann Arbor—and I wanted to prepare for the trip by becoming a vegetarian and doing everything that I thought might be generally accepted as yogic or sattvic. Every day I did my asanas and tried to increase my life force through practising pranayama—the systematic controlling and altering of my breathing. According to my yoga book, *pranayama* would raise my *kundalini* and give me a taste of 'cosmic consciousness'. As I thought about yoga then, I wanted to molt 'my' existing snakeskin—to leave the old separate and selfish 'me' and wake up to whatever might be the non-dual and cosmic experience of a new 'self'.

On the Winter Solstice of 1972, I was at the London train station with a ticket for the Orient Express. This meant I would travel in one train cabin or coach the whole way from Paris to Istanbul. Looking out the window on the Orient Express, I remember it snowing as I passed through Belgrade and reflecting on how peaceful and unified Yugoslavia seemed under the leadership of Josip Broz Tito, the stern-faced President-for-Life.

Turkey—a realization

As the train left Bulgaria and entered Turkey, I realized that unlike my African trip where I was traveling to see new things, my interest was now in learning to see myself in a new way.

I spent the Christmas of 1972 at the Youth Hostel in Istanbul—not far from the famous Blue Mosque. I bought exotic fruits that I had never even known existed, let alone tasted—and shared them on Christmas day in a spontaneous happening of a Christmas dinner with Europeans, Americans, and (always) Australians.

The day after Christmas, I headed south to Cappadocia in the heartland of Turkey, to see the underground city of Kaymakli. In the centuries before the Common Era, the ancient Phrygians had built underground dwellings which Christians later extended to create a multi-levelled city of refuge with elaborate ventilation shafts. I was told that there were around 100 tunnels in this city and many of the tunnels contained storage areas—so during times of persecution twenty thousand people, with food and livestock, could live for years without showing their faces above ground.

The Ruins of Palmyra

I entered Syria by bus and spent a relaxing day at the desert ruins of Palmyra.

I had heard that Fatah had just been forcefully evicted from Jordan by King Hussein, the ruler of that country. Fatah, the main faction of the Palestinian Liberation Organization, had been launching attacks on Israel from within Jordanian-controlled territory and King Hussein now wanted peace with Israel. The result was that the recently expelled Palestinian fighters were pouring into Syria. Being near the Jordanian war zone, this meant that there were few tourists—so I had the ruins (almost) to myself.

I was particularly attracted to the temple of the Mesopotamian god Bel, or *Baal*. The temple was more than 2,000 years old and at various stages in its history had been a Christian Church and then a Mosque. Come the end of August in 2015, this temple was belligerently and explosively rubbed out by ISIS (ISIL) with 30 tons of TNT— leaving only rub-BEL (or is it rub-BAAL?)

Am I a Beatle or a Beetle?

My next stop was Damascus, where I stayed in the Youth Hostel. I was surprised that on my first day there that youths in the street would point at me, shouting: "Chomfous!" As none of the shouters spoke English, I had no idea why I might be a labeled a *'chomfous'*. That night I told the Arab youth who ran the Youth Hostel what I had been called, and he laughingly told me that *'chomfous'* was the Arab word for beetle, and because my hair was unusually long, I had been identified as one of the *The Beatles*. Now I was in on the joke and as I met new people, I would point at myself and say "*Chomfous*". My joke got universal laughter—such was the power of the 'mop-topped' Beatles.

A Sufi Resting Place

On my second day in Damascus I went to the tomb of Ibn 'Arabi (1165-1240 CE)[13]—who was called *Muhyiddin* (Revivifier of Religion) and the *Shaykh al Akbar* (The Greatest Shaykh). At the tomb there were women dressed in black who were wailing and weeping and I wondered why they were crying for someone who had died more than seven centuries ago? To find out, I opened the paperback book of his writings that I had bought in London—the bookstore had a shelf labeled *Mystics of Islam*. I learned that Ibn 'Arabi believed that there can be a perfect human being who is a true expression of divinity, and as examples, he gave Mohammed and Jesus (Ibn 'Arabi had lived the first 35 years of his life in Spain among Christians). To Ibn 'Arabi, humans are engaged in a return to God in a dynamic relationship to the Divine; each is seeking out the other. Ibn 'Arabi's name for this perfect human is an *Isthmus*, because he or she has become a narrow link between the realms of the earthly and the divine.

Opening a dictionary, I found out that an isthmus was the neck of land (*isthmus* is the Greek word for neck) between two large expanses of water. The two most famous geographical *isthmi* are in what are now called the territories of Suez and Panama. On learning this, it dawned on me that where there once stood *isthmi*, there were now canals—it took over seven centuries after Ibn 'Arabi wrote about *isthmi* for both Suez and then Panama to become canals. Seeing that the Panama Canal connects two oceans, I realized that although it was indeed noble to be an isthmus, humans like to make canals where there were once *isthmi*. Looking inside myself, I saw that the canal that I wanted to help construct would join two ways of being–the questing and dynamism in the thought of the West to the tranquility and surrender in the thought of the East.

An Encounter with Fatah

The Fatah headquarters was not far from the youth hostel where I was staying in Damascus and I asked a Nigerian traveler named Mobo–he told me that his name meant 'Freedom'–who was staying at the youth hostel if he wanted to go there with me. He said he was willing. I saw it as an adventure and a way to temporarily align with my mother's pro-Communist anti-Zionist ideology. We stood at the doorway of the Fatah headquarters together and after ringing the doorbell, we were greeted warmly by a Fatah commander in uniform who invited us both inside his building. Once we were all seated, he asked in excellent English why we were there. I took about 10 minutes to tell him about my mother's progressive agenda and that I was sympathetic to struggles against imperialism. I emphasized how I had been a protester against the war in Vietnam (which was still ongoing then). To my surprise, he invited both of us to see the camp where he was training soldiers to prepare for the 'armed struggle' against Israel. Being committed to solving problems through non-violence, I realized that I was in way over my head. I did not want to go to a military training camp where there might be real guns.

So rather than say no, I asked a question to this commander of Fatah–after emphasizing again that I was a progressive who sympathized with his cause, I told him that I was wondering if it would affect his invitation in any way that I happened to be born 'Jewish'. Immediately his face took on an expression that was first shock and then he became highly agitated. I told him that the Fatah literature that I had read had said that they were not 'anti-Jewish' but only 'anti-Zionist'—but this did not lessen his increasing malevolence and I got that our polite dialogue had come to a precipitous and calamitous conclusion. Mobo was tugging hard on my shirt-sleeve and demanding that we leave. When we got outside the building, Mobo said that he could not believe his ears when I told the Fatah commander that I was Jewish; he thought that if we had not left, we both could have been murdered. As there was no mistaking the raw malice in his stare, I could see that Mobo had made a good point. This made me wonder: *Do I have a death wish?*

Lying to get a Visa in Iraq

From Damascus, the next capital was to be Baghdad—when I went to the Iraqi Embassy, I was asked to fill out a questionnaire to get my visa that asked in big letters at the top of the application: *What is your religion?* I remembered that my father had been asked the same question in Berlin by his Nazi professor and I thought that it might be better not to tell the Iraqi government about my Jewish faith—so I consciously told a lie for the first and only time in my travels—I wrote as the answer to the question of what is my religion: *Christian.* I thought it funny that a Muslim government had forced me—for at least a moment—to become a nominal supporter of the Jewish cause named *Jews for Jesus.*

Visiting a Synagogue in Baghdad

I made another mistake in Baghdad in going to visit a synagogue. A lady in the Tourist Information building gave me a map and, in response to my inquiry, matter-of-factly showed me the location of the biggest synagogue in Baghdad. After I went there and politely introduced myself as an American Jew, I found that the two elderly men with whom I spoke were both terrified to be in my presence. I later learned that in 1969 Jews (and others) had been publicly hanged in the main square of Baghdad for being members of an American-Israeli-Zionist spy ring–half a million people had attended a festival organized by the government where the highlight of the spectacle was the hanging of nine Jews. Since I told these elderly Jews that I came from America, they could not know whether or not they were possibly being set up for another death sentence. Here I was, from the very country that according to the Iraqi government had originated the alleged spy ring. I realized that I had again been reckless and asked myself for the second time in a few days: *Do I have a death wish?*

Brave . . . or something else?

In inquiring of myself why I had been reckless in two successive capital cities–Damascus and now Baghdad–two faces appeared before me.

The first face was Jerry Rubin, the most famous Yippie, who had proclaimed to the world that he was a 'Groucho Marxist'. As a proponent of Symbolic Politics that presented an alternative to the Establishment, Jerry was both colorful and charismatic. When I met him at the national convention of the *Students for a Democratic Society* (SDS) in Clearlake Iowa during the summer of 1966, he was six years my elder (I was only 20), and I respected him for his dramatic flourish and his apparent courage. When I had asked him to give me some personal advice on how to lead my life, he looked at me gravely and said these five words:

"Never trust anyone over 30."

He gave me another stare as if he really meant for me to take this advice. I had let this directive sink in and I had lived by them for the seven years since I had met Jerry. I now realized that I had just endangered my life and possibly the lives of others, and for the first time I let myself wonder whether Jerry's advice was not only foolish, but at least the way I had interpreted it, quite life-threatening. I perceived that the part of me that accepted his teaching was trying to die before I ever became 30 years old—and my dying words would be:

"At least I have ended my life still being trustworthy!"

And realizing that I was not ready to die, a second face suddenly appeared in my field of vision.

This second visage was of an elderly Socrates in 400 BCE—he was now 70 years old—and in my mind Socrates asked me these questions (as he had asked the Greek philosopher Xenophon):

What is prudence?
What is madness?
What is courage?
What is cowardice?

(Xenophon's *Memorabilia* I.1.16)[14]

In my Humanities class at Amherst College, I had read how Socrates had once directed these questions to Xenophon. After now doing this Socratic inquiry, I saw myself as lacking in prudence and having more than a little madness. I had been reckless in not politely refusing the invitation to visit the Fatah training camp and also in not saying 'No' to myself before visiting a synagogue where the Jews were being unjustly executed by their government. In both cases, I had endangered the lives of others. In a moment of clarity, I saw this was not courage but really cowardice—I had fooled myself into believing that my mere bravado was actual bravery. I also saw that I was so reckless because I was too cowardly—or possibly too ignorant—to ask myself this question: *What do I really want?*

The Lone and Level Sands of Babylon

To boost my morale after such a stern self-correction, I decided that

I should travel a little over an hour by bus to visit one of the Seven Wonders of the ancient world: *The Hanging Gardens of Babylon*. These were a set of tiered overhanging terraces constructed of baked mud bricks with so many planted trees that it resembled a green mountain. *The Hanging Gardens* existed in the midst of a desert thanks to an elaborate system of irrigation channels from the nearby Euphrates River. Right next to *The Hanging Gardens* was the royal palace of Nebuchadnezzar the Second and it was as his guest that Alexander the Great died at the age of 32 (in 323 BCE). At that time Alexander was on his return journey from what is today called India and he had never lost a battle due to his bravery in being in the very front of his own troops as he led them into every battle. I realized that in my own journey east, I would be following the same path that Alexander the Great had followed around 2,300 years earlier.

Although there was a small museum at the site where the gardens had once stood, there was nothing visible of either any palace or any greenery—where once there had been a mountain of gardens, there was only a great expanse as far as the eye could see of "lone and level sands". Contemplating the passing of worldly power, I thought of the poem, *Ozymandias*[15] written by Percy Bysshe Shelley:

> *I met a traveller from an antique land,*
> *Who said—*
> *"Two vast and trunkless legs of stone*
> *Stand in the desert . . . Near them, on the sand,*
> *Half sunk a shattered visage lies, whose frown,*
> *And wrinkled lip, and sneer of cold command,*
> *Tell that its sculptor well those passions read*
> *Which yet survive, stamped on these lifeless things,*
> *The hand that mocked them, and the heart that fed;*
> *And on the pedestal, these words appear:*

My name is Ozymandias, King of Kings;
Look on my Works, ye Mighty, and despair!"

Nothing beside remains. Round the decay
Of that colossal Wreck, boundless and bare
The lone and level sands stretch far away.

I am Just East of Eden

On the bus to Basra in the south of Iraq, I passed a sign with an arrow pointing to the right that read in bold letters:

GARDEN OF EDEN–6 *kms*

I realized I was in the marshland where the Tigris River was meeting the Euphrates River in the heart of Mesopotamia–which is the Greek word for the meeting of the rivers. In the Bible it says about the Garden of Eden:

> *Now the Lord God had planted a garden in the east, in Eden;*
> *and there he put the man he had formed . . . A river watering*
> *the garden flowed from Eden; from there it was separated into*
> *four headwaters . . .*
> *The name of the third river is the Tigris . . . And the fourth*
> *river is the Euphrates.*
>
> Genesis 2.8-2.14

I knew that these two rivers had met here for thousands of years to create what came to be known as 'the cradle of civilization'.

Why 'the cradle of civilization'? Because it was here around 3,400 BCE that there were the origins of humankind's first written languages. Prosperous agricultural communities formed a fertile crescent of city-states that stretched all the way from the meeting of these two rivers in the Persian Gulf to what today are the Mediterranean nations of Egypt, Israel, and Lebanon.

There are many Garden of Eden myths, and I go along with the interpretation of the early Christians who called themselves Gnostics. *Gnosis* is the Greek word for a knowledge that is intuitive rather than mental. The Gnostics called the serpent in the Garden of Eden ' Sophia' (the Greek word for wisdom) and concluded that the serpent was the one with the true wisdom. To them, God was an arrogant tyrant who threatened to punish Adam and Eve for wanting to become self-aware by eating from the tree that would give them knowledge of good and evil. The Gnostics believed that it was only because Eve was willing to disobey a tyrannical God that humans now have the potential to be free.

When did the Garden of Eden exist? According to religious fundamentalists who deny Darwin's theory of evolution, the serpent was in the Garden of Eden in 4004 BCE. I thought it might be worth getting off the bus to see how the Garden of Eden had fared in a mere 6000 years. However, the bus driver said that there was no transport of any kind down the dirt road to the Garden of Eden and that the bus from Baghdad to Basra only ran once a day. I was still considering what for me would be an easy six kilometer hike—I was young and healthy, I had a sleeping bag and it was still warm in the desert even at nightfall. I asked myself: *If for just one night I make the effort to sleep under the stars in the Garden of Eden, might it not be possible that I could reclaim the innocence that Adam and Eve had lost in this very place?* But when the bus driver told me that he had once been to the Garden of Eden and all he saw was a grove of date palms, that made up my mind not to go. I realized that the Garden of Eden must have gone through just one change too many since Adam and Eve had left—and I stayed on the bus. Even if there might be some truth in the Bible story that the Garden of Eden was humankind's original home, I resigned myself to this sad reality: *You can't go home again.*

Iran

I had travelled through the south of Iraq and crossed the border into Iran. The Iranian border guard while looking at my American passport told me that just minutes ago the news had flashed on his TV screen: "The 36th President of the USA is dead. Today Lyndon Baines Johnson (LBJ) had a massive heart attack . . ." As he was speaking, I thought of how his presidency had met with defeat in the jungles of Southeast Asia. Although LBJ had helped the poor through his War on Poverty and had done much to advance racial equality through pushing through a Voting Rights Act, such significant domestic progress had become eclipsed by his foolish decision to escalate the war in Vietnam.

Leaving the Customs Station, I saw huge fires eerily shooting up into the sky. I understood that the Iranians were burning off all the natural gas that was coming up from the ground while they were pumping out the crude oil. Such a burning of natural gas would be considered highly wasteful in more advanced technological countries and I assumed that the Iranians just lit these fires because they did not have the capital to invest in equipment that would utilize their own natural gas. The fires burned all day and all night with the 100-foot flames shooting up into the air every 100 yards or so for at least the next 100 miles on the road to Shiraz.

Sufi tombs and a Sufi Story

Once in Shiraz, I saw the mausoleum of a Sufi named Musharrif al-Dīn ibn Muṣlih al-Dīn—better known to the world by his pen-name Sa'di (1213-1291 CE). Persian scholars call him 'The Master'. Much of his wisdom was written around his tomb in both Farsi and English. I remember this quotation:

> *The rose and the thorn—*
> *just like sorrow and joy—*
> *are forever linked.*[16]

And from Sa'di's tomb, it was just a hop, skip, and an easy jump –actually it was less than one mile–to another tomb. This was dedicated to Hafez (or Hafiz, 1315-1390 CE). I had read that Hafez is Iran's most celebrated bard–the Persians give him an elevated status comparable to Shakespeare in the West. Unlike Sa'di's tomb which had very few visitors, Hafez's tomb seemed like a festival–there were throngs of people praying, meditating, and some reading his poetry. There were quotations from Hafez throughout the garden:[17]

Fear is the cheapest room in the house.
I would like to see you living in better conditions.

❀ ❀ ❀

Even after all this time the sun never says to the Earth:
"You owe me."
Look what happens with a love like that–
It lights the whole sky.

❀ ❀ ❀

One day the sun admitted, I am just a shadow.
I wish I could show you the Infinite Incandescence which has
cast my brilliant image.

❀ ❀ ❀

I wish I could show you, when you are lonely or in the darkness,
the Astonishing Light of your own Being.

❀ ❀ ❀

When all your wishes are distilled, you will find only two
desires: to love more and to be happy.
And then you will realize that they are the same desire.

❀ ❀ ❀

When I am dead, open up my grave and see the clouds of smoke
that will arise to surround you– in my dead heart, the fire still
burns for thee.

❀ ❀ ❀

Zero is where the real fun starts.
Everywhere else, there is too much counting.

At the tomb I met an Iranian man who told me his version of this
tale about Hafez:

Tamerlane–who ruled all of the Middle East–(he is some-
times called Timur, meaning "iron")–had a tax collector who
informed him that a certain poet named Hafez had not paid his
taxes. Tamerlane summoned Hafez to his court in Samarkand
and once Hafez dutifully appeared before him, Tamerlane told
him that he was not that concerned about his tax payment, but
was quite upset by what he had just read in the first edition of
Hafez's book of poems and pointed to these lines of poetry:

Beautiful dancing girl of Shiraz,
If you would only take my heart in your hand–
I would give all of Samarkand and Bukhārā
For that black mole on your cheek.

Tamerlane had just put a huge effort into beautifying
Samarkand (his capital) and Bukhārā (his finest city), and he
saw insolence in valuing the two jewels of his empire as worth
less than an insignificant mole on the cheek of a dancing girl.
He told Hafez:

I have conquered the greater part of the world to beautify
Samarkand and Bukhārā, and you, oh pitiful wise man,
would exchange these two cities for a mere black mole on the
cheek of a dancing girl.

Hafez responded: You indeed have created great wonders, but
your meanness may have given you your wealth and power. I

have generosity of spirit, but it has reduced me to my present state of poverty wherein I cannot pay my taxes nor even afford to buy a black mole on a dancing girl. I am in your power. Your meanness is obviously more effective than my generosity.

What Hafez is doing here is trying to cleverly side-step the issue of whether or not he is willing to barter away all the splendors of the material world (symbolized here by the "two jewels" of Tamerlane's empire) for the heart of his Beloved (symbolized here by the "black mole" on the Beloved's cheek). Although he tells Tamerlane that Tamerlane's wealth has given him the greater power, Hafez's poetry says the opposite—that what Hafez *really* valued is a wealth that is not outwardly-discernible, but inwardly-discerned through *love*—and that this love in his *heart* was a pyre upon which all that was transient and time-bound would be immolated.

In any case, the way the story goes is that Tamerlane laughed at Hafez's answer and exclaimed: Rāstī Rustī (ﯼﺗﺳﺍﺭ ﯼﺗﺳﺍﺭ) *meaning, "Honest, indeed honest" and excused him from pay-ing his taxes and also gave him enough gifts so he could afford to buy "a black mole on the cheek of a dancing girl".*

After Shiraz, I wandered among the ruins of Persepolis and just a little bit further were the elaborate mosaics covering the mosques of Isfahan. Then in Tehran, I saw that Nishapur was directly on the main route to India. In Nishapur, there were the tombs of two mystic poets: Omar Khayyam (1048–1131CE) and Attar (1145–1221CE). I had bought English translations of their works at that same London bookstore and in my backpack I carried *The Rubaiyat of Omar Khayyam* and the *Conference of the Birds* by Attar.

I love the Edward Fitzgerald translation of the *Rubaiyat of Omar Khayyam*. Two verses from his famous translation have kept appearing in my life at the oddest moments:

The Moving Finger writes; and, having writ,
Moves on: nor all thy Piety nor Wit
Shall lure it back to cancel half a Line,
Nor all thy Tears wash out a Word of it.

A Book of Verses underneath the Bough,
A Jug of Wine, A Loaf of Bread–and Thou
Beside me singing in the Wilderness–
Oh, Wilderness were Paradise enow! [18]

The second verse is open to various interpretations, particularly about the meaning of the word 'Thou'. While some say 'Thou' refers to the divine in the wilderness of his own Being, others argue that this 'Thou' may refer to a romantic affection. After learning that Omar Khayyam was a rebel against all orthodoxy, I prefer the second more romantic guess.

In Iran, I also read an illustrated edition of the *Conference of the Birds*[19]—and was quite stunned by its modernity and its relevance to my own spiritual path. I understood this story of birds trying to find enlightenment in different valleys both as a profound parable and a mystic allegory. What the 30 birds that do survive the 'seven valleys' discover at the end of their journey is that the divine wisdom that they were seeking externally actually lies within and can only be found internally.

Passing through the Nishpuri bus station on the way to Masshad, I realized that I had had enough of tombs and the thought came to me: *I would get off the bus to meet either Omar Khayyam or Attar in person, but both have been dead for over 750 years–they will not feel hurt if I do not visit their tombs–it is my time to visit Jack Fate–he may not know that I am coming, but he does have the virtue of not yet being entombed.* I was anxious about meeting Jack Fate, but I saw that the mission that I had come to complete could no longer be postponed. In order to explain to you, the reader, the nature of my mission, I need to go back to a foggy London morning two months earlier when I was getting ready for my journey to the East.

Visiting a Prisoner of the War Against Drugs

On this cold and foggy London morning, the thought came to me that I wanted to do a good deed while passing through the Middle East. I knew that some of the countries that I was going to be passing through had failed miserably in providing their citizens with their human rights and the thought came to me that it would be a good deed to visit a political prisoner. So that morning I went to the world headquarters of Amnesty International in central London. The receptionist near the front door appeared flustered and did not know what to do with me when I told her about my intention—so she called a superior, who invited me upstairs into his office.

After explaining my intention to this English official—"I want to visit a political prisoner while traveling overland to India"—he surprised me by pulling out a big file and saying that he had just the right man for me. His name was Jack Fate (not his real name) and he was a 27-year old American (his real age was indeed the same as my real age) who had been imprisoned three years ago in Mashhad, Iran—he had been caught by the customs agents at Iran's border with Afghanistan transporting 45 kilos of hashish hidden in a metallic false bottom constructed below his Volkswagen bus. Amnesty International had a report from an Iranian supporter of their organization, who had attended the one-day trial where Jack Fate had been sentenced to 30 years in prison. In an ominous tone, I was told that the prison where Jack Fate was staying served no food to the prisoners—the families of the convicted prisoners were expected to provide their family members with food. The Amnesty official said that every few months he had personally sent inquiries out to Iran asking about Jack's welfare, but that he had never received any response. He went on: "I also personally wrote to Jack Fate's family in Los Angeles, and they were courteous enough to write back to me explaining that they wanted to have absolutely nothing to do with a drug trafficker." He wrote down the address of the prison on the outskirts of Mashhad and told me that he would appreciate it if I did some investigating and sent him back a report. After handing me his business card, he said: "Good luck on your travels" and then he looked down at his desk and I got the cue that our meeting was over.

Now I was staying in a hotel in Mashhad and I was told the next day was a religious holiday called Ashura (the tenth day of Muharram, an important and holy time for followers of Islam) and there was to be a parade down the main street to mourn the martyrdom in 680 CE of Imam Hussein ibn Ali, the grandson of Prophet Mohammad, may peace be upon him. I was told that Hussein was a devout Muslim who had been killed by an evil tyrant. Shi'a Muslims believe that mourning for Hussein is a source of salvation in the afterlife and is to be undertaken in remembrance of his suffering. This is expressed in the common saying: *A single tear shed for Hussein washes away a hundred sins.* I noticed that the date of Ashura on this year of 1973 was on Valentine's Day; it falls on a different date in the Gregorian (Western) calendar every year, as the calculation is made on a lunar calendar. When I arrived at the parade, I saw this gathering was different from anything I had ever seen. There were no women, only a long procession of men with bare torsos. Each one was carrying his own metal chain and all were flagellating and chanting in Arabic. Some of them were whipping themselves while others were beating the man in front of them. All had red bruises on their backs, and some had more than a little bit of blood. I stood out among the crowd in my Western dress and although I was doing nothing but observing, several of the participants did not like me being there—if I had had a camera I think I might have been attacked—and besides more than a few dirty looks, two of the flagellators left their ordered line of men rhythmically painfully lacerating themselves to try to grab me.

As these two men tried to grab me, I disappeared quickly into the crowd and neither was willing to do what they would have had to do to catch me: they would have had to let go of their heavy metal chains.

The next morning I went to the bus station and discovered that there were two buses a day going to the prison where Jack Fate was held and two buses a day returning on the same route—the prison was out in the desert, nine miles from Masshad. I decided to take the trip early the next morning. I showed the bus driver the name of the prison in English written by the gentleman at Amnesty International and he gave me a look of surprise. An hour later, after most of the people had gotten off the bus, he stopped way out in the middle of the desert where there was no bus stop. At first glance, I thought he must have made a mistake as all I could see was the paved road that the bus was travelling on going endlessly through a no-where's land. I thought of the Robert Frost poem called *Stopping by Woods on a Snowy Evening:*

> *My little horse must think it queer*
> *To stop without a farmhouse near*
> *[. . .] He gives his harness bells a shake*
> *To ask if there is some mistake.*[20]

The bus driver saw my quizzical look and pointed out a lone building looming out of the desert far in the distance and indicated by a gesture that this was the place on my piece of paper.

After a long walk in the hot sun, I was at the front door of this prison. There were no guards anywhere to be seen—so I just used the knocker that was on the front door.

Eventually a tiny window opened—all I saw were two eyes—and I explained that I was there to see Jack Fate. I repeated "JACK FATE" louder each time. The door shut without the man saying a word–and I just waited there for five minutes. Then the window opened and there was a different voice that spoke English–again I could see only his two eyes–and the voice said: "There is indeed a Jack Fate here, but you cannot be admitted to the prison without the signature of the Attorney General of Mashhad." Through the eyehole he handed me a paper with the Attorney General's name and address in Roman letters.

That evening I showed that paper to the man at my hotel desk, who said that the Attorney General was one of the most powerful men in the city of Mashhad–he was known to be a personal friend of the Shah, the ruler of Iran at that time. The next morning, I was at a big government building that housed the Office of the Attorney General. To my surprise, the Attorney General was an affable, easy-going middle-aged man. I soon learned he was a graduate of the University of Minnesota and he clearly welcomed the opportunity to speak English. I told him about my life, my travels, and how moved I was by the wisdom of the Sufi poets. After over an hour had gone by, a puzzled look lit up his face. I fell silent and then he asked, "By the way, why are you here?"

I told him how I had visited Amnesty International in London and continued: "I have the name of Jack Fate . . ." At the mention of that name, he interrupted me and said, "Ah yes, Jack Fate. He seemed to be a fine boy. I was the one who was his prosecutor during his trial and I spent a day with him in court–you know, he did have 45 kilos of hashish in his Volkswagen bus."

After a pause, I responded: "The man at Amnesty International said that the prison to which he has been sent does not feed the prisoners . . ."

Again, I was interrupted: "Of course, that is our custom–in Iran, the families of prisoners are the ones to feed the prisoners– that gets the families involved in the redemption of the prisoner–it is because we want to bring them back into society."

And I said: "In the case of Jack Fate, his parents have repudiated him because they look down on him as a drug trafficker—they have refused to send him any money or even to communicate with him."

He exclaimed: "An excellent point! Now that you mention it, you have asked me a good question: 'How is Jack Fate being fed?' I do not know how he is fed but he must be alive—the prison sends me a report every time a prisoner dies. Would you be willing to investigate for me? I would appreciate it if you found out how Jack Fate is doing."

And with that request, he rang a bell on his desk and a young woman in modern Western dress appeared. He spoke with her for a moment in Farsi. After she left he gave me a lecture: "The Shah wants to stop the flow of drugs through Iran—and he asked me personally to try to stop this flow as my city is right near the border between Iran and Afghanistan. Iran is in the center of the biggest drug thoroughfare in the entire world—it stretches from our east and goes right through us into Europe and onward toward your country America. The Shah believes that only harsh sentences will send a signal, a message—yes, a very *strong* warning—to the drug traffickers of the world not to even think of bringing any drugs through our country."

I remained silent and in a moment the young woman appeared bearing a form with five copies—the Attorney General signed the top one with a heavy press of his pen, tore the bottom two off for himself, and handed me the three top identical forms—each in Farsi and with no English. Standing up as he handed the forms to me, he added his business card which was written in both Farsi and English. He said: "This is my address. These forms are a ticket to see Jack Fate. I am interested in what you find. I do wish you good luck in your travels." And with those words, he nodded his head and I got the cue that it was time for me to leave. As we shook hands, we exchanged glances of mutual respect. I noticed that I was really grateful for how honest he had been.

The next morning at the same time, I was knocking at the door of the prison. Again the same little window opened, and this time without saying a word, I stuffed the triplicate forms through the iron bars. Once again, I waited for five minutes, but this time I heard the sound of a bolt being thrust out of a socket, a lock turning, and then the loud creak of groaning metal as the door opened. A well-dressed man in a Western suit with a tie stood before me and said in an impeccable but accented English: "Jack Fate is now waiting for you—you have exactly one hour."

I was ushered into a small white room and there was Jack Fate. He looked at me nervously behind the glass partition that separated us. Before either of us talked, I felt the fear emanating from him—he seemed to be like an animal trapped in a cage who had gotten thoroughly exhausted throwing himself against the bars.

Talking through the middle of the round hole in the glass partition, I told him that I was an American who had gotten his name from Amnesty International and I was on a mission to talk to him and then send them a report. I assured him that I was a mere traveler and had no connection to any agency or any government, and I was curious to hear his story. I asked: "How are you doing?" He told me that he was doing "terribly"—and that he just wanted one thing: "I just want to find a way out of here."

He went on: "I thought that I could get a better life if I had more money. I went to a metal shop in New Delhi and had the workers build an extra metallic compartment beneath my Volkswagen bus. After I carefully wrapped 45 kilos of hashish into Indian newspapers, I put the packages into my newly created compartment, and drove through Pakistan and Afghanistan, but then an Iranian custom's official struck the bottom of my bus with a metal rod and I still remember the slightly hollow sound—and then the customs officials carefully examined the bottom of the bus and indicated to me with a hand gesture pointing where there was a slight bulge. As he pointed, I felt total terror and my whole body began trembling. . ."

After a few minutes pause, I brought up a new topic: "I heard that the prisoners here are not fed. . . ?"

He replied: "Yes, that is true, I am the only one here who does not get food from his family—there are only men in this prison. I have to do tasks like sweeping the floor and other menial tasks for the guards and some of the other prisoners—and then they give me some of their food."

I asked: "Does anyone ever ask for sexual favors?" and he answered, "No, that has never happened."

Again, I brought up a different topic: "Is there any redeeming aspect of your life in prison?"

He paused for a long moment and then answered hesitantly, "Actually, there is. Every morning all the prisoners and all the guards have a daily ritual—we smoke hashish together to begin our day. This is often the only moment of the day when I can forget where I am. The most surprising moment since I arrived here is that on one morning for the daily ritual I saw that the hashish that was brought out by the guards was wrapped in the same Indian newspaper that I had used to enclose the hashish I tried to smuggle from New Delhi—and I realized that here in this prison I was smoking my own hashish."

After that revelation, there was again a few moments of silence. As for myself, I was letting in the ironies of the way Jack Fate had been caught in the middle of an astounding amount of hypocrisy concerning man's quest to get high through the use of substances.

I did make one attempt to give him a gift that failed miserably. I had just finished reading Idries Shah's book, *The Way of the Sufi,* and I wanted to give the book to Jack. I showed Jack the book and told him that the Sufis were Muslims who had been confronted with great hardships—and that they had found a way to go *inward* when "the shit hit the fan". I could see his attention dwindling and I got that all he really wanted was "to find a way out of here"—and that he had zero interest in going *inward*.

To break the tension, I asked if there were any English books in the prison library and he looked at me as if I were crazy, saying silently with the look in his eyes: *You still do NOT get where I am, do you, Mr. Isenberg?*

He then politely told me: "There is no library in this prison." As the Idries Shah book was the only one I had brought with me, I stuffed the paperback book through the open hole—into Jack's reluctant hands which said to me, without using spoken words: *I am starving—so I will take even this tiny morsel of a gift.*

I thought about giving him some of the Iranian money that I had on my person, but I decided against it as I guessed that it might bring him more problems than solutions. It was not obvious to me what he might get in return for any money that I might give him or how it might benefit him. What was certain is that there was not a canteen at this prison at which he could go to buy provisions. He was clearly in hell and I asked myself if anyone, in this world or the next, can ever succeed in making a successful bargain (or is it a deal?) with the devil?

He seemed to want to speak English—so for the rest of our hour, I asked him questions such as what it was like for him to have grown up in a suburb of Los Angeles and where he had actually traveled in India and from where he had procured as many as 45 kilos of hashish to hide in his van. When the hour was nearly up, he told me I was his first visitor in the three years that he had been there and he asked me to write to his parents. I handed him a pen and paper through the little glass hole and he handed me back an address of a mother and a father in an Orange County city that was part of greater Los Angeles.

While I was looking at the address he had written, I heard a knock and a moment later the door opened and the same well-dressed Iranian man was standing there. I took one last look at Jack and then made a hand gesture that said: *Sorry I cannot help you more.* He looked at me grimly and neither of us said another word.

After I left the building–the metal door made the same loud creaking noise as it closed and I heard the sound of a lock turning and the bolt being put back in its socket–I realized that the prison officials had kept all three copies of the triplicate form that I had brought. And this strange thought came to me: *I won't take even one souvenir home from this experience!*

What I said to myself about a souvenir was a lame attempt to tell a joke to myself.

In truth, I did not want a souvenir. I was grateful to have been the witness to someone talking honestly about what it was like to be in hell. The main feeling with which I had while leaving the prison was one of being grateful for the great privilege of being able to have the prison door shut behind me–with me on the outside, rather than on the inside. I knew it was a case of 'there but for the grace of God go I'–meaning that some day I could be inside some sort of prison. I saw this fear as being the source of my lame attempt to joke with myself–I was distancing myself from my own helplessness when confronted by another human being's lack of control over his own fate–as if a souvenir would guarantee me some future happiness.

I spent the next day in the main library of Mashhad writing three almost identical letters–one to Amnesty International, the next to the Attorney General of Mashhad, and then the last to Jack's parents–I had in front of me business cards from Amnesty International and the Mashhad Attorney General along with the piece of paper in Jack's hand-writing. After addressing the three envelopes, I wrote a letter to each telling them that Jack was doing menial work in the prison and had food to eat, but he was not doing well and he would greatly benefit from having more visitors. *I told none of them that Jack's prison guards were allowing him to smoke his own hashish.*

When two months earlier, I had visited the office of Amnesty International, I had been disappointed to be given the name of a drug trafficker rather than what I had requested–a political prisoner. Nevertheless I had just accepted that the name given to me was ordained: that I would do my 'good deed' for a drug trafficker. After spending that hour with Jack Fate, I was surprised to find myself thinking of him as a political prisoner or, more exactly, a prisoner of war in a worldwide war against drugs. As long as we have societies that stigmatize the use of drugs that are used recreationally to get high or spiritually to expand consciousness, drug dealers will make immense profits. The few who are caught are indeed at the mercy of our political systems punishing the human desire to experience alternative states of consciousness.

Through the years, I did my best to follow up on what happened to Jack Fate. After Ayatollah Khomeini came to power in 1979 (6 years after I was in Iran), I read in a magazine that one of the first acts of the newly formed Islamic Republic of Iran was to re-sentence anyone who was in prison for drug trafficking and give them an automatic death penalty. According to the Ayatollah Khomeini, who viewed Western culture as a toxic influence upon his people, these executions were an attempt to purify the populace by killing decadent individuals. The Ayatollah wanted a theocratic rule of jurists who followed the teachings of Mohammed and, in his interpretation of Sharia law, this meant that drug traffickers had no human rights—in fact, they had no right to be alive. According to this article, there were many newly dug mass graves filled with drug-traffickers next to each of Iran's prisons. As I read a little bit further, the article reported that the day before these mass executions, the Ayatollah had released all foreigners sentenced for drug trafficking and given each a free plane ticket to their own home country. Although I never discovered what happened to Jack Fate, I assume that after serving nine years of his 30 year sentence, he was flown back to America.

A Surprise at the Afghan border

At the border between Iran and Afghanistan, a surprise waited for me. As I was going through customs, the customs official brought out three different types of hashish. He explained that they were each of a different quality and came from different parts of Afghanistan. At first, I thought this might be a set-up for a bust—just a few minutes before I had been at the Iranian border where the customs officials were searching people coming from the east for drugs (I was not searched since I was coming from the west)—and here the customs official was trying to make an extra buck by selling hashish. I saw the other customs officials were looking on and as they could see what he was doing, it made the whole scene seem like business as usual. I decided that if I did not buy his product then and there, I would never have the experience of purchasing hashish from a customs official. I bought the most expensive hashish, which was still very cheap and leaving the border, I was already getting high just from anticipation and its overpowering smell.

Stoned—courtesy of a customs officer

In Herat, I did not want to share a chillum with the other Westerners in my hotel as I heard that was a way to get hepatitis, particularly since I knew (coming from a family of doctors) that anyone who had ever gotten hepatitis was at their very most infectious in the period *before* they came down with the main sign of jaundice, the telltale yellowing of the eyes. I had seen Westerners putting a handkerchief over the part of the pipe that they smoked as they passed the pipe around a circle and from what I could see, as the handkerchief was never changed, this meant that the spit was transferred from one person to another. I went to the marketplace with a newly-made friend who I met at my hotel and bought a little pipe and during my first night in Afghanistan, I got stoned for the first time in the many months since I had left the commune in Ann Arbor. I realized that I had forgotten how much fun it was to get stoned and I thought of this title from a Bob Dylan song: *Everybody*

Must Get Stoned! As I am writing this memoir many decades later, all I can remember is the face of my companion—I have forgotten his name—but I do remember the name of the town in which I was staying in Afghanistan: Herat. But under the influence of the substance, Herat changed to its anagram of 'HEART'. I saw within my full name—ELLIOTT ISENBERG—there were the letters both for 'rebelling' and a 'rebellion'. And then without any warning, six letters jumped out of that same full name—Elliott Isenberg—to spell 'LISTEN' and then the same six letters re-arranged themselves to say 'SILENT' and then before I knew it, I received this command (as more letters kept popping out of my name): 'ELI, BE SILENT'. I then paused, thought for a moment, took another puff of the hash, and I realized that my higher self might be giving me some good advice: 'ELI, BE SILENT—LISTEN!!!' I thought that possibly I might be having a non-linear holistic experience. The hashish that I bought from the customs official lived up to my highest expectations.

The Buddha Statues of Bamiyan

My biggest disappointment in Afghanistan was not being able to go to Bamiyan to see the two tallest standing Buddhas in the world. I had heard about these two 6th-century statues of Gautama Buddha carved into the limestone of a cliff only 140 miles (230 kms) from where I was staying in Kabul. The two main Buddhas were respectively 174 feet and 115 feet high (53 and 35 meters). According to the famous Chinese monk and traveler Xuanzang who saw the Buddhas when they were first created, each statue was originally completely covered with gold leaf and precious jewels. When I arrived at the bus station, I was informed that as heavy snow had fallen the previous night on the mountain passes to Bamiyan, all the buses to Bamiyan had been cancelled. I was told that I could make a round-trip excursion on a plane that went to the little airport near Bamiyan for $250, but considering that

I only had $1500 to my name at that moment, that seemed like too big a chunk of my fortune. I thought: *Maybe I will come back some day.*

But before I could come back to Bamiyan, the Taliban (in March of 2001) dynamited and destroyed both statues. Where the tallest Buddha in the world once stood, there is now only a void. Although emptiness—sometimes called *sunyata*—is an object of veneration in Buddhism, I still consider the spiritual work is to see the emptiness in the fullness—rather than to destroy what we do not understand. The reason that the Taliban say that they dynamited these statues is that according to their strict interpretation of Sharia law, it is forbidden not only to enjoy music or television or to play sports, but to even look upon an idolatrous statue. The final proclamation to destroy the statues was made by the official in the Taliban government who was designated as *The Minister for the Propagation of Virtue and the Prevention of Vice.* I can empathize that if I had such a heavy responsibility, I might want to order the use of dynamite to live up to such a lofty title.

A startling but wise comment

The week that the statues at Bamiyan were destroyed, I was in the company of a teacher named Adyashanti who had had an awakening in the Zen Buddhist tradition. In the question and answer period, I brought up the destruction of these monuments expecting him to feel the outrage that I was feeling. Instead, he said that when he heard of these statues being destroyed, the thought had come to him: *It's about time!* Hearing him say that was like a Zen slap in the face which immediately brought to mind the Buddha's teaching on *impermanence.* I was shocked that he was not mourning the passing of these beautiful Buddhist statutes—and that punch line has stayed with me as a reminder that "this too shall pass".

Approaching India through Pakistan

I flowed onward toward India through the famous Khyber Pass and then the three cities in the northern route of Pakistan ending up in Lahore, the last stop in the predominantly Muslim state with Hindu India looming in the distance. A few miles from Lahore was the border crossing from Pakistan to India, and as I approached the crossing on foot, I saw crowds of people. I was told that the border was closed–not indefinitely, but no one knew definitively when it might open again. I spoke to a Pakistani border guard and he told me that the border had been closed "intermittently" ever since the war between India and Pakistan in December of 1971. In that war, Pakistan lost the eastern part of their country which became the new state of Bangladesh.

I spent that night in a sleeping bag near a 10ft-high metal fence topped with barbed wire that separated the two countries–I was told that there were no sleeping accommodations anywhere near the border. When I woke up, I saw around 50 people gathered on each side of the fence waiting to get across the border. Through the metal openings in the fence, I had a good chance to compare all the travelers going over the border–I saw that everyone who was at this border crossing was Caucasian–there was not a Pakistani or an Indian nor even one Asian face. Then I noticed a striking difference between the travelers going *to* India and those coming *from* India. Those going to India looked like somewhat normal Euro-American travelers with back-packs–wearing blues, grays, and blacks–surely a little scraggly and scruffy, but essentially on the verge of being respectable.

The travelers coming from India had an exotic look–the men wore white dhotis and the women yellow, red, and purple saris–no backpacks, only colorful bags strapped over their shoulders–and both the men's and women's eyes had a spacey glazed far-away look. They may just been hungry or tired, but what I projected upon them was a quest described in the lyrics from a song I had just heard Don Quixote sing in the 1965 musical **Man of La Mancha**:

> *"I'll always dream the impossible dream,*
> *And reach for the unreachable star."*

A question of life after death

A stream of thoughts came to me: *This country India that I am about to enter is beyond unusual—look what is has done to these people—as someone with a Masters Degree in sociology from the London School of Economics, I want to ask everyone I meet in India a question—what will that question be?—*and then this question popped into my mind:

> *What do you believe will happen to you at the moment after your death?*

Once I formulated the question, I realized that I was genuinely curious about how people might answer. Still mulling over my question, I suddenly heard a man's voice over a loudspeaker with a Pakistani-English accent: "Please line up at the gate—the border is now open".

That night I arrived at the Golden Temple in Amritsar—the largest and most holy Sikh Temple in the world—and I was given (free) accommodation on a concrete floor inside the grounds of the temple. For the first time in my life, I both took *darsan* and was given *prasad*. As "Westerners" were still not that common in the East, I attracted attention and I soon found myself being grilled in a way that I was in no other country. One Sikh man in a turban asked me: "What is your country?" "How old are you?" "What is your profession?" "Are you married?" "Do you have children?"

I answered that I was an American who was 27 years old and that I was a traveler and that I was never married and had no children. These (to my questioner) were clearly unacceptable answers. He said: "You mean you are a tourist" and I answered that I had already been on the road without a home for over three years. I riposted by asking him rhetorically: "Does not a tourist have a home?" My questioner's biggest upset was that he could not understand how I could be content with my situation of being 27 years old and not be seeking a wife. I responded: "I have had serial monogamy with women—but none of the relationships that I have had up to this moment have worked out" and as he shook his head showing his continuing lack of comprehension, I told him: "Look, we clearly come from different cultures, you have asked me so many questions—so let me in return ask you just one question" and then I asked my new question for the first time:

"What do you believe will happen to you at the moment after your death?"

My questioner quickly made the transition from interrogator to interrogated and answered: "Unfortunately, I will not be able to experience *moksha* as I do not have enough good *karma* to avoid another birth. We Sikhs call such liberation *mukti*, but it is quite similar to the Hindu concept of *moksha*. When I am born again, I do feel fortunate that I have done enough good deeds to be born as a human again—I really don't want to come back as a rat or a pig. What I really want is to leave *samsara*."

During the next eight months in India and Nepal, I asked over 100 people this same question and I was surprised that every time all I got was variants of this original answer. Sometimes people would describe this world as *samsara*—a wheel of birth and death—and they told me that liberation from this wheel, *moksha*, would require more good deeds and then yoga and meditation. In my eight months in the Indian sub-continent, I did not interview one person who wanted to be born again—and yet each in their own way was resigned to their eventual rebirth or reincarnation.

I want to conclude this chapter with a scene related to my singleton question that happened in New York City the same year as I had been traveling in India. When I flew back from India in December of 1973 to temporarily live with my parents, this was my first extended stay in New York City since before I went away to college—which was more than 11 years earlier. I had arrived from India just before the holiday season and so I decided to increase the size of a friend's holiday party (with his permission) by inviting all the friends who I could find who had graduated from Forest Hills High School (FHHS) with me back in 1962. Many of these high school friends I had not seen since the day of our high school graduation. I called up 20 people whose telephone numbers I could still find, and all were interested in my travels, and many said they could make it to the party that was scheduled for the Saturday night between Christmas and New Years Day. From my preliminary telephone conversations, I found out that all my high school friends had finished college and graduate education and they were all working long hours at the early stages of their professional careers—lawyer, doctor, administrator, teacher—and several who I never ever suspected were gay had since come out of their proverbial closet.

Even though I was living with my parents in Queens, the party was at my friend's house in Manhattan. As it snowed the day of the party, I wore my winter clothes—and underneath I had the loosely-fitting white drawstring pants and the equally loose white cotton shirt that I had been wearing the day I flew back to NYC from New Delhi. To be playful, I wanted to show off my Indian identity at the party—not only was I the only one wearing Indian clothes, but when the host served a delicious gooey Fettuccine Alfredo covered in butter and cheese, I was the only one to eat the Fettuccine Alfredo with a hand—I still remember the startled look of my friends who could not verbally express what they were feeling, but their eyes said:

Is this really *happening?*

I non-defensively explained: "It has been over a year since I have eaten with utensils—in India, I just got used to eating with my hands. Notice it is my right hand—no one in India ever eats with their left hand. And I can actually feel the Fettuccine Alfredo with my fingers—eating this Fettuccine Alfredo (a creamy pasta dish) with my hand does help me to enjoy both its taste and its gooeyness."

After I washed my right hand, my friends forgave me for my social impropriety, and I asked them all to gather round into a circle to ask them a single question.

I was going to ask every single person at the party the same question that I asked all those who I had interviewed in India. This was a much more homogenous sample than in India, where those I had interviewed were predominantly Hindu, but there were quite a few Buddhists, and also three Jains, two Muslims, and even one Zoroastrian. Here in my NYC sample, everyone at the party was in my graduating class at Forest Hills High School or the partner of a friend in that graduating class. Because when I graduated from high school, each ethnic group tended to live in their own area and my neighborhood was predominantly Jewish, all of my interviewee subjects were born from parents who were of the Jewish faith.

So (again) the question was:

> *What do you believe will happen to you at the moment after your death?*

Before I tell you their answer, I wonder if you want to guess—I will give you two hints:

All of them gave a very different answer from my interviewee subjects in India—and all said a variant of the same answer.

Have you guessed what my NYC Jewish friends answered?

What they said each in their turn was a variant of this answer:

At the moment of my death, I will be annihilated forever and ever and I am pissed off about this coming annihilation. I could see that each was making a good living, enjoying their lovers, eating out at different gourmet restaurants, excited about the NYC theater and opera, and they were regretful and angry that they could not go on enjoying their good life forever.

The only similarity between my Indian and NYC informants was that all were unhappy with what would happen at the moment after their death—the Indians because they had to be born again and my NYC friends because their good times would eventually be coming to an end.

Before concluding, I want to give an update on how these answers might be changing over time. In my 40 years as a therapist in San Francisco, I had many Indian clients who were working in the tech industry and eventually I asked each of them this same singleton question. All these young techies answered like my NYC friends did in 1973—they saw their parents' belief in rebirth or reincarnation as a superstition and each was angry that they would eventually have to face annihilation.

And many of my NYC friends—those who are still alive—are now dabbling in metaphysics and several are no longer quite so certain as they were over five decades ago that annihilation is what they will face at the moment after their death.

Too bad I could not interview my high school friends who were present that day and have already gone over to the other side or—to use a phrase I first heard in India—'left their body'. These friends could have given me a definitive answer and conclusively have answered my question to tell me whether or not they had been annihilated at the moment of their death. I would be surprised if they told me that they had experienced an annihilation, since I lean toward the Tibetan Buddhist belief that we go through *bardos* (transitional states) after our death and our karma creates and influences our new birth. However, I do not go along with my

Indian friends in their belief that this life must always be a vale of tears and suffering.

Even though the daily news paints a picture of a world where "a hard rain's a-gonna fall"—and storms, both literal and metaphorical, are sure to rage for millennia—I believe the ultimate outcome of our species' evolution remains unknown. If we are to bring about more favorable conditions for our species, our collective wisdom must first recognize the futility of revenge and retribution. We need to embrace the necessity of nonviolent responses to oppression. Is this not the time to outgrow the mindset that "vengeance is mine"? The old belief in "an eye for an eye, a tooth for a tooth" will leave us all blind and toothless.

Evolutionary scientists agree that of all the human species that ever existed, only one—*homo sapiens*—has survived. This species, our species, still a very young species, emerged within the last 300,000 years. The term *sapiens* comes from the Latin word for discernment and is often translated as 'wise'. Yet, to truly earn this designation, we must spend the next half-million years allowing the kindness in our hearts to rule over the fears in our minds. If humanity is ever to release the stranglehold of fear from our collective consciousness, one way is to encourage people to practice mindfulness and meditation.

In my own life, I've found that lessening my own suffering has been helped by a deepening commitment to virtues like kindness, patience, generosity, and self-discipline. Most important to me is to be earnest in practicing non-attachment—this means to me not getting attached to my preferences.

If embraced globally, such a virtuous approach could address many of the world's problems. Imagine, for instance, in the Middle East, where centuries of conflict might find resolution through a shared embrace of spiritual intelligence. Perhaps then, the people of the holy land might all chant in one voice:

From the head to the heart,
Palestinians and Israelis can be smart.

Do you remember at the very beginning of this chapter there was this proverb:

Great minds think alike–
Fools seldom differ.

Do you agree with my worldview? If so, we may both have great minds–but, alas, it is also possible that we are merely fellow fools. Whether you agree with me or not, I know for myself I always have another *think* coming.

4

A restless heart seeks a moment of rest . . .

My desire to be a hero was transmuted into a search for what I thought of as enlightenment in Neem Karoli Baba's ashram in India. Before spending time with this *mahasiddha*, I was easily distracted and quite attracted to any bright shiny object that might appear in the realm of the senses. My time with Neem Karoli Baba was the turning point in my life. I began to regularly ponder this question: "If enlightenment can really happen to me, what can I do to pursue this wake up call?"

> *"You have made us and drawn us to yourself,*
> *and our heart is restless until it rests in you."*
>
> *Augustine of Hippo,* Confessions[21]

Meeting Neem Karoli Baba: the moment before . . .

THE TAJ MAHAL UNDER A FULL MOON! Princess Mumtaz' tomb seemed to shine with its own light and never again would I see such a sign of one man's devotion to his consort. It was almost too much for my senses to drink in and when I walked away I could find no words for what I had seen.

Speech found me again as I met a young Canadian named Jerry Toon in my Agra hotel. To this day, I remain grateful to Jerry. Our chance meeting led me to visit Neem Karoli Baba in his ashram—a fortunate occurrence which led to insights and unfoldings, both subtle and mind-blowing. I did not know then that if my life was like a see-saw where my intentions moved from the worldly to the spiritual, this was the moment where the weight was equal on both sides of the fulcrum.

When I asked Jerry about himself, he was quite forthcoming:

"I am really high right now, and it is not on substances. Have you heard of the book called *Be Here Now*? I just spent yesterday with a guru named Neem Karoli Baba whom Ram Dass described in that book. I know the book said that you will be turned away if you try to see him, but he is actually quite accessible in an ashram only 50 miles (80 km) away in a town called Vrindavan. Vrindavan is the town where the young *Avatar* Krishna played with the milkmaids (*gopis*) and there are now thousands of temples dedicated to Krishna. Vrindavan is a walking town—there are almost no cars—only a few motorcycles and mostly rickshaws and bicycles."

He did not need any prompting to draw a map showing where the Neem Karoli Baba ashram was located, close to the Jamuna River. Westerners could stay in a building, a *dharmsala*, at no cost for food or lodging. Neem Karoli Baba lived with a few Indian devotees and a Greek woman named Draupadi. Jerry told me that Draupadi was beautiful and exotic, and no one knew why she was the only Westerner who was allowed to stay in Neem Karoli Baba's quarters.

Jerry told me: "I believe that Neem Karoli Baba is a pure expression of *Hanuman*, possibly a re-incarnation—Hanuman is the monkey who is the ardent devotee of *Rama* in the Ramayana. Let me call Neem Karoli Baba by the name those of us who were living at the ashram called him—'Maharaji'—which is Hindi for 'great king'. Every day I was living at the ashram I would hear a story of how Maharaji had served another person or I would see such service directly. One time I was frustrated as Neem Karoli Baba was speaking only in Hindi while talking to an Indian man (as that day there was no translator), but I could see the Indian man relax, become more focused, and then wobble his head as he said: 'Accha, Accha, Accha'. Although I did not understand anything that had been said, I could see that there was a transmission of love."

I asked Jerry Toon about Draupadi and he responded: "No one knows why Draupadi is the only Westerner allowed to live with Neem Karoli Baba. None of the Indians will say anything about whatever may go on in that part of the ashram. Draupadi is the most silent Westerner at the ashram; in fact, no one who I knew at the ashram ever heard her speak. Some people say that just like Neem Karoli Baba is a re-incarnation of Hanuman that Draupadi is a re-incarnation of the famous Draupadi in the *Mahabharata*." I knew nothing of this book called the *Mahabharata*—so Jerry told me the story of the Bronze Age princess, Draupadi, and how her honor was saved by a miraculous sari that had no end. I have included this story in the endnotes for those of you who may not know it.[22]

When Jerry Toon finished telling this story, I was more curious than ever to meet both Neem Karoli Baba and the mysterious Draupadi.

Pass over mindfully

I put off my visit to Vrindavan for a day to do what I had already planned: visit Fatehpur Sikri. This Ghost City was created by Mughal Emperor Akbar, the grandfather of the Shah Jahan who built the Taj Mahal. At these 'ruins', I was most impressed by the Buland Darwaza—translated as 'The Gate of Magnificence'—which was not in any way 'ruined'. Its red sandstone was quite a contrast to the white marble of the Taj Mahal. This gate is still the highest archway in the world, the equivalent of a 15-story building. Inside the bridge of the archway was a white marble plaque with a saying inscribed in Persian script that was attributed to the first man of Christendom—Jesus, son of Mary. I will never forget what was written there:

> *Isa son of Mary said:*
> *The world is a bridge that endures but an hour—*
> *do pass over mindfully,*
> *but know there is no spot here*
> *for you to build your resting place.*

Vrindavan Ashram

The next morning I was off to Vrindavan. I quickly found the ashram, thanks to Jerry's map even though there was no address or name on the door.

Dungarees!

To understand what happened next, I must say a word about how my clothing changed while I was in India. When I left India six months after that day when I first entered Neem Karoli Baba's ashram, I was wearing a white loose-fitting shirt with matching drawstring pants. On this day of my arrival at the ashram, I was still wearing the main piece of clothing with which I had left my commune in Ann Arbor: a denim bib and brace overall. Known as *dungarees*, this particular blue work outfit had two adjustable straps that went over the shoulders where two metal fasteners met with two buttons. To make an interpretation of my appearance on that first day, I looked like a hick with a beard.

At the gateway to the ashram, I was met by two Americans each with white loose-fitting shirts with matching white drawstring pants, and each had a turmeric-colored dot on his forehead. One said: "There is no longer room at this ashram". And the other said: "If you want to see Neem Karoli Baba, you can rent a room in town and come for *darshan* tomorrow morning." At that very moment, an Indian woman in her early thirties came to the gate and asked all three of us: "What is happening here?" Before either man had a chance to say anything, I said: "They are saying there is no longer room at this ashram." She gave them both *a look*, gestured to me, and said: "Come with me". She guided me to a big room with no beds, but plenty of floor space, with only a few inhabitants. I learned that the number of people (Westerners) staying had gone from a dozen or so to about thirty during the past month and new arrivals kept coming—probably because *Be Here Now* had become a bestseller. A few of the original dozen had taken it upon themselves to keep these new people out—as they competed for the guru's attention in what I learned was facetiously called 'The Grace Race'.

Marvin

It was a strange feeling to come to this place where I wanted to immerse myself in 'spirituality' and to find—yet again—my friendly nemesis, Marvin Ratner. Marvin challenged me on levels that perhaps I was least keen to address in my spiritual search—non-judgmental compassion being one of them.

I had met Marvin for the first time in a Tehran hotel, then we met again in Herat, again in Kandahar, again in Kabul and once again in Rawalpindi—which I thought was our last 'chance' meeting. Now, here he was in 'my' room.

Marvin suffered from Tourette syndrome: he made loud grunting sounds which drew furtive stares from, for instance, fellow diners when we were eating out. He suffered from nystagmus too: his eyes moved involuntarily from side to side in a rapid, swinging motion. This meant I could never look him straight in the eyes, making it difficult to engage. These two conditions were congenital neurological conditions, over which Marvin had no control, and I reproached myself for my distaste.

But it was the third aspect of Marvin's behavior that really bugged me—Marvin was an 'over-hugger'. He loved to hug and he would always hold his hug more than a moment longer than was either comfortable or appropriate for the 'huggee'—I would see the unfortunate huggee wondering what he or she had gotten into and how they could get out of it without being rude. Marvin never hurt anyone and would always stop the hug when asked—it was just his neediness that affected me. What irks us in others is often something that lives unacknowledged in our own psyche—but I did not think of that at the time.

Marvin had just taken LSD the day before our latest meeting and had "a really good trip". It seemed both the Tourette syndrome and the nystagmus had become less severe and for the first time, he did not try to hug me. He told me that he had been there a week and it was like a resort but without any beds or maid service. Once a day all the Westerners sat on the verandah, big leaves were put in front of them, and then people came by with buckets of mild vegetable curries and put the food on each leaf with a stainless-steel ladle. Each day there was a carbohydrate accompanying the curry, some days there would be rice and on other days chapatis (flatbreads).

I asked Marvin if there were any teachings, and he told me a joke that he had heard at the ashram—the joke was that what was practiced at this ashram was a 'five-limbed yoga':

1) eating
2) sleeping
3) drinking chai
4) gossiping
5) walking about

Marvin said that as far as he could see, there were no formally scheduled teachings and each person was just hanging out, although some people on their own were learning to chant the 40 verses of the *Hanuman Chalisa*, some were learning Sanskrit, and some were doing their daily practice of hatha yoga *asanas* or *chi kung*. As for myself, I decided that nothing was something worth doing.

Neem Karoli Baba (Maharaji): a first encounter

On my first morning, I waited in a group of mostly Western spiritual seekers and devotees—fewer than 50 people. When Neem Karoli Baba arrived, the crowd parted and he made his way to a raised wooden plank platform where he sat in the half lotus position with his bare feet sticking out from big plaid blanket. From now on I will refer to him as Maharaji, as this was how he was addressed. He looked at the group in front of him, and said a few sentences in Hindi and then he looked directly at me and said in a heavily accented English: "What is your name?" I answered: "Elliott". And then he said: "From where do you come?" I answered: "America". He looked at me and said something in Hindi. As soon as I possibly could, I cornered an Indian devotee and asked him for a translation. The Indian man said: "He said that he could see that you are a 'nice, kind, and good person'". My first thought was: *I never wanted to be 'nice', but I do want to be 'kind' and 'good'.* I realized I could not be sure what Maharaji said in Hindi and whether the word 'nice' meant to him what I meant by 'nice'. I did take it as validating that he had seen that I had come to my spiritual path without ulterior motives, and I was gifted with both earnestness and sincerity.

Darshan lasted for about a half hour. Except for the translation that I had asked for after Maharaji spoke to me directly, I could not understand even one word of what was being said.

Two formidable ladies

Being a bit frustrated at not being able to follow the dialogue, I started looking around for Draupadi and sure enough, I found a woman who looked like a Grecian statue standing nobly and quietly in the background. I asked one of the Westerners who had been there for a while: "Is that Draupadi?" And he nodded that it was. She had a dignity and a beauty, though she seemed silent and lost (or found) in an inward space. She did not seem the least bit interested in relating to the people there. All her attention was on Maharaji.

At this first *darshan*, someone pointed to an Indian woman in her late 30s and told me that this woman was named 'City Ma'. I noticed that every part of her clothing was impeccably white and she did not have even a smudge on her sari. I thought maybe she was so clean because she lived in the city and maybe there was another person at the ashram named 'Country Ma' who because of her farming had dirt on her sari. Later I learned that this Ma was a *siddha* in her spiritual attainment and perfection, and that she had no relationship to any 'city'. I eventually learned that *siddhi* might refer to psychic powers, but this word might equally refer to many spiritual attainments. When I asked around to learn if Siddhi Ma had any super-normal powers, each of the several people I asked said that as far as they knew, the word 'siddhi' in her case did not refer to powers, but only spoke to her level of spiritual realization. I must take full responsibility for my mis-innerstanding of the name of Siddhi Ma. Siddhi Ma was indeed a true 'siddha'—yes, a master in the art of loving—and I mistook her for being a mere woman of the 'city'. I got how I was projecting my own level of ignorance onto a happening that was indeed sacred and holy.

The Etymology of Takhat

Besides *siddhi*, I learned another new word that first *darshan*. Someone referred to the wooden plank platform upon which Maharaji sat as a *takhat*. After I inquired, an Indian devotee told me that the word came from the Arabic word *takht*, meaning 'throne'—and by extension, it had come to be used in modern Hindi for any raised platform associated with authority.

Neem Karoli Baba (Maharaji): the second encounter

Maharaji's sleeping quarters were the setting for the next *darshan*. We were all sitting beside the *murti* (the statue of Hanuman) when to my surprise an Indian devotee opened a gate that led into Maharaji's private quarters and told us to enter. There was Maharaji sitting on a porch in front of his room with his eyes closed and continually touching each of his four fingers in his left hand with the thumb of his left hand and then doing the same with his right hand—all the while whispering quietly. There was more space here than near the *murti*, so we created a big circle around him and watched him for 10 minutes in silence. Then Maharaji opened his eyes, gave each of us a look, and without speaking a word gave a signal to an Indian devotee that we were to be shepherded out of his living quarters. But before we were ushered out, many of the devotees began 'taking the dust of his feet' which were sticking out from his blanket. I kissed his feet too—that was the only time I ever touched Maharaji. I learned later that it was only Westerners who mistakenly kiss the feet of a guru—the usual custom is to touch the feet with one's forehead.

After we were back in our living quarters, I asked a long-time devotee what had just happened. He told me that while Maharaji was touching each of his fingers, he was whispering the name of Ram (God). My informant said that someone had once seen Maharaji's diary and it was just the name of Ram (in Sanskrit) repeated on each and every page.

My first few days at Vrindavan

Westerners lived in a hotel-like white building with several large rooms. I had found out from Jerry that this building was called a *dharmshala*—a resting place for pilgrims or spiritual seekers. Every afternoon at the ashram professional musicians would sing the *Hanuman Chalisa* (and sometimes other Indian chants) and we could hear their voices all day over the loud speakers. I spent my first days there practicing the 4th limb of the so-called 5-limbed yoga, meaning all I did was gossip. I found out about the lives of the other Westerners staying at the ashram, most of whom had been in India for quite a while; and I learned there were so many different spiritual paths, so many ways to do yoga, and so many different parts of India. There were, too, so many different stories about Maharaji, particularly about his *siddhis*, which in his case really did mean supernormal powers.

Neem Karoli Baba: some facts

There are few written records, but here is what I was told of his life-story: Maharaji (Maharaji is a combination of three syllables: *maha* meaning great, *raj* meaning king, and *ji* which is a universal term of respect in Hindi) was born around 1900. He married in his early teens, but soon left home to wander India as a sadhu or holy man. After 10 or more years, his father located him and persuaded him to return to their home village. Maharaji became a householder and the father of three children. He left home again in 1958 to become a wandering sadhu, often living in the caves of northern India, and only settling for weeks in ashrams like the ones in Vrindavan or Kainchi Dham as they were being built by his devotees.

Siddhis, Mahasiddhas, and a miraculous train ride

In 1958, the 'miracle' occurred that gave Maharaji his name. Because he did not have a train ticket, the conductor stopped the train where there was no station near the village of Neeb Karori (a few hours from Vrindavan). But after kicking the *sadhu* off the train, the conductor found that the train would no longer start. Eventually the conductor figured out that it would be a smart move to allow the *sadhu* back onto the train. Maharaji agreed to board the train on the condition that the conductor would request that the railway company would build a train station where he was thrown off the train and also ask conductors to not demand tickets from *sadhus*. The conductor agreed to make both of these requests to his superiors and Maharaji boarded the train saying:

> *I do nothing.*
> *God does everything.*
> *Is it up to me to start a train?*

The train did start after he boarded. And that is how he got his name: *neeb* meaning 'foundation' and *karori* meaning 'strong and firm'—and Maharaji was to be 'a strong and firm foundation' for many of his devotees. Today there is not only a train station at Neeb Karori, but in that town there is also a Maharaji ashram.

Now I have to introduce a new word: *mahasiddha*. As mentioned before, *maha* is both the Sanskrit and Hindi word for 'great'. When the word is placed before *siddha*, it refers to a being who is by definition rare. Although there are many people who are *siddhas*, in all of India there were considered to be only around a dozen *mahasiddhas*. None of the *mahasiddhas* owned worldly possessions. Maharaji did keep a wool blanket wherever he went, but that was the extent of his baggage, whether at home or traveling. He changed his blanket every year and his 'inner circle' devotees vied for the honor of providing the new blanket. And Maharaji was unusual among those dozen *mahasiddhas* in that he would often leave the Himalayas and come to eat and sleep in the homes of his devotees on the plains of India. His inner core of devotees would keep a room in their homes for him so that they were prepared for his unexpected visits. Many rich people in India became his devotees and would even contribute to his temples or *dharmshalas* (like the one where I was staying). Even though he had an open invitation to visit palatial mansions, he preferred to make the rounds of the two ashrams that had then been built for him and make surprise appearances at the homes of a few inner core devotees. Having a visit from Maharaji—the 'great king' of India—would be like getting a visit in England from the Queen or possibly in America from Martin Luther King. Not an everyday event, and clearly memorable.

Until the late 1960s, Maharaji was not in the media or the public eye, but was known throughout India by those who kept themselves informed through their informal networks about India's own secret national treasures—the *mahasiddhas*. At this time, Maharaji was unknown in the West as he had never written a book and had no interest in any publicity, either Indian or foreign. Some of his disciples were in the government of India, some were the richest men and women of India, some were movie stars, but not one of them had any interest in telling the world about their guru. Maharaji's life changed dramatically in 1967 when Ram Dass became his disciple. The very first edition of Ram Dass' *Be Here Now* (published in 1971) had this paragraph about Maharaji's ashram:

Now in the temple, or around Maharaji, there were eight or nine people. Bhagwan Das and I were the only westerners. In fact, at no time that I was there did I see any other westerners. This is clearly not a western scene, and in fact, I was specifically told when returning to the United States that I was not to mention Maharaji's name or where he was, or anything. The few people that have slipped by this net and figured out from clues in my speech and their knowledge of India where he was and have gone to see him, were thrown out immediately . . . very summarily dismissed, which is very strange. All I can do is pass that information on to you. I think the message is that you don't need to go to anywhere else to find what you are seeking.[23]

When I first read this paragraph in Ann Arbor in 1972, I guessed that Ram Dass was telling a white lie to try to protect Maharaji from being overwhelmed by Westerners. Once it became clear to me after reading *Be Here Now* that indeed Maharaji was a true *mahasiddha* (with *siddhis*) who was alive and well and living in an ashram in India, I thought: *"How is it possible that Maharaji would not welcome a sincere seeker?"* However, Ram Dass' warning that Maharaji might not be available did have the good effect on me of slowing down my journey significantly; not knowing if I would really find Maharaji at the end made me attentive to savoring each moment and much less focused on getting to find him at the expense of experiencing the process of getting there. I wanted to begin my practice of "being here now" in the here and now.

In his 'specialness', I see Maharaji as having the same problem as Jesus Christ. Both transmitted love, but what most people wanted more than love was the spectacle of miracles. The motto of the Maharaji ashram was:

Had ye but either faith or love, ye would not need miracles.

In the Bible people also come to Jesus wanting a miracle and Jesus tells them:

Unless you people see signs and wonders,
You will never believe. —John 4:48 NIV

What Jesus wants is for people to surrender to the divine will even if there are no signs and wonders. *Not my will but thine be done* (Luke 22:42 NIV). Jesus' message is that real freedom is in cultivating a faith in the power of love that does not need signs and wonders. This problem of wanting miracles more than love occurs because miracles, one interpretation of *siddhis,* are a much greater spectacle than just plain ordinary human love. In fact, when they do arise, they are indeed spectacular. If you are an actual witness to a *siddhi,* such as the materialization of objects

out of thin air, watching someone being healed from a lifelong ailment, or even simply having your mind read, you may experience
your mind being blown.

As far as I could see, there were no dogmas or doctrines at the
ashram of Maharaji. The only directive was not a set of beliefs,
but a suggestion that the best place to hang out was in the heart
(rather than in the head). The idea was that the head could be a
terrible tyrant, but when the mental energies were channeled into
service, the head could become the servant of the heart. Maharaji's
motto was:

> *Love all*
> *Serve all*
> *Remember God*

And then he would sometimes add: "Feed people." When
Westerners had a private meeting with Maharaji and asked him for
advice, more than one Westerner was told that their minds were
too scattered and cluttered and that the best thing that they could
do for themselves is to quiet their mind by practicing a Buddhist
meditation practice known as *vipassana*.

To the small extent that there was a set of beliefs at the ashram, it could be best illustrated by this story from the *Ramayana*,
one of the most important Hindu scriptures. In this tale, Rama is
God—an incarnation of Vishnu—and when his wife, Sita, is stolen
away from him by a villainous *rakshasa* named Ravana, a monkey
named Hanuman comes to her rescue. In the Ramayana, after
hundreds of pages of heroic efforts and many a battle, Hanuman
finally succeeds in bringing Sita back to Rama. Once success is
assured, Rama asked Hanuman this question: " Who are you?" and
Hanuman responds with these words:

> "When I know who I am, I am not separate from you (God)—
> When I forget who I am, my only aim is to serve you."

And although I never directly witnessed a *siddhi* or a miracle, I heard story after story that seemed quite miraculous as I was practicing gossip, the 4th limb of the '5-limbed yoga'. I found the ashram gossip enjoyable and seemed to be filled with great tales. I was both intrigued and fascinated by these tales. To give one example, an Indian devotee told me that he was sitting with Neem Karoli Baba in one city, and then he called up a friend who was a fellow devotee in another city hundreds of miles away and both he and his friend were shocked to discover that at that very same moment Maharaji was in each of their rooms. I had a perverse thought on hearing the story of this 'miracle' that I did not share with my Indian informant: *Would it not be an even more impressive miracle if you had put Maharaji on your own telephone and your friend would have put Maharaji on his phone, and he could have had a telephone conversation with himself from two different cities?* Clearly, as a Western atheistic rationalist who believed in the laws of a materialistic science, I had to make a huge stretch to understand how such an event could conceivably or even might conceivably take place.

The British geneticist J.B.S. Haldane wrote (in 1927):

I have no doubt that in reality the future will be vastly more surprising than anything I can imagine. Now, my own suspicion is that the Universe is not only queerer than we suppose, but queerer than we can *suppose.*[24]

In this universe that is "queerer than we *can* suppose", many orthodox defenders of materialism theorize that there was indeed one moment where matter was materialized. The commonly accepted name for this moment is the Big Bang (although I prefer to call it 'the Big Stretch' as it seems to me the phrase the 'Big Bang' implies that there was some material that was there to explode). Before the Big Stretch, the *initial singularity* was one super force that combined the four fundamental forces of nature:

1) gravity
2) nuclear strong force
3) nuclear weak force
4) electromagnetic force

This singularity of seemingly infinite density contained as a potential all the mass and space-time of the universe. This means that the Big Bang was not an explosion *in* space, but rather the creation *of* space itself at speeds faster than the speed of light (and as time did not yet exist, why not?). To make a long story shorter: after its initial expansion, the universe cooled down sufficiently to allow the formation of matter in the form of particles and later simple atoms.

The reason for this digression is to point out that in the currently most widely accepted scientific hypothesis about the origin of the universe, there is an analogy to the *siddhi* in which there is a materialization of matter.

The interesting similarity between the moment of the Big Stretch (or if you must, do call it the Big Bang) and Maharaji's consciousness is that both existed in a world where there was no previous time. Ram Dass described Maharaji's consciousness as having no relationship to these thought-forms relating to the past: guilt, shame, regret, resentment, blame, or even a whiff of a complaint–he was solely in the 'power of the present moment'. Similarly, another scientific name for the Big Stretch (or Big Bang) is the 'day without a yesterday'.

These are the best two sentences that I could come up with to describe what I witnessed at the Maharaji ashram:

> Eternity appears to be playing with time.
> I got a glimpse of eternity breaking into time.

Over the years I have come to believe that Maharaji did have supernormal powers and that these powers came from being in a 'moment without a yesterday'. In his case, he also lived in a world where there was not a worry in the world because tomorrow never comes—what Ram Dass called *Being Here Now* or, if we switch the letters around, it can also (in equal truth) be called *Being NoWhere.*

Before I say anything more about the *siddhis,* I would like to mention one refrain that I heard over and over again as coming from Maharaji himself. Supposedly after many of his 'miracles', Maharaji would tell the one who witnessed it: "I am nobody. God did it!" and then at other times he often would tell people not to try to imitate him by cultivating such powers. The teaching was that these siddhis could just as easily be used foolishly or even malevolently. Several times I heard people repeat Maharaji's teaching that if there ever comes a moment where you are offered a *siddhi,* give your utmost energy and most intense concentration to refuse that power. I was told that in Maharaji's view, such powers were only gifts when they come unsought and you have no desire for them; Maharaji saw that the most common result of desiring and then eventually acquiring any siddhi would be insufferable ego inflation. What I understood is that a true devotee does not want to cultivate the desire for power and control that comes from unhealthy stimulation of the third (*manipura*) chakra; rather that devotee wants and embodies the capability to feel gratitude in all circumstances. A grateful flow is a gateway to the fourth chakra (*anahata*), where the devotee can realize the powers of love and compassion.

Patanjali's Teachings on the Siddhis

To begin to understand what I was hearing about *siddhis* day after day, I began reading the section in *The Yoga Sutras* of Patanjali where he discusses what he calls the eight supernormal powers. In Patanjali's view, these powers can arise from five different sources:

at the moment of birth, through meditation, through mantra, through austerities, or through taking mind-altering substances. Patanjali does not frame siddhis as supernatural in the Western sense, but as latent potentials of consciousness unlocked through intense yogic discipline. These are Patanjali's eight categories of *Ashta Siddhis* ('ashta' is Sanskrit for 8):

- **Aṇimā:** the power to reduce the size of one's body so that one can become "smaller than the smallest" (associated with invisibility)
- **Mahimā:** the power to expand the size of one's body so that one can become "larger than the largest" (associated with invincibility)
- **Garimā:** the power to increase one's weight by will to become "heavier than the heaviest" (so one becomes an object about who one can say in the terms of the olde Negro spiritual: 'We shall not be moved')
- **Laghimā:** the power to become "lighter than the lightest" (as is a feather) or to have no weight (associated with flying and levitation)
- **Prāpti:** the power to attain anything, including to know the thoughts of others or to move objects anywhere or to even be in more than one place at the same time (associated with telepathy, teleportation, clairvoyance, clairsentience, and claircognizance).
- **Prākāmya:** the power to obtain any goal or any object that is desired
- **Iṣiṭva:** the power to master the forces of nature: creation, preservation, destruction (associated with miraculous healings and even raising the dead)
- **Vaśitva:** the power to hypnotize, charm, and enchant celestials, humans, demons, animals, birds, reptiles, insects, and even trees (associated with the taming of

wild animals and also having the charisma to start a new religion)

When I read about the first two *siddhis*, I thought of the beginning of *Alice in Wonderland*. I knew that Alice became very small after she drinks from a bottle that says "DRINK ME" and then gets very big after she eats from a cake that says "EAT ME". She repeats the process and then she adjusts her 'dosages' one last time, so as to spend the rest of the tale quite small. Part of the appeal for the reader in learning how Alice changes her size so often might be the spiritual desire not to be limited by the laws of time and space. I also thought that Lewis Carroll might be prophetic in that many a modern *psychonaut* finds a psychedelic bottle that says "DRINK ME" and they drink and then they find a cannabis cake that says "EAT ME" and they eat –their motive may be to explore what they might experience outside the rules and ruts of their everyday life.

Three Possible Miracles?

I want now to tell you three stories of what happened while I was at the ashram that some might consider 'a miracle'. None of these three stories satisfy the inner critic in my mind because I do not know all the facts and each depends on knowing what was in some-one else's mind. The first two depend on the testimony of people I met at the ashram and the last one is my own experience, but I cannot know what was in the mind of Maharaji as he (seemingly) read my own mind.

To better understand what happened, it will be helpful to understand the physical geography of the Vrindavan ashram. There were essentially three main structures: the quarters where the Westerners would eat and sleep, the quarters where Neem Karoli Baba would eat and sleep, and in front of the entrance to where Maharaji ate and slept, there was a *murti* which was a big beautiful lifelike statue of Hanuman. This statue was the size of a human and he was created with such penetrating eyes that I was often sure that this statue was quite alive. Next to the Hanuman *murti*, there was the *takhat* where Maharaji sat and there was space for 50 people standing around him. During my two weeks there, Maharaji never came over to the Western sleeping quarters, but I saw him nine times near the *murti*, once being followed by 30 disciples going down the road in front of the ashram, and once as I have already mentioned inside his own sleeping quarters.

Miracle ONE?

The first of what I am calling 'miracles' happened after I had been at the ashram for three days. Even though Maharaji had appeared the morning after I arrived (when I had been asked the two questions), he did not appear for the next two days. Each of those two days after a group of around 30 of us waited near the *murti* for an hour or so, word came down from inside Maharaji's quarters that he would not be appearing that day. I got to know a friendly American guy named Scott and he told me that even though he had seen Maharaji several times before I had arrived, he was complaining that for the last two days he had waited without getting to see Maharaji. The story he told me was that on that very afternoon he was "pissed off" (as he phrased it), but as he was passing the building next door, who should he see sitting right next to the *murti* but Maharaji. Maharaji was behind a locked gate about 30 feet from him talking to two Indian devotees. The thought arose in Scott's mind before he remembered that his own mind was being read: *I don't think that Maharaji is really properly doing his duty as a guru. Why does Maharaji not show up for work each morning and even now he is putting a locked gate between us?* To Scott's terror, Maharaji looked at him directly for a very long time and then pulled his blanket around his body, nodded to his Indian devotees, and started slowly, slowly walking directly toward Scott. After Maharaji opened the gate (which was not locked), he took another step closer to Scott and moved his face closer and closer until they were eyeball to eyeball, with Maharaji holding his stare directly on Scott for a very long moment. *Not a word was spoken*. And then Maharaji turned around and slowly walked back. According to Scott, this blew his mind and he kept telling the story to everyone he met for the next week: "I see that the gate was only locked in my mind—the gate was never really locked. Yes, it was only locked in my mind—Maharaji's love was always there."

Miracle TWO?

The next 'miracle' happened during a morning *darshan* at the *murti* after I had been there for around 10 days and the group for *darshan* had been steadily growing—now there were around 50 people and an Indian *sadhu* was sitting right next to Maharaji. To put the story in context, I had asked if I could contribute some money as I was getting free room and board, but I was told that a Westerner had tried to put a large sum of money on the *takhat* and Maharaji had just given the money back to him. I gathered there were rich Indians who gave Maharaji money—I heard the hostel where I was sleeping was built as an offering by a rich Indian industrialist, but there was no donation box or any clear way a Westerner could make a contribution for his or her own upkeep.

This being the case, I was quite surprised when during *darshan* Maharaji focused in on an American 21-year-old woman who had just arrived at the ashram and asked her for money. I later learned that she had spent almost all her money ($240 or at the then exchange rate the equivalent of £100 sterling) to buy the ticket for the bus from London to New Delhi. There were no hotel costs on the journey because everyone slept in an old rickety bus that had moveable seats that could be stacked up each night. Visas were still free at the borders if you had an American passport. And she had come to the ashram with a crumpled up Rs100 rupee note at the bottom of one of her pockets—according to her, that was all the money that she had in the world. What I saw with my own eyes is that Maharaji zeroed in on her and after she told him her name and country, he repeated several times that she was now to give him "Ek sau Rupayeh!"–by that time, I knew enough Hindi to figure out these words meant Rs100 (one hundred rupees). After she heard his demand and saw his gesture that she was to give him something, she looked around like a terrified animal–she had not told anyone that she had a 100 rupee note–and I could see that she really did not want to give Maharaji the money. But everyone around her told her that she just had to obey the guru–so she took the crumpled-up note from deep within her front pocket and reluctantly handed it to one of the people near her who was most insistent that she had to give her money to "the guru". That person went up to the *takhat* and handed the still crumpled up note to Maharaji.

Maharaji then gave a teaching–the only word I understood was *Maya*–but he repeated that word three times with more emphasis each time: "Maya! Maya!! Maya!!!" As Maharaji did say a few sentences in Hindi after he repeated "Maya", I felt I had to find out what he said–so I imposed myself on an Indian man standing next to the *takhat* and said: "*What* did he just say?" I was told that Maharaji had just said that said: "All money is maya and that one always had the money that one needs." I knew that maya was the Sanskrit word for 'illusion' (with the possible secondary meaning of being 'only an appearance'). According to my informant, Maharaji continued (as he handed the American woman's Rs100 note to the *sadhu* sitting next to him) with these exact words: "When you need money it comes; when you do not need it, it goes." The *darshan* went on for another five minutes and then Maharaji left, along with almost all of the devotees.

I looked around for the American woman and I saw her with downcast eyes looking down at the ground, sniffling, and almost ready to burst into tears. Several of us went up to her and that is when I learned that just yesterday she had been dropped off from her cross-continental bus in New Delhi–and all she owned then besides a small backpack was a map to the Maharaji ashram and Rs100. She told the small group around her: "Now I have just lost my hundred rupees. I feel so far from home with not even one rupee." One of the devotees suggested that she could beg for money by asking everyone for a contribution. Her response was: "You mean it is all *right* to beg?" The devotee assured her that everyone had seen what had just happened and it was certainly all right now, but it would even be all right in the future whenever she might need money. When she came into my room an hour later, I saw each of us were giving her some money and I gave her Rs10—at the exchange rate of that time, that was worth a little more than $1, but in terms of prices in India then, Rs10 could buy six meals or around three nights in a hotel. When I bumped into her again that evening, I asked her how much she had collected in total and she said "162 rupees". And then she asked me a question: "I told no one that I only had 100 rupees–I had only arrived here a few minutes before I met Maharaji–how did he know that all I had was 100 rupees?" When I shook my head and did not even try to answer her question, she continued with a happy look: "All this morning I was thinking: 'What to do? I only have 100 rupees'. Do you think that he actually read my mind? Isn't that a miracle?"

Miracle THREE?

In the story that is now to follow, this last seeming 'miracle' does not speak well of my upbringing. One afternoon a few days before I left the Vrindavan ashram, I was walking by the building where Maharaji lived and I saw him sitting silently near the *murti,* surrounded by only half a dozen devotees–all foreigners. As the gate was wide open, I joined them for this quiet contemplation. I could see that Maharaji's eyes were closed and everyone was just being present in stillness. After a few minutes, I could see that the other Westerners were enjoying the silence more than I was–what

I wanted more than 'mere' silence was a teaching. Eventually Maharaji opened his eyes and one of the devotees asked Maharaji in English: "What words of English do you know?" Maharaji imitated himself by repeating the only two English phrases that I had ever heard him say: "What is your name?" and "From where do you come?" As he said these two phrases, the thought popped into my head: *"Huh! That is all he knows of English. I am actually more educated than him."* Suddenly he looked directly at me and pointing a finger directly at me said in a loud exclamation: "JAO!" (Hindi for "GO!"). I could feel my face turning a bright red and I slunk away.

Before the crimson of my blush had disappeared, I intuited that the thought that had gotten me busted had come from my Western conditioning about what it meant to be 'educated'. I perceived that I had (falsely) identified education with what the mind knows–while giving so little recognition to the (true) 'knowing' of the heart. And even in my limited concept of education, Maharaji actually knew more English than I knew Hindi–he clearly understood a complex question about what English words he knew before he had imitated himself saying the two phrases that were his standard inquiry when a new Westerner appeared.

All that happened to me is that I had to leave that specific gathering and there were no consequences after that moment of expulsion. During the two weeks I had been in Vrindavan, I had already seen several 'JAO-ings'–in each case, a man had been 'JAO-ed' who it appeared was not doing anything but sitting there–and in each case the man who had been told to leave was allowed to come back for the next *darshan*. I asked several of these men why they had been 'JAO-ed' and they each said that all that they had been doing is thinking 'negative' thoughts. I can see why Maharaji never accepted any of the many invitations that came his way to come to America–Maharaji would have to do too much work if he had to do a 'JAO' every time he discovered a negative thought in anyone's head in America.

Taking My Leave

A few mornings later, I woke up and realized that it was now my time to leave the ashram. I had never seen the Himalayas and several people had told me that April and May were the best months to go to Nepal to do the Annapurna trek. Marvin had already said goodbye to me a few days before and I realized that there was no one at the ashram to whom I felt connected or to whom I wanted to say goodbye—people were connected to Maharaji and not to me and I had the perception that no one would even notice that I had left.

I decided to be moving on at the break of dawn. As I was leaving, I was about to pass the building next door with the *murti* and who should I see standing there on the road in front of that building but Draupadi. Although she had been at every *darshan*, she had never spoken a word and we had never talked. As I approached her, Draupadi did give me a nod of recognition and as I wanted to hear her voice, I said: "I am going to Nepal today." And she shook her head from left to right in a way that would mean "No" in America, but I knew it meant "Yes" in Greece. And realizing there was nothing else to say, I just said: "Good luck!" Again, she nodded her head, but this time with more heart-felt energy and she made a gesture with her hand that meant to me that what you wish for me I also genuinely do wish for you. I was on the road again—and never did hear the voice of Draupadi.

Kainchi Dham

After leaving the ashram in Vrindavan, I spent the next months hiking in Nepal. I stayed in Kathmandu for six weeks and came back to Kashmir in the far north of India to undertake a pilgrimage to Amarnath. Leaving Kashmir, I was hiking in the foothills of the Himalayas near the Indian town of Manali and who should appear but Jerry Toon. He was the same Canadian whom I had originally met in Agra who had drawn for me a map to the Vrindavan ashram of Maharaji and told me the story of Draupadi and her ever-lengthening sari. After I expressed my gratitude for his having told me about the Vrindavan ashram, he was just as informative as before and told me that he had just spent the entire month of August at another Maharaji ashram in Kainchi. Jerry explained to me that although the village where the ashram was located had the name of Kainchi, the ashram was called *Kainchi Dham*. He said Kainchi meant 'scissors', so named because even before the ashram was built, there was a valley there where the where the confluence of two rivers had the shape of scissor blades. Jerry went on to tell me that the scene at *Kainchi Dham* had been different from that of Vrindavan since the day a big shipment of LSD had arrived there from the USA. Several of the devotees had begun taking high doses of LSD regularly and had become both unruly and rowdy. Jerry said that this chaos had come to a head just last week when late on one afternoon he had witnessed an American who was wearing only a blanket (he was tripping on LSD) leap onto Maharaji's back, pulling Maharaji backwards, and almost dislodging Maharaji's own blanket. In the process of making his great leap forward, he lost his own blanket and lay splayed and displayed in the center of the ashram as naked as the day he was born—except for the 108 large *rudraksha beads* that were still hanging around his neck. All present knew that this was an egregious break with Indian customs. The next morning the male Indian devotees of the ashram came around to where the Westerners were staying and told everyone that they had to pack up and leave Kainchi Dham immediately. When a few people protested that they were innocent and had done nothing, they were told that if they waited

144

a month, their request to return would be considered—once they agreed that they would not bring any mind-altering substances into the ashram. Jerry told me that the humorous label applied to the forced evacuation of the ashram was *'The Great Cleanse'*—and similarly people had designated the devotee's jump on Maharaji's back as *'The Great Leap Backwards'*.

For the second time, Jerry Toon drew me a map, but this map was much easier to follow—all that I had to do was tell a bus driver to stop at *Kainchi Dham* around nine miles from Nainital. Jerry drew the ashram on one side of a bridge with a stream going under that bridge and the bus traveling on a wavy paved road.

I arrived at the ashram on Sunday, 2nd September of 1973. When I crossed the white bridge, I sat down and spent a good while listening to the current and watching the water move around the rocks in the stream. Walking into the ashram of whitewashed cement buildings, I was amazed that I was alone. Compared to the bustle of the ashram at Vrindavan, this was a ghost town.

I just sat with my backpack near to the *takhat* in *Kainchi Dham* and I decided to send out friendly feelings to Maharaji. To my surprise, out came Maharaji with an English 'Ma' lady. I noticed that the 'Ma' was wearing an impeccably clean white sari. I politely told Maharaji that I would like permission to stay. There was a silence that lasted more than a minute as Maharaji looked me over and then I saw him look carefully down at my backpack. I wondered if he was doing a drug scan to see whether my backpack had any LSD, but I knew that I had brought only a sincere desire to learn how to *be here now*—and no substances. Eventually he spoke to the Ma in Hindi and pointed up a hill to a place where I could stay. The Ma and I walked silently together and eventually came to a cement lodge. Before we entered, she said, "There will be *darshan* tomorrow in the morning." And then she left me alone.

I opened the door and I saw a room that could comfortably fit eight people. There was no furniture, just a cement floor with a door that closed tightly and glass windows on each of the four sides of the room. I had a sleeping bag and my other clothing served as a mattress. I went to sleep overflowing with gratitude. I felt I had found a home.

My First *Darshan* at Kainchi Dham

I went down to *Kainchi Dham* the next morning for my first *darshan* in this new ashram. Three professional musicians were in the back room and the ashram's loudspeakers were playing the Hanuman Chalisa. I saw that I was the only Westerner there; Maharaji had not yet appeared and there were five Indian devotees moving about near the *takhat*. I spoke to one of them, who was not talking to anyone else, and he told me that his name was Krishna Kumar Sah, but I should call him KK. He had known Maharaji for 33 years having met him in 1940 when KK was just five years old. He told me that he had done a life-long study of the wisdom of the *siddhas* who had lived deep in the Himalayas and he had met many of them in person.[25] As he spoke, he suddenly looked sad and explained that he was still mourning the death of his beloved sister, Janaki, who had died a month ago. KK described how angry he had been that Maharaji did not use his siddhis to save her from dying an untimely death in her thirties, but he had slowly come to accept that it was Janaki's karma to die so young. Today was the first time he had come to Maharaji since her death. Talking to KK, I felt as if I were being included in a family that had been surrounding Maharaji for many decades.

Then Maharaji came out and as Maharaji was seating himself on the *takhat*, KK bent down to take the dust of Maharaji's feet with his forehead. Because there were so few of us, we were seated as six men in the front row surrounding the *takhat*. In the back were Siddhi Ma and a few other women devotees all dressed in white saris who formed a half circle. Draupadi was not there and after inquiring, I had learned that when her two-year Indian visa had expired, she had gone back to Greece. As I was the only Westerner in the front row of the *darshan,* all the talk was in Hindi—so I just meditated on the sound of the language with my eyes closed. Then suddenly I heard Maharaji stir, and I opened my eyes to see that he had moved his position into a more upright half-lotus pose. He then pointed at each of the men in front of him (including me), then pointed his finger toward himself, and lastly he pointed at KK. He proclaimed something in Hindi as he pointed his finger at each of us and I could see by the expression on everyone's face that they were all quite shocked by what Maharaji had just said. I politely waited until Maharaji had left to ask KK what had been said that had so surprised everyone. He said that Maharaji had pointed at the five of us men—including me but not KK—and said that each of us would die—and then Neem Karoli Baba had pointed at himself and said that he too would die—and then he pointed at KK and he said quite loudly and definitively:

"KK thinks he will *not* die."

I asked KK what he thought Maharaji meant and he said what came to mind is that presently he still feels so strong and healthy that the thought had popped into his head just a few days ago (which by his tone I knew that he realized that it was a thought that had no basis in truth): *I will not die.*

Finally I get a Teaching

I decided not to let KK off quite so easily—partially because he was so childlike and because it was such a pleasure to be talking to someone who spoke such good English. I said: "A moment ago you told me that you studied with the *siddhas* of the Himalayas—as we both realize, these are very wise men—could you help me understand what Maharaji was saying when I was at the Vrindavan ashram five months ago?" After he nodded his assent, I told him the story of how Maharaji had demanded the 100 rupees from the young American woman and had repeated the word 'maya' three times: "MAYA! MAYA!! MAYA!!!" and then had given a speech that money was maya, only an illusion. KK saw my sincerity and maybe he even saw I also had a childlike side—so after pausing for a moment, he spoke for quite a while. This is some of what he said:

"Everyone might use their own mind to give their own interpretation of what might have happened. This is my interpretation. The ego with all its desires and fears is like the shell of a walnut. The tasty meat inside is like the feeling of being connected to those whom we love. In this ashram, we value the nut and throw away the shell, but both the nut and the shell are nothing but an experience—meant to come for a moment and then pass away. We suffer like I am suffering now when we get attached to those whom we love. Where is my sister Janaki now? Yes, she is in my heart. And where will I be after I too die? When Maharaji is in the mix, you can never be sure of what he is teaching. I think Maharai is pointing out that love is the greatest power. The wealth of the world has no value if it is not connected to a deep love in our own heart. Power comes from love, not the other way around. Attachment is the greatest block. Clinging to money comes from a lack of faith in God. God does everything. Money is a passing show—an appearance. The only real power is love."

Finally, I had gotten a teaching. The main immediate effect of this teaching was that I had a strong craving for walnuts. A few days earlier when I had been at a market not far from Kainchi, I had seen a woman selling walnuts, so I went back to her and bought a whole kilo of walnuts. I found a stone right near my *dharmsala* that was shaped like a perfect V and I would place each nut in the middle of the V and then with one bang from a rock, it would open up and I would have a taste treat. I wanted to experience in each walnut the shell and then the nut. While I looked at each shell, I would try to imagine a different desire or a different fear (in my head)—and then while eating the nut I would try to experience a connectedness to a specific person who I loved (in my heart). Before I tasted the nut, I would look at it carefully and do a meditation on how it looked so much like a brain and I would ask for wisdom. I still have never tasted better walnuts than those that I bought at that Himalayan market.

Meanwhile two or three people were arriving at the ashram each day. Many arrived on a plane from the West with only a cut-out photo of Maharaji from the book *Be Here Now*. Once their plane had landed, they would show the photo to everyone they met and each would eventually find someone who knew Maharaji and tell them how to get to his ashram. Indians love to be helpful. A common story that these seekers would tell me is that after a careful reading of the book they had intuited that Maharaji was a genuine *mahasiddha*—so getting to meet him while he was still in a body had become a top priority.

A thought experiment

Now I want to take you along on a thought experiment. Imagine you are Maharaji and because you have had *siddhis* for over seven decades, you are given a strong transmission from your intuitive faculty that in a very short time that your destiny is to leave the body. What would you do with this knowledge? My guess is that this transmission did come to Maharaji on Sunday, 9th of September of 1973 and I will now tell you what I saw.

The last *darshan*

Late on Sunday afternoon, we Westerners were beginning to settle in for the night. By now, there were eight people living on the same floor where I had been alone just one week before. That morning there had been the usual *darshan* with Maharaji and we had already been fed that afternoon. However, someone came running up the hill, and said to us: "Maharaji wants to meet with everyone!!!" That meant we were to go down to the *Kainchi Dham* a second time in the same day—immediately. This was the first time in my stays at both ashrams that there had ever been two darshans on the same day.

When about 30 people were gathered around the *takhat* with the Ma's standing behind, Maharaji came bounding out of his room and after a moment of silence, he zeroed in on two American women who had just arrived. After asking them their names and from where they had come, he found out that one of them spoke Hindi. A long Hindi dialogue ensued and the only Hindi which I could understand was the name of 'Sai Baba' (which was repeated several times)—I knew that Sathya Sai Baba was a guru in South India who had the *siddhi* of materializing *vibhuti*. *Vibhuti* is made of dried cow dung that has been burned to ash as part of a Vedic ritual—however, Sai Baba was known throughout India as being able to materialize *vibhuti* from his fingers without making a fire. When at the request of Maharaji, the two women left to get their *vibhuti*, someone who understood Hindi told me that Maharaji had just asked them to bring him the urn of *vibhuti*, which they had told Maharaji they had just seen Sai Baba materialize from thin air a few days before. When they returned, they put the urn in front of Maharaji on his *takhat*. I took a look at the *vibhuti* and it was not quite to the top. Maharaji put his hand in the *vibhuti* and with the ash put a vertical *tilak* on the forehead of the people in the front row and then indicated for all of us (like myself who were in the back row) to come forward for our *tilak*. But because the people in the front row were not asked to move and we had to lean over to be near Maharaji, some ash landed in our hair and then some on our face and some also just fell on the floor. After he finished with us, he indicated to the Ma's in the background to come forward and after a path was cleared for them, he put a vertical *tilak* on each of their foreheads. Lastly, he smeared a single line of *vibhuti* horizontally across his own forehead that went from the top of his left eyebrow all the way to his right eyebrow. So much *vibhuti* had been distributed that his own blanket had lost its hue and color and had become ashen gray. After giving all of us a final look, Maharaji wrapped his blanket higher on his body and went back into his room. That was to be the last time I ever saw him.

Once he left, it was now getting dark, and when I looked down into the urn that he had left behind, I could not believe my eyes when I saw that the *vibhuti* was now at a much higher level in the urn than when the two women had first placed the urn in front of him—and the thought arose in my mind that this particular urn might contain an infinite mountain of ash. No one there had a camera, but if a picture had been taken of the devotees who remained steadfastly in front of Maharaji, they were each covered in so much ash that they would have each come out in the photograph looking like ghosts.

Going back to my room as the sun was setting, I thought to myself: *Was that really a miracle that the ash was higher in the urn after so much was placed on each of the devotees? But the fact is that I never touched the ash before it was distributed and it is just possible that the ash was packed much more tightly in the beginning? Maybe it just looked like there was more ash at the end than at the beginning because the tightly packed ash was just loosened up after Maharaji stuck his hand in the urn. And then when I last looked at the urn at the end, it was getting dark—is it not even vaguely possible that I mistakenly thought the higher level of ash was from the shadows cast in the fading light of the sunset? I am no longer sure if what happened can be authenticated as a 'miracle'.*

The next afternoon—Monday, 10th September—we were told that there would be no *darshan*, and rumors were circulating that Maharaji had left Kainchi with a young Indian boy named

Ravi Khanna. And then on Tuesday the 11th, there was a virtual flood of rumors—that Siddhi Ma and all the mothers had left the ashram at the break of dawn when they had received a phone call that Maharaji had left his body in the early hours of the morning. For whatever reason, I (wrongly) contended that this story was a rumor. In Vrindavan I had witnessed a day of hysteria around the fate of Maharaji when he had left for a day and rumors had begun to spread that he had left his body—the rumors only stopped when he had showed up for *darshan* the next morning. Because I did not believe the rumors and it was also clear that there would be no *darshan* at the ashram, I decided to spend the afternoon ever so slowly—really slowly—doing my walnut meditation.

Did I finally get myself an authenticated miracle?

When I had already been doing my walnut meditation early in the afternoon, for about an hour, I saw a devotee running up the hill waving a piece of paper in his hand. While he talked, I put my elbow on the ground and held the rock in the air above the next walnut. When he stood in the middle of us, I saw that his face was covered in tears and he breathlessly read what it said on the paper in his hand. The telegram said: *Maharaji left his body at 1:15 this morning in Vrindavan. The body will be burned tomorrow on Wednesday. Come immediately to Vrindavan.* And having finished reading the telegram, the messenger started sobbing.

I realized that my contention that it was a rumor was completely wrong. A shiver went down my own spine and I just let my arm fall without any intention and as my arm fell, the rock in my hand landed on the next walnut waiting in the crevice of the stone. To my amazement, I saw that the shell had opened and there was *no nut inside.* I looked carefully all around the rock to see if just possibly the nut might have flown somewhere on the ground, but there was *no nut to be found anywhere.* Eventually I finished all the other walnuts and each and every one of those remaining walnuts did have a nut inside the shell.

I asked myself: *Did I finally get myself an authenticated 'miracle'?*

Addendum the first: The next summer

The next summer I heard the story of Maharaji's last hours from Ravi Khanna—you may remember him as being the young Indian boy who had left the Temple with Maharaji on Monday morning. The occasion for meeting Ravi (as he asked to be called) was we were both attending the very first summer school advertised throughout America that was meant to celebrate the opening of the Naropa Institute (in Boulder, Colorado). For two evenings of each week, Ram Dass was there telling stories about Neem Karoli Baba and the yogic path to spiritual awakening, and then giving his Hindu wisdom. On alternating nights, Chögyam Trungpa was talking about how to overcome 'spiritual materialism' and the tantric path to spiritual awakening, and then giving his Tibetan wisdom.

One afternoon during that first week at Naropa, a few of us who had been with Maharaji asked Ravi Khanna to tell us his story of the last days of Maharaji. The gist of what he said was that on Monday the 10th he had taken Maharaji to see a heart specialist in Agra and the doctor had given Maharaji a clean bill of health. Then on that same evening of the 10th after he bought a train ticket for both of them to come back to Nainital (which was near Kainchi), he had been asked by Maharaji to make an unscheduled exit from the train at the town of Mathura (only 40 miles/60 kilometers from Agra). While Maharaji sat on the steps in front of the train station of Mathura, he began convulsing and sweating, and when Ravi touched his hands and arms, Maharaji's body felt extremely cold. Ravi thought he might be having a heart attack. At Maharaji's request, he took him to Vrindavan (only 10 miles/16 kilometers from Mathura). Once in Vrindavan, Ravi took Maharaji to the emergency room of the Ramakrishna Mission hospital. Maharaji looked unconscious, and the hospital staff gave him an injection, put a blood pressure measuring band on his arm and an oxygen mask over his face. Just a moment after they had finished putting on all this medical apparatus, Maharaji roused himself and sat up and pulled the blood pressure measuring band off his arm and took the oxygen mask off his face and looked at each of the doctors and said: "Bekar!" (Hindi for 'useless!' meaning that these measures will not work). He then repeated this mantra three times—each time in a lower pitch:

JAYA JAGADISH, JAGADISH HARE!!!
(HAIL TO THE LORD OF THE UNIVERSE!!!)
Jaya Jagadish, Jagadish Hare!
(Hail To The Lord Of The Universe!)
jaya jagadish, jagadish hare
(hail to the lord of the universe)

And then he lay back and his breathing slowed down until he was no longer breathing at all. Maharaji had left his body. Ravi was given the body and he got helpers at the hospital to take it to the Vrindavan Ashram (where six months before I had first met Maharaji). In the morning, Ravi sent out the telegram that was read to me on the slopes above Kainchi Dham, where I had been eating my walnuts.

Maharaji's symptoms did not fit the usual profile for a heart attack. At the hospital all the monitors showed that his pulse was quite normal without any fluctuations. The doctors, not knowing the true cause of his death, wrote on the death certificate that he died from 'a diabetic coma', which is clearly a misdiagnosis as Maharaji had never been diagnosed with diabetes nor was he in a coma when he pulled their medical equipment off of his body. If I were trying to diagnose the true cause of Maharaji's death, I would say it was Maharaji's moment to come home after serving his sentence in what he would jokingly refer to as 'Central Jail'.[26]

Neem Karoli Baba's death—like his life—remains a conundrum permeated by a riddle inside an enigma all wrapped inside the great Mystery.

Addendum the second: Two Dreams five years Later

These last two dreams took place five years later.

I entered a PhD program in psychology almost five years to the day after Maharaji's *Mahasamadhi*. The name of the graduate school was then the California Institute of Asian Studies (CIAS), but before I graduated the name was changed to the California Institute of Integral Studies (CIIS).

In that first week of classes, I met a half-dozen people who were to become my life-long friends—and I had two dreams with Maharaji.

In the first dream, there was a man on a *takhat* imitating a false guru saying just take this herb and you will find enlightenment and then who should appear but a fat naked midget with absolutely no neck and this midget told me (to my great surprise): "You never knew it, Mister Isenberg, but Neem Karoli Baba is actually your guru."

Waking up, I realized that the midget had spoken the truth. A little while after I had the dream, I came upon a painting of a look-alike fat naked midget without a neck in a book on Hindu Gods and that midget had the name of *Vamana*—the dwarf incarnation of Lord Vishnu.

Then a few days later, I had a second dream and this time Maharaji himself appeared and asked me if I wanted a name. Before I tell what happened in this dream, I have to say another word about my relationship with the names that I have received in my life.

While I had been at each of the Maharaji ashrams, several people had asked for a private darshan to receive a name from Maharaji. After these individuals had come out of their private meeting with Maharaji, all the ones I spoke to had received a name that had ended in either a *das* or a *dass* (these are two spellings of the Sanskrit word *dasa* which means servant or one who serves). Because I was rebellious and did not want to follow any normal path in getting a spiritual name, I did not want to become a *das* or a *dass*—so I had never asked for a private meeting during which I might get a new name.

Then during the first week of classes at graduate school when I had this dream where Maharaji asked me if I wanted a name from him, I had just begun introducing myself for the very first time in my life with my Hebrew name Eliyahu. This was the name I received before birth, but until this week at a new graduate school, my identity had always been as an Elliott.

My research showed me that Eliyahu אֱלִיָהוּ had two of the holiest Hebrew syllables. The 'Yah' is Jehovah which implies the beingnesss of I AM as when God says in Exodus 3:14: "I am that I am." The 'El' is Hebrew for the Lord, and implies that which is mighty and powerful. Many of the Hebrew prophets had 'El' in their name—Ezekiel, Daniel, Samuel, Elisha, and of course Elijah. The Jews had also even given their 'El' sound to such Christian archangels as Michael (bestowing strength), Gabriel (the messenger), Raphael, (the healer) and also Uriel (the wise). And in the Kabbalah, Haniel is the feminine archangel who bestows divine grace. Even though my name literally means means 'Jehovah is He who is the Lord', I came to translate my name more figuratively as **Reality Rules** or **Beingness Rules** or even **I AM Rules**.

Getting back to my second dream. I was very excited (in my dream-body) to see Maharaji in his dream flesh for the second time in a week after not having seen him at all (even in my dreams) for five long years. In the dream, after Maharaji asked me if I was finally ready to receive a name from him. I surrendered totally and said: "Yes, I am." And he said: "Your name is . . . " (then as my heart raced in suspense, he concluded with the name):

". . . *Eliyahu*".

Addendum the third:

As you may remember if you were an attentive reader of this chapter, I was greeted at the Vrindavan Ashram by Marvin Ratner who had just taken LSD.

I thought I was through with Marvin when he left the Ashram (before I did), but then it was my fate to meet him one last time in Asia. I was doing my ablutions at 2 am in the loo of my Kathmandu hotel two months after I left Maharaji's Vrindavan ashram (this was now May of 1973). I chose one of the three doors, and I was letting go of my thoughts of the day. Suddenly the toilet door (that had no lock) was pushed inward and I shouted: "I'm in here!" And then I heard a familiar voice that said, "Elliott" and I was being hugged. It was Marvin and he was bursting with joy to see me. I realized at that moment this great truth: *Resistance is futile.*

As that was to be Marvin's last day in Kathmandu, I helped him bring his bags to the airport and we even exchanged addresses for the very first time.

Then I saw him again four years later when I was passing through Berkeley from where I was living in Hawaii. Marvin was selling jewelry on Telegraph Avenue and I realized I could easily pretend that I did not see him as he was pre-occupied with a customer, but I just accepted that *resistance is futile.* And after we talked for a moment, there was a mutual recognition that we would both soon be in NYC. I ended up meeting his parents and sister by accepting his invitation to come for a dinner at his NYC home (in Brooklyn) where Marvin had grown up.

Are not the ways of karma mysterious? Now more than five decades after the events described in this chapter, the only one who I had met at either of the Maharaji ashrams to whom I still talk to regularly is Marvin Ratner.

To call it a 'miracle' that I met Marvin seven separate times in Asia (in five different countries) does not reflect my true feeling. I do see it as a quite remarkable coincidence and I do accept that coincidence is God's way of remaining anonymous. I connect this to a word created by Carl Jung: *synchronicity*.

The way karma unfolds is truly part of the great Mystery, and Neem Karoli Baba taught me that at the heart of this Mystery is the power of love. Little did I realize when I left the ashram that Neem Karoli Baba would have a long-lasting, sometimes imperceptible, remarkably indestructible influence throughout my life. I now knew that it was possible in the human condition to not only experience, but also to manifest a love that is unconditional.

1. *Elliott with his mother (1947)*

2. *Elliott with his brothers (1948)*

3. *The three brothers (1950)*

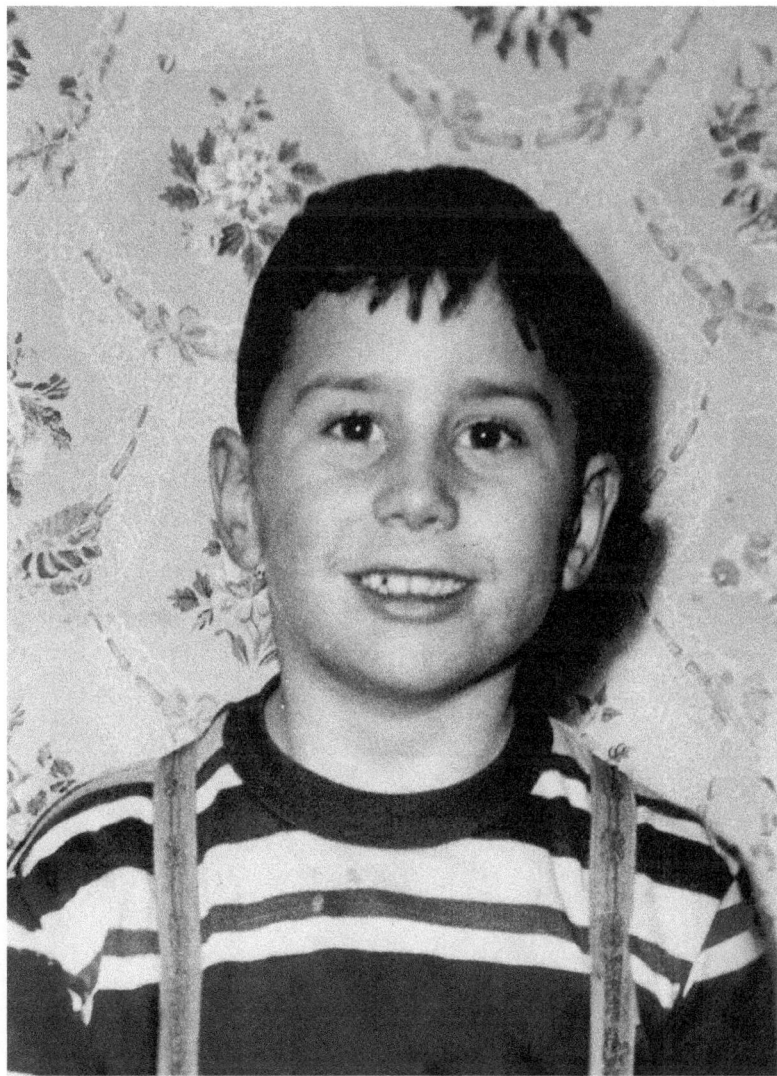

4. *The boy (1953)*

5. *Frieda and Morrie (1954)*

6. *Elliott in Hawaii (1977)*

7. *Barbara at Fort Jesus in Mombasa, Kenya (1970)*

8. *Elliott at Fort Jesus (1970)*

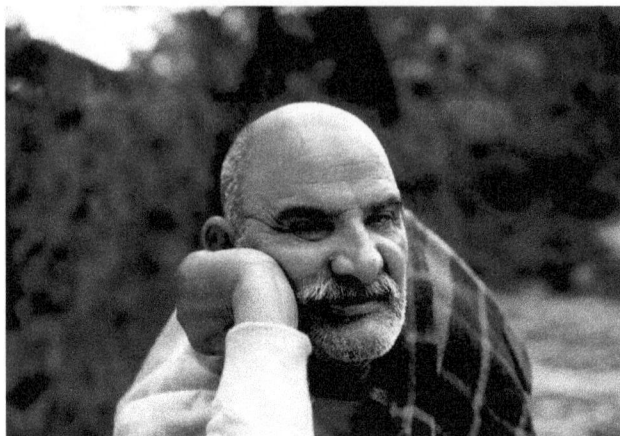

9. Neem Karoli Baba (1973)

10. Ravi Khanna, Neem Karoli Baba, and Draupadi (1971)

11. *Elliott arriving in San Francisco (1978)*

12. *Elliott in a Tai Chi class with Judyth O. Weaver (1980)*

13. *Elliott looking up (1980)*

14. *Morrie yawning at the very spot where he will be buried (1999)*

15. Morrie visiting his own gravestone the month before he died (2003)

16. *Sunyata in Almora, India (1973) Copyright © by Maggie Hopp*

17. *Tibetan lama and artist Drugu Choegyal Rinpoche (1992)*

18. *Allyson and Alex Grey at The Chapel of Sacred Mirrors (CoSM) in New York City (2006)*

19. Byron Katie (1997)

20. Adyashanti (2006). This photo was taken by Peter Scarsdale.

21. Karl Renz (2007)

22. *Ramana Maharshi (1940)*

23. *Nisargaddatta Maharaj (1975)*

24. Ram Dass (2018). This photo was taken by BeQui Frankel.

25. The elephant is 3 days old (2019 in Thailand). This photo was taken by Joanie McGovern.

26. The tiger is — hopefully — tame (2019 in Thailand)

27. Elliott in a devotional moment (2021) by Vinny Olimpio

28. Taken on a morning walk in San Francisco (2022) by Vinny Olimpio

29. Steve Forrest (2018). This photo was taken by Jeff Turner.

As
you
thinketh
in
your
HEART
so
will
you
BECOME

Fuck **E**verything

And **R**un

Face **E**verything **A**nd **R**ⁱ_s^e

Forgetting **E**verything's

All **R**ight

Forgive **E**nemies, **A**bolish **R**esentment

False

Evidence

Appearing

Real

"You can only see what you believe – nothing else is possible."

When
the fear
arises,

the fear
makes
what

the fear
is saying
appear

to
BE
THE
TRUTH

30. *Warrenton, North Carolina in July 1963: The sign is not referring to "white" laundry.*

31. This photo appeared in Marshall McLuhan's **The Medium is the Massage**. Elliott is walking out on the far left and Secretary of Defense Robert McNamara is on the podium (June 1966)

32. A commune in Salisbury, Rhodesia in March of 1971. Martin on the far left gave Barbara and Elliott their first LSD. (This photo of the commune was sent to Elliott at his home in NYC as a greeting card and neither Barbara nor Elliott are in the photo.)

33. My family in August of 2000. I am the only one dressed in black. Edward and Howard are (left to right) 1st and 3rd in the back row. My father is seated in the center of the photo with my mother seated next to him.

34. *The psychedelic commune called Millbrook near Poughkeepsie New York (1966)*

San Francisco Chronicle

SFCHRONICLE.COM | **Sunday, November 1, 2015** | PRINTED ON RECYCLED PAPER | $1.50 ★★★★

S.F.'s only gun shop sells its last weapon

Final holdout in city closes its books with sale of Colt .45 to Mission man

By Lizzie Johnson

The last gun from the last gun shop in San Francisco has been sold — without a single bullet.

Elliott Isenberg, 70, wouldn't have known what to do with ammunition anyway. He was printing flyers at Copy Central on Mission Street last week when he noticed the signs in the windows of High Bridge

Arms: "Final sale!" and "Closing Oct. 31!" He went inside for a look and left with a receipt for a Colt .45.

"Thanks for supporting the last gun shop in San Francisco," the receipt read. The handgun cost $1,221.25. Isenberg, who lives in the Mission, had never even held a gun before, let alone owned one. But he's the last person to buy a firearm legally in San Francisco.

"It's almost more of a work of art than it is a weapon," he said in a thick New York accent. "My purpose is nonviolent. It's a beautiful gun, and I feel like it's in the spirit of what San Francisco is. It somehow feels right."

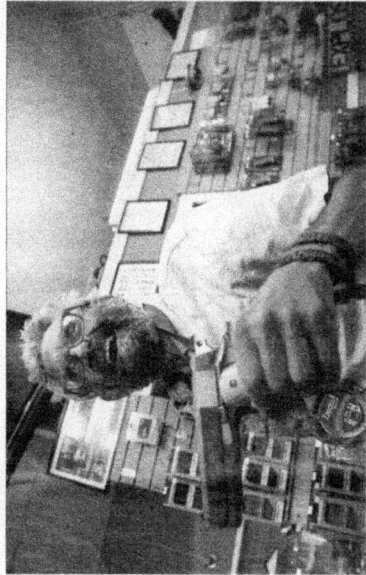

Santiago Mejia / Special to the Chronicle

Elliott Isenberg holds the Colt .45 he bought at High Bridge Arms. Isenberg didn't purchase any bullets to put in it. "It's almost more of a work of art than it is a weapon," he said.

35. Elliott buying the last gun ever to be bought legally in San Francisco, California (2015). Almost ten years later, he still is yet to acquire his first bullet.

36. Elliott posing for Vinny Olimpio to show what he looked like while writing this book (2023)

5

Can a noisy mind get a glimpse of THE GREAT SILENCE?

Yes, and how many years can the river 'Elliott' exist before he flows into the ocean 'Eliyahu'?

Yes, and how many years must a mountain exist
Before it is washed to the sea?
And how many years can some people exist
Before they're allowed to be free?
Yes, and how many times can a man turn his head
And pretend that he just doesn't see?
The answer, my friend, is blowin' in the wind
The answer is blowin' in the wind
                    —Bob Dylan, *Blowin' in the Wind*[27]

AFTER NEEM KAROLI BABA LEFT HIS BODY, all of us living at his ashram in Kainchi were invited to Vrindavan to be there for the burning of the body on the very next day—September 12th, 1973.

Those of us who did not choose to go to the cremation in Vrindavan all gathered at Neem Karoli Baba's *takhat*, but now there was no master. A framed photo of Neem Karoli Baba had been put in the center of the *takhat*, and each of us were absorbed in our own quiet space. I decided to leave the next morning for my first meditation course.

Earlier that day I had asked myself what I really wanted and the answer came up: *I want to learn how to meditate.* I had gotten a flyer that said that a Burmese meditation teacher, Satya Narayan Goenka (known as S.N. Goenka), was giving a 10-day intensive meditation course in the village of Nalanda starting on September 20th. Looking at the map, I saw that Nalanda was in the state of Bihar and not that far from Bodh Gaya, the village where there still exists the descendent of the Bodhi Tree (*ficus religiosa*) under which the Buddha sat when he got enlightened 25 centuries ago.

Meditating near the ruins of a Buddhist university

Four days later I was greeted in Nalanda by the director of what was then called the Pali Institute (now known as Nava Nalanda Mahavira). He was a friendly man and when I asked him to tell me about his Institute, he explained that although this Institute had been created in 1951 to bring the study of Buddhism back to India, this was the first time (the year was 1973) that they had invited a meditation teacher to give them instruction on how to do vipassana meditation.

The director told me that Sariputta (Sariputra), one of the Buddha's two main disciples, had been born, achieved enlightenment, and then left his body here in Nalanda. One thousand years after Sariputta's death, the town had become the home to the biggest Buddhist University in the world. For the next seven centuries—from the fifth to the twelfth century CE—many of the most famous teachers of Buddhism had come there to do their teaching. Among the most renowned was Padmasambhava (whose name means 'born from a lotus'). He taught at Nalanda in the eighth century and left to continue his teachings on the Tibetan plateau where he is viewed as a central figure in the transmission of Buddhism to Tibet. When I asked the director what had happened in the twelfth century to end the university, he said that the Muslim general, Muhammad bin Bakhtiyar Khalji, had ordered his
160

army to massacre as many members of the university as they could find during a jihad in 1193 CE. He did this because he believed that since all Buddhists were infidels (given their religion had no God), they did not deserve to be alive. Once the killing was over, he had his soldiers spend several months burning the millions of books in the university's library.

After talking to the Director, I took a short walk to the ruins of this great university. At the ruins that day, there was no one else there. I just wandered around the grounds with so many crumbling red brick structures. What came to mind was a saying about the ephemerality of all material things: *this too shall pass*. I noticed myself experiencing a moment of melancholy.

The course began in the meditation hall with 20 Indians and eight foreigners—all English-speaking. Goenka's wife was sitting near him in the front of the hall on his left. Goenka's first words were: "Rare is it to be a human being, rarer still to have heard of enlightenment, and even rarer still to pursue it." Then he taught us a practice he called *anapana*—a bare attention to the sensation of the natural breath at the tip of the nose where the breath was entering and exiting from the nostrils. Although I attempted to observe the sensations as instructed, I could not keep my attention focused for more than a minute without the constant repetition of this jingle that I had heard quite often in my childhood in a TV commercial:

AJAX ... boom boom!

THE FOAMING CLEANSER ... boom boom boom boom!!!

AJAX ... boom boom!

THE FOAMING CLEANSER ... boom boom boom boom!!!

As the jingle would not go away and stayed with me hour after hour, I knew that I was in trouble. The next day Goenka offered to have a private meeting with anyone who was having difficulty with the course. I put my name on the list. When the time came for my interview, I told him about how I really wanted to meditate, but I was being pursued by a jingle and sang the jingle to him. When I finished, there was a long pause and I feared he was going to tell me that I was a loser in the practice of meditation, but instead he said: "It seems to me like a mantra about cleansing. Are you not trying to clean up your mind?" As he said this, I felt a wave of relief. And then he continued: "And is not Ajax a hero of great strength in Greek mythology?"

I could feel I was in the presence of a wise and comforting being, and I immediately went enthusiastically back to the meditation hall. To my amazement, the jingle never appeared again—not even once. I came to believe that it was just my mind's way of rebelling against the discipline, and once the disciplinarian was seen as merciful, my mind became (more) obedient.

Years later I was on another meditation course with Jack Kornfield and he told the group that he had an original obstacle to his meditation practice in Thailand because he continuously would hear a commercial jingle for Alka-Seltzer:

PLOP! PLOP! FIZZ! FIZZ!

O What a relief it is!!!

PLOP! PLOP! FIZZ! FIZZ!

O What a relief it is!!!

It amazed me how these jingles could penetrate so deeply into the unconscious.

Each morning Goenka would begin singing Pali chants at 4:30 am—this was half an hour before our first silent group sitting at 5 am. I would draw near him because the sounds coming from him were so heavenly and melodious. Goenka sounded like a man who had found inner peace.

After three and a half days of *anapana*, he changed the directive and told us to do what he called 'sweeping'. This required a systematic body-scan from the top of the head to the bottom of the feet—staying with the sensation in each part of the body for as long as possible. As *sweeping* had more variety than *anapana,* I was able to stay with this for longer periods of time. And luckily, there was a walking meditation between sittings—hour after hour, I watched my feet as I said these words during each step: "Lift... Push... Place... "

Each evening, Goenka would give his talk of the day. His voice reverberated throughout the meditation hall without a microphone. He said that the central messages of the Buddha's teachings were about the cause of suffering and how to end that suffering. I remember one day he waxed eloquent talking about the Four Noble Truths:

Dukkha—the truth of the existence of suffering

Samudaya—the truth of the origin of suffering in craving

Nirodha—the truth of the cessation (end) of suffering in non-attachment

Magga—the truth of the path to the cessation of suffering.

And then on other evenings, he would talk about the nature of existence. I learned that *vipassana* was the Pali word for 'insight' and that the Buddha's three main insights that characterized all phenomena and beings were . . .

Dukkha (unsatisfactoriness)

Anicca (impermanence)

Anatta (no self—the absence of any essential self or soul)

What Goenka emphasized is that it was important to find out who we are before the moment that we would eventually physically die—'to die before you die'. I resonated with this philosophy because it seemed so practical—and it was based on an experiential method—sitting quietly and getting used to studying my own mind. I began asking myself whenever I felt uncomfortable: *"What is my mind doing that is creating distress at this moment?"*

I also noticed that all three of the Buddha's insights were in English spelled with six letters. Since 3 X 6 = 18, I was proud that my new path had 18 letters. 18 or Chai (חי) is the number for 'good luck' in the Jewish religion (since the two letters of chai in the Hebrew alphabet—the 8th letter *Chet* (ח) and the 10th letter *Yod* (י) add up to 18—and the word *chai* means alive, or living). I thought of myself for the first time as a BuJew—meaning a Jew who is a Buddhist. And already I knew that all religions were pointing to the same ineffable Beingness that could not be captured in concepts.

When we were allowed to talk freely after the 10-day meditation course came to an end, a friendly fellow meditator asked me what I planned to do now. I told him that I wanted to continue meditating in nearby Bodh Gaya and he suggested that I get further meditation directives from Acharya Anagarika Munindra, whom he called Munindra-ji. I asked him for an address and he said everyone in that village would know who he was and I could just ask anyone.

Being Silent in Bodh Gaya

The next day I took a bus from Nalanda to Gaya, and then hired a rickshaw diriver to take me from Gaya to Bodh Gaya. Bodh Gaya was a small village, but was also the Mecca for world Buddhism. It seemed every Buddhist country had a temple made in their own national style. In the center of the town was a descendent of the original Bodhi tree beneath which the Buddha attained enlightenment. Nearby was the Mahabodhi Temple, an impressive structure 180 feet high (55 metres) that had been there in various guises for over two millennia.

Just as the friendly man had told me, the first person I spoke to in Bodh Gaya gave me directions to where Anagarika Munindra was living. When I knocked on the door of his bungalow, he was already speaking with another Westerner. I asked if I was interrupting and he indicated that I was welcome and invited me to join the meeting. He began by asking me why I was there, and I told him that I wanted to cultivate a meditation practice. I told him about my travels and my desire to find mental peace. I explained that I was angry at the injustices in the world and that I had been deeply affected by the murder of the European members of my family by the Nazi State during the Second World War.

Munindra told both of us that we were in luck—that a young teacher named Joseph Goldstein was about to begin teaching a 10-day intensive retreat at the Burmese Vihara. Munindra said that this would be the first course that Joseph ever taught, but that he would be there as a back-up if we ever got confused about the teachings of the Buddha. Munindra asked us if we knew the *metta* practice in Buddhism, and I told him that I had been introduced to that practice during the tenth day of my Goenka course. He said that *metta* might be particularly useful for me, and I could practice sending friendly feeling not only to all sentient beings, but also to those toward whom I still felt anger. I remember him looking at me directly in the eye for just an instant and then saying: "Now is the moment to take responsibility for what is in your own mind." As we were leaving, he gave us both one last piece of advice: we might get the most out of a meditation course if we made a vow to remain absolutely silent for the entire 10 days.

Before the course began, I decided to take a walk to the Mahakala Caves in the Dungweswari Hills, not far from Bodh Gaya. Here the Buddha had done his ascetic practices for six years with five other ascetics before he came to the Bodhi Tree the night before enlightenment. I found a few friends who wanted to do the flat seven mile (12 km) hike. As the water was warm and there were no sharp rocks, I chose to cross the Niranjan River near Bodh Gaya in bare feet. At the cave, there was a Tibetan Temple. When its Tibetan guardians saw we were respectful, they let us proceed to the actual cave without a guide and we decided to commemorate the success of our journey with a meditation. Once I sat down, I felt a current electrifying my body. The electricity just kept increasing in strength until I was shaking intensely—and then as suddenly as it came, the vibration ceased. I fell into a deep silence.

Three days later the course began in the meditation room of the Burmese Vihara. To my surprise, Joseph instructed us to be attentive to the breath in a different place from that suggested by Goenka: rather than notice the breath at the tip of the nostrils, Joseph suggested that it was best to pay attention to the sensation of the rising of the abdomen during the in-breath and falling of the abdomen during the out-breath. He also suggested that, although most of the attention should be on the bodily sensation, it might be useful in order to better maintain our focus to count the breaths from one to ten—and then just start over again. Joseph said that the mind was like a wild monkey who liked to grab different tasty fruits by swinging through the tree branches—but it was only through discipline and concentration that the mind could become stronger. I remember him saying: "Be relaxed, but not casual."

The big event each day was Joseph's talk in the evening. I loved the clarity of these talks and how Joseph's directives often suggested the importance of being aware of 'craving'—which he would also call 'clinging' and 'grasping'. Like Goenka, he emphasized that the Buddha's teachings were all about the cause of suffering and the ending of suffering. He said that it was a noble pursuit to develop a mind which 'clings to nought'. One day he expanded on what the Buddha himself meant by *dukkha*:

> The word *dukkha* is made up of the prefix *du* and the root *kha*. *Du* means bad or difficult. *Kha* means empty. Empty here refers to the empty axle hole of a wheel. If the axle fits badly into the center hole, we get a very bumpy ride. This is a good analogy for our ride through *samsara*.

He said that, since birth and death were inevitably a set of opposites—even though they were not in opposition—it was best to begin the practice of learning to lessen the attachment to our bodies. I remember him saying: "Do not get attached to your body—you will have to leave it some day."

Nothing exciting happened during the entire ten days. The emphasis was always upon purifying the mind through cultivating wholesome ways of thinking. I remember being impacted by a lecture about 'wanting' and how Joseph pointed out that there were many words for 'wanting' in *Pali* (the language spoken by the Buddha). In *Pali*, one could differentiate between three meanings of wanting: there was intention itself (*chanda*), secondly a noble type of wanting that would bring liberation (called *kusala-chanda* or *dhamma-chanda*), and lastly a greedy type of wanting which was the craving that would bring upon suffering (called *tanha*). Joseph's point was that the problem was not 'wanting' itself, but upon which form of wanting we put our attention and intention.

One morning Joseph gave each of us a raisin and we spent a

good amount of time eating the raisin mindfully. After looking at the raisin and feeling the raisin, we eventually put it into our mouth, and did the first bite. The directive was to every action slowly . . . slowly . . . slowly . . . First in the chewing, and then in the act of swallowing. As I was swallowing, I realized that I had lived 28 years of my life and had never even once been attentive to what it was like *to swallow.* Before that moment, I had always been thinking of the next bite before even noticing that I had ever swallowed.

Move Slow and Let Awareness Grow

Once an elephant walked by right outside the gates of the Vihara and as I wanted to obey all the rules and not leave the grounds, I pressed my face up against the gate and watched this majestic animal walk by slowly . . . slowly . . . slowly . . . That elephant is still walking by in my mind. I find it quite amazing how an image can get so imprinted on the mind's eye.

There were three times a day when we could eat—at tea early in the morning, the big meal of the day (rice and veggies) at noon, and then an optional snack late in the afternoon. I thought I would try living like a Buddhist monk and take my last meal at noon. Because I was eating so little and never leaving the grounds of the Vihara, I felt super-energized and would often wake up in the wee hours of the morning when it was still dark. At that time I would slowly do my walking meditation around the grounds—hour after hour, I would watch my feet move forward and I would repeat: "Lift . . . Push . . . Place . . ."

I was rigorous in observing the 10-day silence. I felt I was heading to complete success when on the 7th night I was walking around the grounds as usual. Suddenly around 3 am, right next to me, there was a super-loud metallic sound of someone shaking the locked metal gate. Before I could remember my vow of silence, I said in a startled voice: "Who's there?" The answer came back in a foreign language, but on getting closer to the gate, I recognized the Burmese *chowkidar* (caretaker) of the Vihara—he was drunk and he had gotten locked out of his own Temple. As I opened the gate, I felt a moment of sadness that I had broken my perfect silence. The thought came to me that I should not let what was really good be spoiled by a craving for perfection.

Meanwhile the *metta* was going really well. It did make me feel much lighter emotionally. I would only do it for about an hour of the many hours that I was spending being attentive to my breath. Wanting my empathy to be broad-minded and impartial, I spent at least an hour each day sending these thoughts to the leaders of the Nazi Party:

> *May you be free of pain*
> *May you be free of suffering*
> *May you be joyful*
> *May you be peaceful*
> *May you be happy*
> *May you be liberated*
> *May you be enlightened*

And then I would see an image in my mind's eye of first Adolf Hitler, then Joseph Goebbels, and lastly Heinrich Himmler—and I would send each of them a friendly feeling. Each had left their body when my mother was almost five months pregnant with me. I did ask myself whether the threesome might still exist in some (post-body) energetic form—and if they were indeed still hanging around in the *akasha*, I wondered if my sending them friendly feeling might in some way be assisting them in letting go of their hatred.

The next day Joseph's talk was about *metta* and he said that a 100,000 times greater benefit to another sentient being than any material gift would be a single thought of friendly feeling. I decided that it was unfair to send all my *metta* to Nazis, so I began sending the same energy to my parents, my brothers, my sisters (non-biological), my friends, my classmates, and any who might wrongly believe that I was their enemy. And then I included the animals, the fish, and even the insects. (I did ask for a dispensation to kill any mosquito that was trying to bite me as long as I sent that creature friendly feeling as I killed it.)

The Unbearable Lightness of Being

On the last day I experienced a lightness that I had never known before in my life. It appeared that I no longer had any enemies. To give this a metaphor, if the anger that had been boiling in my being for decades could be compared to water in a tank, somehow a plug had been pulled toward the bottom of the tank and all the long-boiling water had come gushing out. In my mind, I could not find any guilt or shame, any regret or resentment, nor even a whiff of blame. I was so focused on the present moment that I could not even find a future—or anything to create a worry. It felt like there was no thinker in such thoughts as these:

Giving and receiving, but no giver and no receiver.
Winning and losing, but no winners and no losers.
No one to hold on to any projection.
And surely no one to own those projections of 'I', 'me', or 'mine'.
Just grace and gratitude . . . and then more grace and gratitude . . .
and then yet more grace and gratitude.
Who was there to own such grace and gratitude?

It was as if I had always been under a cloudy sky and now the clouds had just parted and the sun shone forth:

Here comes the sun,
Here comes the sun, and I say

It's all right
Little darling, it's been a long cold lonely winter
Little darling, it feels like years since it's been here

Little darlin', I feel that ice is slowly melting
Little darlin', it seems like years since it's been clear [28]

A letter arrived from my younger brother Howard before I left India worrying if I was ever to return from my travels. The letter contained a poem composed by him called *'Something More'*—it was written to the rhythm of Edgar Allan Poe's *'The Raven'*:

Something More

He wanted something else again
Besides the daily war;
He hated the quotidian,
And wanted something more.

He traveled through lands old and new,
And sampled all their store;
But still his search he did pursue;
He wanted something more.

He travelled far from kith and kin,
And many wonders saw;
But though in strange lands he had been,
He wanted something more.

He did not know for what he yearned;
Its shape he could not draw;
But still within he burned and burned—
And home returned no more.

In a moment of inspiration, I wrote him back a last verse for his poem:

> *This lad no longer has an aim*
> *Yet meditates galore;*
> *With a sigh he doth exclaim:*
> *"I wish for nothing more!"*

Even as I wrote this verse, I knew it was composed by a noisy mind that had had merely a glimpse of the Great Silence. I still wanted 'something more'. Even if I had seen a light at the end of a long tunnel, deep down I still believed the story that there was indeed 'something more' that I needed if I ever was to be whole.

At the time I compared myself to a river that was flowing toward the ocean. And I saw that if the ocean represented wholeness, there was still much of me that wanted an identity and dreaded merging with the ocean. Would not letting go of my identity as a separate individual be a loss? In my discomfort, I was soothed by a poem that has been named *Fear*.[29]

> *It is said that before entering the sea, a river trembles with fear.*
>
> *She looks back at the path she has travelled,*
> *from the peaks of the mountains,*
> *the long winding road crossing forests and villages.*
>
> *And in front of her, she sees an ocean so vast, that to enter there*
> *seems nothing more than to disappear forever.*
> *But there is no other way.*
>
> *The river cannot go back.*
> *Nobody can go back.*
> *To go back is impossible in existence.*

The river needs to take the risk of entering the ocean,
because only then will fear disappear,
because that's where the river will know
it's not about disappearing into the ocean,
but of becoming the ocean.

6

"Tsunami!!! Grab a coconut tree!!!"

In Hawaii I had the opportunity to test out my inner peace and found that it was easily trumped by the (very natural) visceral, all-consuming fear of bodily annihilation during a catastrophic natural disaster. From that fear, I quickly learned lessons that might never have been available to me had I not gone to the depths of terror in a moment of overwhelming despair.

And what did you hear, my blue-eyed son?
And what did you hear, my darling young one?
I heard the sound of a thunder, it roared out a warnin'
Heard the roar of a wave that could drown the whole world

—Bob Dylan, *A Hard Rain's A-Gonna Fall* [30]

TO MOVE THIS STORY FROM INDIA TO HAWAII, let me do a little space-time orientation.

You Can't Go Home Again

After the experience of a quiet mind in Bodh Gaya, I lost interest—but only 100%—in continuing my travels. And where was there to go but home—and in my case, that meant a room in my parents' house in Queens of New York City. I arrived home just before the lighting of the candles on the first night of Chanukkah in December of 1973. I stayed in New York for over three months, meditating about four hours each day. Even though I was more peaceful than ever before, this was upsetting to my mother who wanted me to be more ambitious in getting on with a career and to make a beginning on the path of eventually giving her grandchildren. One morning I was peacefully meditating when my mother came into my bedroom and loudly shouted: "You are nothing but a zombie! All you do every day is stare at your *pupik!*" (The word *pupik* is Yiddish for belly button and rhymes with 'look it'.) As I just continued to meditate with closed eyes and did not move, she screamed: "You are nothing but a vegetable!!!" And slammed the door. Although I felt hurt, I could empathize with my mother's frustration. I felt like singing her my own rendition of these lines from Bob Dylan's song "It's Alright, Ma (I'm Only Bleeding)"[31]:

Although the masters make the rules
For the wise men and the fools
I got nothing, Ma, I'm only meditating

I eventually realized that New York City was no longer my home. I had spent the last few years in the tropical climates of Africa and Asia, and this was a particularly cold winter in New York City. Once I left NYC, I traveled for many months visiting friends in New Mexico, Arizona, California, Oregon, and Washington. In November of 1974, I boarded a plane with a one-way ticket to Hilo on the Big Island of Hawaii. I had never been to Hawaii, but I had heard that the air and water of Hawaii were the purest in the USA, and I was looking for an island where I could feel both warm and safe.

Good Luck in Hawaii

And I was in luck. Who should I coincidentally meet at the airport of Hilo but a friend who had meditated with me in Bodh Gaya who

175

had the new name *Yongdu*—in India, he had called himself Ward Holmes. Yongdu told me that he was part of a Tibetan Buddhist group that was transforming an old abandoned Japanese temple into a Tibetan temple in an area called Wood Valley near the town of Pahala in the southern part of the Big Island. Like a true dharma buddy, he said that if I was willing to help in that transformation, I could get free 'room & board' for the next few months.

And I did labor diligently for those three months. Mostly, I assisted in painting the wooden boards of the abandoned Japanese temple with the color scheme of Tibetan Buddhist temples: red, yellow, and green. Kalu Rinpoche arrived in early February with three other Tibetan monks and an excellent Western translator. Kalu was 70 years old and he looked tranquil and wise. With Kalu present, I 'took refuge' in what are called the *Three Jewels*: the *Buddha,* the *Dharma,* and the *Sangha.* From what Kalu said, I gathered that the highest good of Buddhism was *bodhi*—which could be translated as 'enlightenment' or 'waking up'. By taking refuge, I was dedicating my life to finding a path (the *dharma*) to wake up by aligning myself with the community of people (the *sangha*) similarly inclined to such an awakening. I thought of the *Three Jewels* as a tree where the *Buddha* is the roots, the *Dharma* the trunk, and the *Sangha* the leaves.

Camping Out in an Idyllic Spot called Halapē

Eventually I made my home in Hilo. I lived in voluntary simplicity and worked as a substitute teacher in the public schools of Hilo. Loving the outdoors, I made a whole new set of friends who were interested in exploring the beaches and hills of the Big Island. One of my favorite places was called Halapē—which is the Hawaiian word for that which is 'lost' or 'missing'. Halapē is a campground in Volcanoes National Park right on the ocean beneath a 1000 foot (300 meter) cliff called Pu'u Kapukapu (Hawaiian for 'forbidden hill'). There was no road for a motorized vehicle to get to Halapē over miles of black lava. Because Halapē could only be reached on foot or on horseback, it remained unadulterated by civilization.

The first time I visited the campground at Halapē, I found it to be idyllic. The temperature was always mild. The Park Service had built shelters where water that ran off the shelter-roofs was stored in adjacent catchment tanks to give campers an abundant supply of rainwater. The shelter was in a coconut grove. As I had become skillful in wielding a machete to split open coconuts, I would have at least one delicious coconut each morning. I could swim out to a tiny island in the ocean called Ke'ā'oi—Hawaiian for 'sharp islet'. Studying the letters in the name Ke'ā'oi, I figured this might be the only time I could visit an island whose name contained each of the first four vowels of the English language. On the way to the island was a serene lagoon where I could put on my face-snorkel and see the endless profusion of colorful fish—and even turtles—that were everywhere near the shoreline of Hawaii. Knowing that it was good to balance my diet, I had brought an ample supply of vegetables and brown rice, and when others arrived, we shared food and stories in lively camaraderie.

In one Night, two Earthquakes

My second visit to Halapē was on the Thanksgiving weekend of 1975. This time my hike was sponsored by the local chapter of the Sierra Club and I went with a group of eight. Along the Puna Coast Trail from Kalapana, the eight-mile hike was along a path that was well-marked and well-maintained. Since we were walking over a giant lava field that was windy and hot, I felt that I had arrived at an oasis when I saw Halapē with its sturdy shelters next to water tanks amidst a coconut grove and right next to the ocean. Many people had already arrived—there was a troop of six Boy Scouts with four leaders, two sets of couples, and also nine fishermen who had brought down nine horses. We had hiked in on the Thursday of the Thanksgiving holiday, and after a relaxing

Friday, an earthquake woke us all up at 3:35 am on the Saturday morning. It was just a single jolt and startled us, but since all seemed peaceful, we each drifted back to sleep. Then there was a much stronger earthquake at 4:48 am—unlike the first one, the shaking did not subside and it continued on . . . and on . . . and on . . . for at least 30 seconds. Although I was in my sleeping bag, the trembling ground was heaving and jerking my whole body about in a rhythmic motion. Little did I know I was soon to experience the single most intense moment of my life.

While the earthquake was still happening, I heard a loud deafening thunderous roar—it seemed the entire cliff right behind us called Pu'u Kapukapu was land-sliding. As soon as the ground stopped shaking, I jumped out of my sleeping bag to stand up and began shouting as loud as I could: "LANDSLIDE!!! LANDSLIDE!!!" I feared that boulders might be bounding through the coconut grove. As the sound of the landslide began to subside, I could hear a different sound coming from the opposite direction: a rumble from the ocean. Even though it was still dark, a waning crescent moon over the water permitted me to see. All I could make out was that the water level of the Pacific Ocean was much lower. I said to myself: *The Pacific Ocean is disappearing. Where could it be going???* But then far in the distance I saw a high swell coming steadily towards the shore. Knowing that this meant trouble, I asked myself: "Do I have a right to refuse this experience?" The only experience worse than being caught in a tsunami is seeing an enormous wave rushing toward you and realizing there's absolutely nothing you can do to escape your fate. I felt terror rise from deep in the pit of my stomach. I knew that I was directly in the path of an unstoppable tidal wave.

A Tsunami comes to Halapē

My Sierra Club companion let out a blood-curdling shriek: "TSUNAMI !!! Grab a coconut tree !!!" Although there were coconut trees everywhere, I tried to grab the trunk of the coconut tree that my friend was holding onto and I accidentally grabbed the trunk of his body along with the trunk of the coconut tree. Within a second, warm ocean water rushed in gently up to our waists. I watched my tent and my sleeping bag disappear, but I felt in some way this was rather neat. I thought: *Some day I know this will make a great story.*

Then the water surged out of the ocean with an unimaginable power, the pressure so strong that it felt like the force of many firehoses right up against my body. As I was facing the ocean, my neck was being pushed back land-ward. I yelled: "I CAN'T HOLD ON!!! I CAN'T HOLD ON!!!" The next moment I noticed the water was above my head and I went unconscious. Still to this day I do not grasp why I would go unconscious—there was no pain in my body—all I can guess is that the astronomical level of biological fear inside my mind was the pre-condition for a blackout.

When I regained consciousness, I was instantaneously wide awake—and I experienced myself in a time warp, a bit like a latter-day Rip Van Winkle who after he had been asleep for 20 years might wonder what was this strange new environment in which he now found himself. I could recall that ages ago I had been holding on to a coconut tree when the water had risen higher than my head and I could not hold on—but now what I saw was that the coconut grove was rapidly receding into the distance. Being taken inland by a swift current, I said to myself: *Yes, this is indeed a tsunami. This really is not too bad—the water is warm and since I am a decent swimmer, all I have to do is find a way to make sure I am not taken back out to sea when this wave eventually recedes.* As I said this to myself, I was dragged down by the downward spiraling vortex of a whirlpool. I used all my might to struggle to rise to the surface. However, I was being both whirled and twirled around as if I was at the bottom of a drain being swirled into oblivion. Once I could not hold my breath any longer, I noticed that as I continued to breathe, what was being drawn into my lungs was not air but water. As I was (involuntarily) gulping in more and more water, I had the chilling realization that I had lost control of the situation. I knew that this might be the day of my death and I thought of the exact words that Joseph Goldstein had said in Bodh Gaya two years before: "Do not get attached to your body—you will have to leave it someday."

To my amazement, this thought produced not even a single mini-instant of calm or tranquility—in fact, it seemed totally useless in bringing me any peace of mind. A biological mechanism had kicked in and all of me—all 100%—wanted not to be drowned. Words fail me as I try to describe the immeasurable levels of panic that began in the pit of my stomach and moved on to engulf my entire body. Now I was not only breathing water, but it felt like I was being thrashed around inside a washing machine. My mood changed from panic to despair. In this despair, I just assumed that this was the end of my life's journey—I mentally gave up the ghost. Even though I gave up on my struggle for survival, my mind remained frozen in fear. My body could not resist taking an occasional breath, sucking more and more ocean water into my lungs. Then my mood turned even darker—I was experiencing pure terror—I had never felt such an intense feeling. All the panics that had been previously known were like mere molehills—next to this towering monolithic mountain of stripped and naked terror—now nothing remained but an unadulterated fear, visceral and amazingly primal and pure. My mind no longer contained thoughts—time disappeared—but consciousness abided as I witnessed the intense horror of suffocation. I could not stop breathing, and with each breath, drawing more water into my lungs, my insides exploded.

And then I found myself tumbling over a waterfall.

Later I realized that the tsunami had taken me into a crevasse—a deep open crack in the lava that had been created by previous earthquakes—it was about 15 feet (4.5 meters) deep and

30 feet (9 meters) across. No longer being propelled landward by the tidal wave, I coughed out the salt water in my throat. I looked around the crevasse in the pale moon-light and began shouting the same words I had last shouted right after the earthquake before I went unconscious—"LANDSLIDE!!! LANDSLIDE!!!" I was on a big boulder and without seeing where I was going, I took a step in the dark and fell down several feet and landed on my left knee, causing a sharp pain. And now that I was at the very bottom of the crevasse, I was again in water, but this time the water was only knee-deep. I could see where I had previously been on top of a large boulder that was above the waterline. As I could see a waterfall pouring into the crevasse, I crawled back up upon the same boulder and from there I could reach the ocean side of the crevasse. As the water continued to pour down over my head, I climbed up under the waterfall and found that while grabbing a protruding rock tightly with each hand, I could press my mouth near to the side of the crevasse and take a deep breath. I consciously took in a very, very, very, very deep breath. Even though I had been breathing for a full minute, now for the first time I became aware that I REALLY was breathing. That first really deep conscious breath was the most ecstatic breath of my life. And the thought simultaneously arose that I might actually survive to tell this tale.

As the stream of water that continued to fall upon my head lessened to a mere trickle, I climbed up the inside of the crevasse to peep out at the landscape. I could see the water was drawing back to the ocean, and there was a dead horse right in front of me and myriads of fish still flapping about on the land. In the distance, the trunks of the trees of the coconut grove were submerged under water and all I could see were coconut fronds.

And then from right below me, I heard a cry that was less than human—the sound was at the same time both a wail and a moan. I looked at my watch and its hands had stopped at 49 minutes after 4—one minute after the record-books say that the second earthquake had come to Halapē at 4:48 am.

Am I Alive?

Still in the dark, I came down from the crevasse and approached the sound that was wailing and moaning. I should mention that I was both naked and shivering. I was naked because I liked to sleep in the nude in my sleeping bag. I was shivering not because it was cold, but because my body was in shock. A voice came from the wail and the voice asked me a question:

"Uh . . . Am I alive? Uh . . ."

—but the question was more like a wail and a moan than a regular question—it sounded like:

Uuuuuuuhh . . . .
Aaammmm I . . .I . . I . . .aaaaaaaaaaaaaa . . .
lll . . . . . . .iiiiiiiiii. . . .ve . . . ve . . ve?
Uuuuuuuhh . . . . .

To be honest, I had the thought from the moment that I took my first breath that there was a possibility that I could have drowned and that I was just imagining that I was still alive. I was naked, shivering, my watch had stopped, my glasses were gone, and everywhere there were shadows in the spooky dark of the first light of dawn—might these not all be 'signs' that I was actually now a dead being in the underworld? I wondered how I could prove to myself that I was really in the land of the living. I asked myself: *Is it not possible that I might now be dead?* I did want to answer the question from the moaning man while trying to be fully in my integrity and confessed: "To tell you the truth, I do not know whether either of us is still alive."

As the day dawned and the world lit up, I could see for the first time the man who was in the crevasse with me. He was lying on his back and still moaning. Eventually the moans stopped and when he sat up, he complained to me that he should not have almost drowned because—according to the guidebooks—he had done all the right things the moment after the second earthquake. Being a (white) native of Hawaii and a fisherman, he knew that a tsunami was in the offing after such a big earthquake. He had immediately started running and he had just gotten to the edge of the crevasse—around the length of 3 football fields or about 1/6th of a mile (250 meters) from the ocean—when the tsunami hit him from the rear and threw him into the still empty crevasse. He had been drowning as all the water filled up the crevasse, but his life had been saved when the water emptied out of the crevasse's southern opening into the ocean.

Talking to him, I realized that by staying so close to the ocean after such a big earthquake, I had done the 'wrong' response according to the guidebooks. Of course, a guidebook could not have known about a crevasse that would prevent any escape. In my case, my ignorance prevented greater harm—I had still been holding onto the coconut tree while the crevasse had been filling up with water. Both of the people who died in this tidal wave had done what the authorities said was the 'right' action in running away from the ocean the very moment the earth had stopped quaking.

Would you say that I had Good Luck at Halapē?

I realized how lucky I was. The coconut trees were arranged like bowling pins behind me and I was the bowling ball being thrown landward at an unbelievably fast speed—even a slow tsunami goes about 200 miles per hour. If my body had struck any of these bowling pins (coconut trees), it would have indeed been a strike—like "Strike! You're out!!!"

I spent an hour with the fisherman and then the Boy Scouts descended upon us. They told us that they had found the body of their scoutmaster Dr. James Mitchel under a big boulder not far from me in the crevasse. Each boy-scout had his own story—and none of them had been badly hurt. My favorite story was that of a Boy Scout who had scrambled to the top of his shelter after the earthquake and once the tsunami hit, the shelter had been completely obliterated, but the aluminum top of the shelter became his surfboard and he said by riding on top of the tsunami wave, he had the most exciting surfing ride of his life.

One of the Boy Scouts saw that I was still shivering—so he guided me out of the crevasse toward the ocean and left me sitting naked on a big rock in the hot sun while he went to try and find Michael Cruz, a missing fisherman. Michael had last been seen running away from the ocean before the big wave arrived. (Never has he been found.) I sat there in the hot sun and thought of all the events of the day. I was surrounded by dead fish that looked quite beautiful in their multi-colored luminescent skins. I could also see a dead horse not far away and several other horses that had been killed because they had been tied to coconut trees; they were just floating in the ocean next to their respective coconut trees with what had become nooses around their necks. I pondered that if the ropes tying the horses to the trees were lassos or lariats designed to tighten under strain, the horses might have lost consciousness from the severing of their spinal cords once their necks broke—long before they even had a chance to drown.

There were odd pieces of clothing and some shreds of tents and sleeping bags. I saw that the islet called Keʻāʻoi was much lower and now only had its highest rocks above the Pacific Ocean. I decided to go inward—so I just closed my eyes and put my knees up to my chest and to my amazement I started laughing hysterically . . . with the sound of a madman. This laugh was neither joyful nor a response to anything that was funny, but 100% a mechanical release of tension that had been stored in my body while drowning. To imitate this laugh in writing, it sounded like:

HEH HEH HEH . . . . . (pause) . . . . .
HUH HEH HUH HEH HUH HEH . . . . (long pause) . . . . .

.. HEH HEH HEH HEH HEH HUH HEH HEH HUU
HUU . . . . (pause) . . . .
HUH HEH HUH HEH HUH HEH

This went on with lessening intensity for around an hour. Even though the day was quickly warming up and my unclothed body was fully exposed to the sun in a cloudless sky, my body continued to shiver. Never before in Hawaii had I shivered when doing nude sun-bathing.

I began to wonder if anyone even knew there were campers who needed to be rescued down here at Halapē. I figured that if no one came today, I would have to sleep in the nude that night with neither sleeping bag nor tent. I devised a plan where the survivors would eventually send a few healthy Boy Scouts back to civilization to find rescuers. I still had the knee injury from the moment I had fallen inside the crevasse—there was no blood or visible wound, but the knee continued to swell, and I knew I was in no shape to take an eight-mile hike.

The Rescue

Then in the distance I heard the gentle hum of a one-engine plane and I could see the plane was heading right toward us. The Boy Scouts started using scraps of tents and even their own T-shirts to wave bright colors frantically toward the sky. The plane did three horizontal loop-de-loops over our campground and then I knew rescuers would soon be on the way. As everyone's timepieces had stopped, there was no way to keep track of time, but I knew it must already be late in the morning.

And then early in the afternoon our rescuers arrived from the *National Park Service* in their own helicopter. A Park Ranger came up to my rock—he saw me huddled naked and still shivering and he asked me: "Could you use a jacket?" I said: "Yes." And as he took off his own jacket with his name on the front and the words 'National

Park Service' on the shoulder patch, he said: "I will need this back." And I responded: "No problem. I really do appreciate the loan."

He said that he was classifying people according to their injuries and I showed him my swollen knee and he told me my classification was: 'UNINJURED'. I realized that I had never been more injured in my 30 years, but I understood that all injuries are relative.

And then an hour later a military helicopter arrived and the military man yelled out: "Only the 'INJURED' on this trip—another helicopter will be here soon for the 'UNINJURED'." I just stayed put on my rock and saw a man with a branch still sticking out of his ribcage enter the helicopter. A few of the Boy Scouts marched in a solemn procession carrying the body of their Boy Scout Leader Dr. James Mitchel to the helicopter. As they were transporting this corpse, I had a self-centered thought when I wondered if it was fair that a body should be allowed to fly out before me—if he was dead, did he *really* deserve the privilege of being classified as 'INJURED'?

The same military helicopter returned about 1½ hours later and all the 'UNINJURED' climbed aboard by going up a few metal steps. As there were no seats inside, we sat together on the floor. It was great looking out the window and seeing Pu'u Kapukapu from the air. I eventually realized that we were being taken to the hospital at Kilauea Military Camp (KMC) near the visitor center of Volcanoes National Park. I now had the National Park Service jacket covering my torso, but I realized that the jacket only went down to my *pupik* (did you remember that this is Yiddish for bel-ly-button?) and I was naked from the waist down.

When we got to the helicopter landing pad at KMC, I was surprised to see around 30 people waiting at the helipad. I later learned that the news had gotten out to Hilo that there were dead campers at Halapē and the families of the various campers had come to KMC to see if their loved ones were among the living. I also saw a man who I recognized—the photographer for the Hilo newspaper, the *Hawaii Tribune-Herald*. I had a fantasy that he would take my photo naked from the waist down and this photo could go all around the world and I could connect with all my friends in other countries. I had no shame about being naked and the tsunami gave me a perfect excuse in the eyes of the law for not being arrested for either exhibitionism or indecent exposure.

To make it possible for him to get a better photograph, I waited to be the last one to leave the helicopter. The photographer lifted his camera, ready to take a picture, but the moment before he could snap the shutter the military man who was guiding me down the first step down realized that I was naked from the waist down and shouted: "GET BACK into the helicopter." The military man joined me inside the helicopter and said: "Take my jacket and put it around your waist." As he was taking off his jacket, I concluded by the three chevrons on the shoulder insignia of the jacket that his rank must be Sergeant. After he saw me firmly tying his jacket around my waist, he said: "I will need this back." And I said: "No problem, Sergeant. I really do appreciate the loan." And I caught a glimpse of him judgmentally shaking his head as I descended the stairs of the helicopter. The photographer was now nowhere to be seen and I lost my opportunity to become famous (or infamous).

I was quickly ushered into a big waiting room with all the other 'UNINJURED' and their families. Not present were those classified as 'INJURED'—and also the corpse was not here. I realized that the first trip of the military helicopter had been to Hilo, where there was a well-provisioned hospital and a morgue, and it now made sense that the corpse had been taken before me. I let go of my grievance that I had been treated unfairly.

For the first time that day, I saw the time—a clock on the wall said it was 3 pm. I did a quick calculation and concluded that it had been a little over 10 hours since the tidal wave.

I explained to a nurse standing there that the clothes I was wearing were not mine and I had to return them. She quickly saw my dilemma and gave me a big navy green blanket imprinted with the letters 'KMC'. As I wrapped the blanket around me, the National Park Ranger appeared and I handed back his jacket. When a moment later, the Sergeant arrived, I was still covered in the KMC big blanket, and it was easy to return his jacket.

The Eggshell Mystery Solved

I was just meditating with my eyes closed when the same nurse came by and called out: "Who wants food?" She broke me out of my meditative trance. I realized that up to this moment that I'd had nothing to either eat or drink since I had been so rudely awakened by the tidal wave in the first glimmerings of dawn. I raised my hand and said: "I do." She handed me a sandwich and I looked inside the two pieces of bread and saw egg salad. I was suddenly ravishingly hungry and greedily took a bite of the sandwich—and I could not understand the next sensation—it felt like I was eating eggshells, rather than eggs. I said to myself: *I cannot believe this!!! Here I am a survivor of a deadly tsunami and this hospital cannot do better than serve me an egg salad sandwich that is filled with egg shells!!!*

I decided I wanted to examine the food in my mouth. As I realized that this would be too disgusting to do in public, I went to the men's room and took the food out of my mouth and looked at the egg salad that I had been chewing upon. To my surprise, I could not find even one shell. Quizzically, I opened my mouth in front of the mirror and I saw that between each and every tooth there was a tiny seashell and that my tongue and throat were covered with even bigger sea-shells. What came to mind is that I had once seen the lines from Shakespeare's *The Tempest* on the gravestone of Percy Bysshe Shelley (in Rome) that made reference to him drowning in a storm at sea off the Italian coast when he was around my age, 30 years old:

Nothing of him that doth fade,

> But doth suffer a sea-change
> Into something rich and strange.
>
> Ariel's song, The Tempest [32]

I realized how close I had come to suffering a 'sea-change'. Not being in a sentimental mood, I did not want to keep these shells as a souvenir of my early-morning swim. I thoroughly rinsed my mouth and spit out the shells. Guess what? Once I cleaned up my own act and took another bite of the egg salad sandwich, there were no eggshells.

The Hippie has no clothes

I went back to the waiting room and a very tall doctor was asking if any of us had any injuries. I showed him my swollen knee and after a close examination, he said that I had to go to Hilo Hospital for an X-ray to see if a bone might have been broken. Then it was time for everyone going to Hilo Hospital to get into a big van. The ride was a gift from KMC and the American tax-payer—all of us had already donated all of our money to a tax-deductible charitable organization called the Pacific Ocean and there was no way any of us could have paid our own way for a taxi.

As I was leaving the hospital, I was going out the front door with the big navy green blanket that said 'KMC' around my torso. The receptionist at the main door saw me leaving and said to me politely: "Sir, your blanket is military property—you are not allowed to take that beyond the door." I started to hand her back the blanket and she said in a loud startled voice: "*SIR, YOU ARE CERTAINLY NOT ALLOWED TO BE NAKED ON MILITARY PROPERTY!!!*" So I re-wrapped the blanket back around my torso and just stood there staring at her wordlessly as if this were a chess game with my quizzical expression saying: *Madam, it's your move.* She just stood there flustered for a full minute and then told me: "I am going to see if there is any provision in the rule book about

189

what to do when a patient arrives naked at the hospital. I am sorry, but the blankets are counted each week, and if any blanket is not accounted for, I have to pay for the blanket out of my own salary." (The thought arose of paying her for the cost of taking this KMC blanket with me, but then I realized all my money had already been taken by the Pacific Ocean.) When she saw I had no solution for her dilemma, she went to the reception desk and took out this huge book which said: "HOSPITAL REGULATIONS FOR KMC". This felt like some comedy routine and I just could not believe that she would ever find such a regulation about what to do when a naked tsunami victim might arrive at her hospital.

Meanwhile the van waiting outside the door began honking as the driver perceived that one of his passengers was still missing and he wanted me to hurry up. The very tall doctor on duty heard the honking horn and on coming into the room saw me waiting there with the blanket and the receptionist frantically looking in different sections of the rule book for a provision that would match this situation. He said to the receptionist: "What's happening here, Miss Jones?" And Miss Jones explained: "This patient is naked under the blanket and it is against regulations to let him leave KMC with the blanket and I will be held responsible for any missing blanket. I am now looking at the rule book to try to find the provision in the REGULATIONS that might approximately match this situation of where a naked man arrives at our hospital." The (very tall) doctor raised his eyebrows and I saw that he could see the comic potential in the moment and he said gently to her: "I will donate my second pair of pants to this gentleman." And with that, he went back to his room to get his donation and after I changed into his pants, I soon discovered that the pants legs went way down quite past my toes. I thought to myself: *Beggars can't be choosers.* I thanked the doctor profusely—he had at least covered my nakedness.

At Hilo Hospital, the X-rays showed that no bone had been

broken and the doctor explained that the swelling would begin going down in a few days. As the hospital was a mile from my home and I had no money for a taxi, I decided to walk the distance. With no shirt and no shoes and quite a limp . . . no one in Hilo even noticed that I looked the slightest bit peculiar.

The head of the Hilo chapter of the Sierra Club—who at the last moment had decided not to come on the Halapē hike—was waiting for me at my rooming house. He treated me to my first real meal of the day as we spent a sweet evening together. I was so grateful for having survived and excitedly told him all the happenings of the day. We both had a good laugh about the receptionist's frantic effort to find a regulation pertaining to the dilemma of what to do with a naked man covered by HER blanket.

The Nightmares Come

That night I had a nightmare of a wave coming out of the ocean, engulfing me and drowning me with its water and I woke up in a sweat. Every night that week I had another tsunami dream. The last dream of the week was the most dramatic (and traumatic): in my dream, I had finally gotten to the highest point of a mountain in Switzerland—it looked like the Matterhorn—and guess what?—a wave swept up the entire slope of the mountain and carried me away from its very pinnacle.

Although I was to live in Hawaii for 2½ more years, in many ways this experience terminated my stay there. I could never again sleep near the ocean without having at least a mini-nightmare. I still believe that Hawaii has both the air and water in America that is the purest, but I now felt in the cells of my body a terror that was equally unadulterated and pure.

What the books say about this Tsunami

I now want to conclude and tell about the events that happened in the early morning of Saturday, November 29th, 1975 with the gift of hindsight.

All the Boy Scouts survived, but their leader Dr. James Mitchel had been crushed under a boulder in the crevasse. Michael Cruz had been washed out to sea and the search for him had been called off in a few days. The fisherman who was in the crevasse with me never recovered his full breathing capability as half a pound of sand was discovered in the alveoli (tiny air sacs) of his lungs and lung specialists declared there was no way to remove this sand—he had been swallowing sandy seawater for around a minute before the water had left the crevasse.

Both the earthquake and the tsunami were caused by a sudden movement of the sea floor off the southeast coast of Hawaii. According to seismic instruments, the first earthquake had a magnitude of 5.7 on the Richter scale and the second was a 7.2. While the tsunami was coming into Halapē, red hot lava had begun to fountain 30 feet (10 meters) high along a fissure on the floor of the Kilauea Caldera. Because the resulting lava flow came so early in the morning, no tourists had been injured. Young active volcanoes expand horizontally as they rise vertically, thereby becoming unstable as chunks of land can break off the slopes and slide unto the seafloor. Halapē fell 12 feet (3.5 meters) as it slumped seaward during the earthquake—and the Big Island gained a few acres as the south flank of Kilauea moved into the ocean. The spot where I had been camping six feet above sea level had fallen the full 12 feet—so once the land had stopped shaking, my sleeping bag was now six feet *below* sea level. During the moment that I was screaming: "LANDSLIDE!!! LANDSLIDE!!!"—because the land had already descended downwards into the ocean—I was actually at a lower elevation than the entire Pacific Ocean. As the slope of the volcano had broken off, the ocean had been pushed back about 1 mile (1.5 kilometers). One could make up a story to personify what happened next: "The ocean did not like being pushed around by a mere chunk of earth that showed no respect for its clearly demarcated boundary, and being in a foul mood, came back with an unforgiving vengeance."

The coconut trees had lost all their fronds up to the point of 20 feet (6 meters)—so this is the figure given for the height of the wave. After the land subsided, all of the roots of these palm trees were below sea level, so it was just a matter of time until the salt water would kill all these trees.

A tsunami is defined as a wave created in a large body of water by a sudden disturbance—such a wave-like swell can be caused by an earthquake, landslide, volcanic eruption, or even a meteorite impact. The word 'tsunami' combines the Japanese words 'tsu' (harbor) and 'nami' (wave). The highest tsunami ever recorded was in the Lituya Bay in Alaska where a rock landslide created a wave that was 1,720 feet (524 meters)—this is the height of a 145-story building. Tsunamis that have a chance to build up in the ocean are often around 100 feet high when they meet land.

What I went through is now called by the history books: *'The Kalapana Earthquake of 1975'.* Although the swells coming toward Hawaii from earthquakes in Alaska are both higher and more destructive, this Kalapana earthquake has the reputation in those history books of having created the most destructive locally generated tsunami in Hawaii during the 20th century and so far into the 21st century. The last comparable locally generated tsunami anywhere in Hawaii occurred not far from Halapē in 1868, and that was similarly caused by a seaward traveling land mass pushing back the ocean after an earthquake.

Compassion

I felt compassion for the two fellow-campers whose lives ended on that Saturday morning—and also for the fisherman in the crevasse with me who in one minute contracted a life-long case of silicosis. Usually it takes decades for smoke or dust or sand to accumulate in the lungs before such a slow build up can create this lifelong ailment. However, it is a rather unusual occurrence to be under a turbulent Pacific Ocean breathing sand-filled water for a full minute.

Lessons Learned in a Camping Spot called Halapē

This Thanksgiving camping trip that was so interrupted by a big wave now happened 50 years ago. I look upon these events as a great teaching. Being terrified in the face of death showed me that I had lied to myself about my level of spiritual evolution. I see *denial* as a form of lying:

> Don't
> Even
> Notice
> I
> Am
> Lying

I realized that before the tsunami I had not known myself well enough to perceive how truly attached I was to this particular body. Ever since Bodh Gaya, I had been telling people that I had no fear of death. I thought that I had figured out that in essence who I am is 'consciousness'—so what did it really matter when I left my body? I had also told myself that according to the laws of karma, I would just get a new body and be reborn again anyway. In my mind, there was the thought that it did not matter when I died—yes, how little I knew myself before that day. Although I definitely would never want to re-live this experience, I am still deeply grateful that I gained a lesson in humility.

A new way of holding reality became an axiom of my emotional landscape. What died in the dawn's early light of that Hawaiian morning was the belief that I would one day somehow find a secure resting place in the world. This insight resonates with this teaching found in the Bible:

Foxes have holes, and birds of the air have nests;
but the Son of man hath not where to lay his head

—Luke 9:58, KJV

I do have a playful way of expressing this insight when on rare occasions I feel moved to tell my story of the earthquake that spawned a tsunami. I only do this when my audience is logged out of the electronic noise and emotional static of our media age and there are no people coming and going. I have found that the telling often elicits an emotional response from those who hear it —I guess that they feel a dose of that terror that I experienced when such a big wave forever changed my sense of security.

If you are ever to hear me tell this story in person, you will find me concluding this tale by saying the word 'tsunami' in a rather peculiar way—I will (mis)pronounce the word as if it were 'tsu-NO-me'. I will tell you how this 'me' got really terrified when he feared that he might leave his body and become a 'NO me'.

7

Can a Dane create new words for the English language?

I learned so much from the quiet, unassuming Dane, known as Sunyata. The Silence in the atmosphere around him could hardly have been more different than the commotion that always seemed to surround Neem Karoli Baba and yet . . . they both inspired me to seek within for THAT which does not change.

Never the Spirit was born.
The Spirit shall cease to be—never.
Never was time it was not.
Ends and Beginnings are dreams!
Birthless and deathless and changeless
remaineth the Spirit—
forever.
Death hath not touched It at all,
dead though the form,
the house of IT—seems!

Sir Edwin Arnold
The Song Celestial, Chapter 2 (1885) [33]

I MET EMMANUEL SORENSEN WHEN HE WAS 90 years old and I was less than half his age. He gave me great support and inspiration during the last three years of his life. Besides becoming my friend, he challenged and illuminated my mind with a new way of using words.

He had been given the name 'Sunyata' by Ramana Maharshi in a telepathic initiation while sitting silently in front of Ramana in Tiruvannamalai, India. He neither asked for this initiation nor was it given to him—it just happened. These are the five words of the initiation:

We are always aware sunyata.

Sorensen took these words as initiation, blessing, recognition, mantra, and also his name—from then on, he always referred to himself as 'Sunyata'. When he received the telepathic communication, he did not know the meaning of *sunyata*. However, he soon discovered that *sunyata* is a Buddhist concept pointing to the 'emptiness' that is 'full'—or, to use Sunyata's way of translating his new name, 'full solid emptiness'.

Sometimes *sunyata* is also translated as 'the void', the void being the undifferentiated background out of which all apparent entities, distinctions, and dualities arise. The idea here is that although people, things, or events may appear on the outside to be separate, real, and substantial, they are actually—when *innerstood*— interpenetrating, ephemeral and insubstantial.

After Sunyata had left the ashram of Ramana Maharshi for the first time in 1936, Ramana had referred to Sunyata as a '*janam-siddha*'—this is the Sanskrit phrase for a 'rare-born mystic'. As Sunyata had never heard of a 'mystic' before Ramana Maharshi had used this word to describe him, he began an inquiry to try to find out the meaning of this word. What he eventually discovered is that a mystic is an individual who intuits what is true from inside his own being rather than from the surrounding environment. What made Sunyata 'rare-born' is that he was born as a mystic and never had to follow a spiritual path to attain this inner-directedness.

In his childhood he was not extroverted and enjoyed being a quiet observer. His parents made few demands on him. The only interruption in his solitude was to go to a one-room country schoolhouse in the north of Denmark that taught him the basics of reading, writing, and arithmetic. As he was left alone much of the time to play with the animals on the family farm, he was never much conditioned by societal norms. His own predisposition was to be the witness and he never wanted to accumulate possessions, achieve success, or even find a mate.

To just jump ahead in my story, the way I got to know Sunyata was through weekly question-and-answer sessions on the Alan Watts Society's houseboat docked in Sausalito just north of San Francisco. For Sunyata, every question was seen as legitimate and greeted with acceptance and even approval. One evening a new-comer at these gatherings grilled him about his sex-life (after all, the in-thing in San Francisco of the 1980's was to go *tantric*—which for many people at that time meant combining spirituality with sexual union). Sunya (this was his nickname) answered that he only had sex during one week of his entire life—and he told us what happened. Living in England when he was in his mid-twenties, his two best friends were a couple and when the man was killed in the First World War, the woman in the partnership said it would help her to get over her overwhelming grief if she could 'make love' with him. He agreed and they had sex. After Sunyata told us about this sexual experience that had transpired over 60 years earlier, he was asked: "So what do you think about 'sex'?" With a twinkle in his eye, he responded: "It's not as good as meditation".

Before I tell the story about how I met Sunyata, I want to outline the six words that Sunyata formulated that might have a chance of entering the English language. As you will see, all these words come out of a worldview well known to those who are famil-iar with the spiritual traditions of Advaita Vedanta, Buddhism, and Taoism. My own guess is that the first of the six words might become popular, and I am curious how many might one day find their way one day into a dictionary. Here are the six words that

Sunyata formulated and used in his life:

1. Innerstand

For Sunyata, the most crucial word to describe his own consciousness was *innerstanding*—which he defined as 'intuitive awareness' or knowing by identity. In *innerstanding*, there is an identity with what is intuited or known that causes a momentary dissolution of the boundary between subject and object. What he saw was that English had no word to describe the type of knowing that can occur when there is intuition combined with empathy.

> *To understand is mental and intellectual—*
> *which means to 'stand under'—*
> *this means to be burdened by mental conceptions.*
> *This prevents one from grasping the truth.*
> *I do not want to be understood or overstood,*
> *but only innerstood.*[34]

2. Awaring

Sunyata wanted to make 'aware' into a verb because he saw awareness as always in movement and never static. He would break the rules of English grammar by talking about how he was always *awaring*. It made no sense to him that 'to aware' was not a common verb in the English language. 'Knowing' was just too cerebral for his taste. Just as he would rather *innerstand* than understand, he would rather have *Self-awaring* than self-knowledge. As he wrote:

> *A man who seeks truth will never find it.*
> *Truth is in what IS and that is the beauty of it.*
> *The moment you conceptualize it,*
> *the moment you seek it,*
> *you become agitated,*
> *and the man who struggles*

cannot innerstand that we have to be still
—inwardly still—
to aware THAT.
I AM is always aware.[35]

3. Innerstance

Innerstance is a companion word to *innerstand*. *Innerstances* are the set of attitudes and beliefs that one brings to any situation. Positive innerstances—like equanimity and loving-kindness—can predominate even in painful circumstances. And, just as importantly, negative innerstances—like fearfulness or timidity—have the power to become self-fulling prophecies and thereby create the circumstances of our life.

Sunyata's primary innerstances were of acceptance and gratitude and he was capable of apperceiving with joyous ease all the circumstances that life might present. Here is a taste of his own writing concerning his way of seeing the world:

Instead of understanding, there is *innerstanding*.
'Know' and 'understand' are too mental—
I'd rather use 'sense', 'intuit', 'aware', and *'innerstand'*.
Instead of circumstances, there are *innerstances*.
This I AM *innerstands*, everywhere.
Why criticize or judge God's handiwork?
I never made any plans—
the Plan is there
and we can fit in
with joyous ease
and delightful uncertainty.[36]

4. Headucation

Sunyata would ask us not to mis-take schooling for education. To assist us in avoiding this error, Sunyata coined the word *headucation*—he defined this as the conditioning that is imposed on an individual that draws them away from their heart and intuition. He saw that headucation was typical of much traditional schooling throughout the world. Sunyata would often say he had the good luck of having escaped the learned ignorance of headucation. In his life, this meant that he had only made it up to the eighth grade in the small country schoolhouse near his family farm in the north of Denmark. About himself, he said:

I was never *headucated.*
The mind did not develop—
I never had to go to school.
The mind is so troublesome here in the West—
you are so mental.
In India, there is intuitive awareness—
innerstanding.
Indians are not mental in the Western sense of the word.[37]

Sunyata's view was that it was the way that the mind was headucated that was one of the sources of ego-consciousness. He saw the ego as the belief in a separate self, and this belief was conditioned into a child through language. Sunya told us he could best commune with humans before their second birthday. Sunyata's way of innerstanding his own life was that he was born without a sense of being a separate self:

Written to our Self,
the naughty word-symbols 'I', 'me', and 'mine'
do not occur.[38]

When Sunyata was asked how he viewed other people, he answered for him there were no others, but only the Self. Because Sunya was born without a sense of being a separate self, he never had the self-centered desires that characterize most of humanity. He viewed these self-centered desires as imprisoning the true Self. In his innerstanding, this prison was made by the ego.

Sunyata thought it was hopeless for an individual to try to do a prison break by killing or destroying the ego—particularly because in his view the ego was nothing more than a conditioned set of beliefs that was not 'real enough'. Was it not the ego itself that was trying to eliminate the felt sense of an 'I', 'me', or 'mine'? Sunya's view was that the intention to get rid of the ego would only work to strengthen that very ego. He saw the path of freedom was for the individual to become ego-free rather than ego-less—this meant to be free *in* the ego rather than to be free *of* the ego. In fact, Sunyata saw that it was necessary for most people to have a sense of a separate self to survive in the world, but he thought it was possible to direct that ego to cultivate Self-knowledge. When we arrived at being 'free *in* ego', we would still have a 'me'—but that 'me' could engage in a quest to discover that which does not change.

5. Ego-ji

Sunyata would also say that as long as the ego appeared to be real in our minds, we ought to treat it with respect and he coined the word 'ego-ji' to show this respect. The word ego-ji is a combination of the Indian suffix '—ji' which is put at the end of names in Hindi to show respect and then the word 'ego'. For instance, in India, 'babaji' is a combination of the Indian word for father—'baba'—and that same suffix for respect: '—ji'.

Sunyata discerned that this ego that so enslaved most of humanity was only a passing phenomenon. True education would illumine ego-jis so that they would be able to recognize their true nature as the Self. To use one of his favorite phrases: "Ego-oblivion is Self-awareness." His proof that the ego was only a story is the axiom upon which he built all of his thinking:

That which changes is not real enough.

In Sunyata's consciousness, the world manifests as a complementary set of opposites:

birth and death
pleasure and pain
joy and sorrow
success and failure
creation and destruction

Every life contains these opposites, as depicted in the yin-yang symbol. What does not manifest is the field in which these opposites appear. Sunyata saw suffering as coming from an ego's argument with reality. Sunyata once quoted from Nisargadatta's book, *I Am That*:

Suffering is due to non-acceptance.
When pain is accepted for what it is—
a lesson and a warning—
and deeply looked into and heeded,
the separation between pain and pleasure breaks down;
both become experience,
suffering when resisted, joyful when accepted.[39]

In Sunyata's experience, it was possible to be aware of and then integrate the opposites into a dynamic harmonious whole.

"Men say: Time passes. Time says: Men pass." Because egos come and go, we cannot find lasting happiness in what is impermanent. For Sunyata, all satisfaction that is physical, emotional, or mental can only be temporary. There is no lasting satisfaction to be gained by pursuing the desires of the separate self; more 'real' than such a pursuit is to become aware of the energy which activates insentient matter called 'the body'. Sunyata called this all-pervasive and eternal energy that activates insentient matter 'the Self' or

'I Am'. As identification with the ego lessens, there is less and less mental activity—and Sunyata called this innerstance 'Silence'. To him, Silence did not mean the absence of sound, but the intention to still desires, efforting, and willfulness. In this stillness, there would come an attunement to the voice of intuition.

Depending on the context, Sunyata presented four different notions of the 'ego'—it might be best to think of each notion as being true at a certain level of a pyramid of increasing awareness leading to awakening. On the lowest level, the ego that is greedy and arrogant creates dis-harmony through selfishness; on the next, the efforting of a disciplined ego in pursuing its own self-interest might be useful in realizing any goal that it sets; then on the next level, this same efforting might be perceived as an obstacle to 'the peace that passeth understanding'; and finally, at the highest level, there is the *innerstanding* that the ego simply does not exist as an autonomous entity independent of the Self. Sunyata would often say:

> Effort was the helper—Effort is the bar
> Ego was the helper—Ego is the bar. [40]

All these different notions were implicit in Sunyata's respect for the power of the ego —or what he would playfully refer to as 'ego-ji'.

6. WU!

Often there were puzzled faces at the gathering, and at those moments Sunyata would often look directly at the puzzled person and make this sound:

WU !

'WU' is a word (or is it a sound?) that Sunyata defined to simultaneously mean both *Yes* and *No*. He would often gently utter this sound when he had finished a sentence or when people around him looked puzzled. Sunyata got this word from the Chinese Zen tradition where a common answer to a koan can be the sound *Wu!*–which he said simultaneously means *Yes* and *No*. And in honor of this word *Wu*, he called his own higher self by the name *Wu-ji*, but he spelled this name without the hyphen–thus Wuji:

Wuji *innerstands* in affectionate detachment.
He intuits and is filled with gratitude and wonder.
He apperceives that he is birth-free, body-free, time-free, and death-free.
Wuji is also ego-free in non-dual Oneness or Wuness.
YourSelf and mySelf are identical.
I know this, but egojis do not.
This is all the difference and it cannot last.
Wu! [41]

Back to Eliyahu's story

We now move from Sunya's time-free and space-free reality to resume the story of a certain ego-bound individual named Elliott. As you may remember from the last chapter, when Elliott's lungs had begun filling with salt water, his initial panic had moved into despair, and then escalated into pure unadulterated terror.

I got it was time to apply for a Doctorate in Psychology on the mainland. After never having gotten sun-burned in three years, I reluctantly realized that I had to let go of my milky coffee-hued skin that the Hawaiian sun had coaxed forth from the Palestinian deep in my genes. I used my credentials from Amherst College and the London School of Economics to apply for admission to the California Institute of Asian Studies (CIAS), a graduate school in San Francisco. This school had a Buddhist meditation teacher from Burma on the faculty and was committed to finding the commonality between Eastern and Western philosophies. Once accepted and enrolled I met many students and teachers with whom I shared a rapport and I made new friends. To my surprise, the school needed a Financial Aid Officer and I used my organizational capabilities to assist those attending this institution to get student loans from the Federal Government. I artistically placed the capitalized phrase "MAY ALL BEINGS BE HAPPY" at the bottom of all the government financial aid forms.

A Sudden Appearance of the Trickster

Our institution came up for accreditation during my tenure as the Financial Aid Officer. If we failed, we would no longer be eligible for student loans from the Federal government and as we had no endowment, that might mean the end of CIAS. In those days my hair was down past my shoulders, I had a huge beard, and I only wore drawstring pants. I knew this might not be suitable attire to impress the Accreditation Committee. I felt it was my duty to do a total make-over. I went to a barber and emerged clean shaven and with a crew-cut. With the addition of a three-piece suit that I had last worn 15 years earlier at a wedding, my transformation was complete.

At our first meeting with the Accreditation Committee, I carefully placed myself between the Committee on one side of the room and my fellow administrators on the other side. When we were all comfortably seated, my friends from CIAS thought I was on the Accreditation Committee. When we began our meeting by formally introducing ourselves, I said my name with each syllable pronounced distinctly—El-li-ott I-sen-berg, Fi-nan-cial Aid Of-ficer. I soon heard loud guffaws from the CIAS part of the room. I could see many of my friends who were in the room shaking their heads in disbelief—and the Accreditation Committee never had a clue about why there was such a commotion. (Yes, we were accredited. And yes, I loved playing the trickster.)

The Devil Made Me Do It

When it was time to write a doctoral dissertation, I had a meeting with Ralph Metzner, the Academic Dean of the Institute. I knew that Ralph had been teaching at Harvard along with Richard Alpert (Ram Dass) and Timothy Leary and that the three of them had been pioneers in the movement that had brought psychedelics into the forefront of world consciousness. Although Ralph was a proponent of the responsible use of psychedelics, he also had rigorous academic standards.

When he asked me what topic I wanted to explore in my doctoral dissertation, I told him that I was interested in learning more about "the Goddess and the forms in which She might manifest in our time". He asked me why I had this interest and I said: "Because she is a force to oppose evil." And he said: "I want you to do your doctoral dissertation on evil." My initial reaction was to resist anyone telling me what to do because I thought that I had the right to pick my own doctoral dissertation topic. But when I really listened to his suggestion and became less reactive, I realized that I didn't really know what evil was and that I could sink my teeth into such an exploration.

I told my father about my conversation with Ralph. My father was enthusiastic about having his prodigal son become a doctor so he was willing to support me for up to two years while I explored 'evil'. This meant I was able to get 'an honorable discharge' from my job as the Financial Aid Officer to work full-time on a doctoral dissertation.

Meeting Mister Nobody

Just as I was beginning my dissertation, I saw a poster that there was a man named Sunyata talking at gatherings on a houseboat that was once owned by Alan Watts. Watts had died a few years before (in 1973) and his followers had taken the money that had been left in his estate to travel to India to bring back to America 'an enlightened sage'. Who these followers eventually chose to bring back to America was a Danish mystic named Sunyata.

Having brought him back alive, the Alan Watts Society was

advertising the presence of Sunyata in posters all over the Bay Area. The happenstance that brought me to the first gathering was seeing a poster that proclaimed in big print this phrase: DANCE WITH THE VOID. In smaller print, the poster said that there would be a question-and-answer session with 'a rare-born mystic' at a certain day and time on the Alan Watts houseboat in Sausalito—just north of the Golden Gate Bridge. When I arrived for the evening gathering, Sunyata hadn't yet entered the meeting room of the houseboat, so I sat on a cushion and waited patiently for his arrival.

Eventually, I saw a purple swirl of clothing enter from the back of the room. Moving gingerly yet nimbly, he found a pathway through the people sitting on the floor. His appearance was striking and other-worldly; around his head was wrapped a large lavender turban; he wore loose-fitting Indian-style pants and a shirt of the same light purple hue. He sat upon a chair facing those who had gathered that evening and began the meeting with a few moments of silence. Then, speaking softly with an ever so slight Danish accent, he told the story of how when the Nobel-prize winning poet Rabindranath Tagore had come to recuperate for six months where Sunyata had been working as a 'simple gardener' at Dartington Hall in England, there had been a quiet rapport between them.

Tagore had invited Sunyata to come to India "to teach Silence". He took up the invitation when he was 40 years old and had travelled overland through Europe and then by the long sea voyage from Egypt to India. His visit turned into a four-decade residency in a simple hut on what came to be called 'Crank's Ridge' near Almora, in the Himalayas. When he was 88 years old, he said that he had been 'kidnapped' by the Alan Watts Society from the home where he said he would have contentedly died. He concluded his self-introduction by telling us that he had "nothing to teach and nothing to sell" and then asked for questions. In his answers, he would often smile and tell jokes, and he always seemed to be radiating gentleness and playfulness. He was quite relaxed and exuded an air of confidence.

Being present with Sunyata that first evening, I experienced the eloquence in his Silence. I felt a huge release of tension. Sunyata was like an ocean-bound river that was always murmuring cheerfully no matter what scenery might be passing by—just to sit by that river gave me a calm sense of detachment and inward peace. I experienced Sunyata as being in his heart without any pretense of trying to prove that he was a 'somebody'. In truth, when I first met him, he was wearing a large button that said: MISTER NOBODY.

At graduate school, I was surrounded by highly intellectual people and I knew that a doctoral dissertation was an enterprise that would require a sustained mental energy. As my mind was already getting over-heated with all these theories about evil, I had the thought that it would be a perfect counterpoint for me to regularly spend evenings with Sunyata. Although writing the dissertation necessitated being highly cerebral, each week I would take a one evening break from my research to learn from Sunyata about a more heart-full way of experiencing the world.

During a private meeting with Sunyata, I asked him if he knew of Neem Karoli Baba. He told me that Maharaji had come along with many devotees to visit him at his mountain retreat on Crank's Ridge in Almora. I asked Sunyata what he felt about the day, and he said that it was "the noisiest day" that he had ever spent on Crank's Ridge. I wondered if he was saying that his *preference* was for Silence, but then I remembered he had said that it was only the ego that was attached to its *preferences*.

The Sunyata Gatherings

The gatherings were all somewhat similar but often there would be a unique twist. Each week I would hear the same story about how he had been "kidnapped" from his Indian hut and that he had "nothing to teach and nothing to sell". And then one day Sunyata told us one reason he had agreed to come to California was that before the First World War, he had regularly attended lectures in London by Annie Besant of the Theosophical Society. One of her themes was that a 'New Race' was going to be born in California during the 21st Century. He said that if a 'New Race' was about to be born, he wanted to be there to witness the birthing.

The same small core group of devotees attended each of the gatherings—we were 'the regulars'—and then there would always be a few newcomers. Many gatherings had a spark of humor because most newcomers could not intellectually comprehend the philosophical viewpoint that was being presented. Basically, Sunyata would say that if we put less emphasis on what we wanted and paid more attention to our true nature, an inward space would inevitably open where we would be capable of 'awaring' an ever-present inner realm of grace.

I remember one evening a young man told a story about how his girlfriend had just broken up with him and he was so very anxious and could hardly sleep and asked Sunyata what he should do to find peace of mind; after a pause, Sunyata asking him in a very quiet puzzled voice:

"Why would you continue to want anything
that you could no longer have?"

The young man looked totally perplexed and mystified, and I could see that he could not understand what Sunyata was saying. The room fell into a long, deep silence and, like most of the new-comers who came to these gatherings, this young man never came back. In fact, of the 20 people who I personally invited to meet Sunyata so that they might have an experience of being in the presence of 'a rare-born mystic', only one person returned for a second meeting. Sunyata had no flash and no showmanship and the most common reaction from those I invited was: "Thanks for inviting me to see that sweet old woman." The reason that they mistook his gender is because he was very soft-spoken and like many healthy people in his 90's, he had become quite androgynous. Out of curiosity I had purposely decided not to say whether he was a man or a woman and to just tell the people who I invited to the gatherings that he was 'a rare-born mystic'. My aim in not revealing his gender identity was to see if they would perceive him as a man or a woman. It must have been his gentleness that resulted in most perceiving him as 'a sweet old woman'.

As I was doing my doctoral dissertation about evil, I decided to ask Sunyata about his views on the subject. I had a hint of what he might say because how often he would repeat this saying:

"All is right that seems most wrong."[42]

When I finally asked Sunyata specifically about evil, he gently told me of his own *innerstance:*

"Evil is not real enough."

Once I had finished my doctoral dissertation in 1983, I was awarded a Ph.D. in Psychology. While writing the dissertation, I had discovered that I enjoyed writing. In the summer of 1984, I told Sunyata that I would like to write a book about him and asked him if he would be willing to assist me? I knew that in his 93 years he had only published a few small articles in Indian journals and no book had been written either by or about him. When I arrived at the gathering the next week, Sunyata brought in a stack of papers which had much of his writings of the last few decades.

Sunyata Leaves His Body

Within less than a month after giving me his writings, Sunyata was hit by a car and died a few days later. I felt I had lost my best friend and cried with tears running down my cheeks for a full day and then I grieved for many months. I had lost what had been an easy and dependable access to peace of mind.

Co-editing a Book About Sunyata

A year after Sunyata's death, I was talking to Betty Camhi, a friend who had been Sunyata's secretary. She asked me: "Would you like to co-edit a book about Sunyata?" I was enthusiastic about the idea. Working one day a week with Betty, it took almost two years to complete a workable manuscript. Our joint creation centered around one long autobiographical essay that Sunyata wrote in 1945 called *Memory*. Sunya had picked this title *Memory* because it was his translation of Socrates' word *anamnesis*—usually translated as 'recollection'—which Socrates used to describe his own remembrance of the wisdom that he possessed before he was born. In this essay, Sunyata tells his life story—of how he only briefly identified as an ego—and describes what it feels like to be in a life-long state of ego-free consciousness. What motivated Sunyata to write the essay is that he was trying to figure out how it happened that he never completely lost touch with a pre-natal awareness of wholeness, unity, and dynamic living harmonies.

Once Betty and I had created a workable manuscript, we were surprised at how difficult it was to find a publisher. I sent the Sunya manuscript to seven different publishers in the USA who each specialized in spiritual books—this was before the Internet, so each was a hefty package. Each of the seven eventually did answer and what came back from each of them was essentially the same message (here I am combining a few of their responses):

> *Thank you so much for sending us this beautiful manuscript. I found it quite moving to learn about such an un-known amazing 'rare-born mystic' who had lived in the USA for a few years. However, as you do acknowledge, Sunyata is now dead.*

Our editorial staff has a policy of no longer accepting books for publication that are written by spiritual teachers who (through no fault of their own) happen to be dead—we have found that none of them sell.

Our policy is also that we never return manuscripts—so this concludes our relationship.

We wish you the best of luck.

I shared my sadness with an Amherst College classmate of mine who knew about the publishing world—his name was Richard Grossinger and he happened to be the owner of North Atlantic Books. He said he would look at the manuscript. When we met the next week in Berkeley, this is what Richard said:

Thank you for this beautiful book.

North Atlantic Books has a policy of never publishing books about spiritual teachers who are not famous and are also dead —we have found that these books do not sell.

However, because we have been friends for over 20 years since we sat near to each other in Leo Marx's English class during our freshman year at Amherst, I will publish your book.

Sunyata: The Life & Sayings of a Rare-born Mystic came into the world with a big party on the day that would have been Sunyata's 100th birthday: October 27th, 1990.

Sunyata's Second Book

A few years after we finished the book, Betty went to India and eventually she went to visit the ashram of Ramana Maharshi, the enlightened master who had telepathically given Sunyata his name. At this ashram, she met an Indian gentleman who asked her the name of her teacher and because she had told so many people in India the name 'Sunyata' and not even one had ever

213

heard of him, she resisted by saying: "He is quite unknown." When the man insisted, she said: "Sunyata". The man's mouth fell open and he was totally startled. Sunyata was his guru and he was writing a book about Sunyata. In fact, they eventually figured out that Gurubaksh Rai, the Indian gentleman, had called Betty on the telephone three years earlier when he had seen the book that Betty and I had edited. Betty was now invited to live in the home of Gurubaksh Rai for the next few months—being treated like a queen by his wife and daughters. Eventually a second book of short essays by Sunyata came out that was called *Dancing with the Void: The Innerstandings of a Rare-born Mystic.*

Do You Grok the Meaning of Innerstand

Have you ever heard of the word *'grok'*?

When I once told a science fiction buff about the concept of *innerstand,* he exclaimed: "I *grok* you!" What he meant by his answer is that *innerstanding* is very similar to the way Martians talk about *'grokking'.*

I found out that *'grok'* was a word introduced to the English language by Robert A. Heinlein in his 1961 book *Stranger in a Strange Land.* [43]

Grok is defined by Heinlein as understanding intuitively with the feelings—without the use of the mind. When one *groks,* one comprehends so thoroughly that the observer merges with that which is observed. To *grok* something is to make it part of your identity. Like intuition, it is experienced in a single brief flash. In the book, humans from Earth could not understand the word *grok* because they were so used to understanding with their minds rather than through their hearts or intuition.

How similar to Sunyata's meaning of *innerstand* !

However, there was another meaning to *grok* in this science fiction novel. In the Martian language spoken by the main charac- ter, *grok* also means 'to drink'. Martians use the drinking of water as a simple example of how two entities that are separate become merged—the water becomes part of the drinker and the drinker part of the water. What was separate becomes one identity. If someone wishes to be friends on Mars, they do a ritual to become 'water brothers', and words like these are said in such a water ritual: "Who shares water shares all. With water of life we *grow* closer. May you never be thirsty. May you always drink deep." Water brothers *grok* that where there was duality, there is now no longer any separation.

Although Sunyata knew nothing about this novel, there is a way that in his *innerstanding,* he was asking us to drink deeply of the Self—that part of us that is not separate from that which is ever-lasting. In Heinlein's novel, *grokking* always came with a moment of joy. Similarly, Sunyata would say that he who *innerstands* can get a glimpse of *sat-chit-ananda*—which he translated as 'being-awareness-grace' or 'being aware of grace'.

Do you *grok*?

Sunyata's two Prophesies

Even if Sunyata was birth-free, body-free, time-free, and death-free, he was not prophecy-free. Sunyata made two prophecies in his life.

The first prophecy was about his 100th birthday party:

Do not forget the date of Wuji's birthday party in 1990:
amidst the music of the spheres and
Wuji's droll antics,
ambrosia, amrit, and soma juice will be served.
Wuji makes no effort to be *under*stood or *over*stood
as he *innerstands* awarely —
and so he can shout:
mere knowledge is no more than
mere learned ignorance and mere happiness.[44]

I confess that Betty and I chose the date to have the publishing party for Sunyata's book (we considered ourselves to be his servants) so as to make this prophecy come true. Since the party was scheduled for the exact day of his 100th birthday, many of Sunyata's friends gathered on that day for a joyous occasion. After a few minutes of silence, many of us who knew Sunyata shared stories about how they were deeply grateful for the contribution that he had made to their lives. Even though there were no drugs or even wine at this birthday party, we mere mortals were favored by the gods to imbibe an ethereal feast of 'ambrosia, amrit, and soma juice'.

Here is the second prophecy in Sunyata's own words:

> *Innerstand.*
> It will be a new word in the dictionary.[45]

It is already almost 35 years since Betty and I had the book party on Sunyata's 100th birthday, and this prophecy has not yet come true. The word *innerstand* is still in no dictionary on planet earth.

Let me introduce another two concepts, *protologism* and *neologism*. 'Innerstand' and 'innerstances'—and also 'headucation'—are *protologisms*. A protologism (from Greek *protos*, meaning 'original' and Greek *logos*, meaning 'word') is a brand-new word coined to fill a gap in the language. Whoever coins such a word hopes that it will become widely accepted and eventually flow into everyday usage. Then, once a word becomes accepted, it graduates into being a *neologism*. A good example of a recent *neologism* is the word *grok* from *Stranger in a Strange Land*—it can now be found in dictionaries.

We will have to wait to see if the word '*innerstand*' ever does enter a dictionary.

What I learned from Sunyata

I am attempting to sum up what was most essential in Sunyata's teaching to me in as few words as possible:

No body wants to hear that that they are a nobody.
No ego wants to release its separateness.

It appears that no matter what anyone says, no one really wants to be no one.

Society conditions us through *headucation* with the one rule that must be followed in order for us to love ourselves in the dream—we must be thoroughly and wholeheartedly made to believe that who we really are is the character we appear to be.

Society does this conditioning through stories, but it never teaches us that no story is true.

When the belief in the story that we are a separate person is seen though, the divine takes over.

Tat twam asi.
Thou art the Self.

Once it is known and *awared* that who you are is merely a character in the play and all that happens is the Self, you can wholeheartedly embrace what has been, is, and always will be the truth—that in the Absolute Reality, you will forever reside and abide as a nobody.

There are four quotations which I heard Sunyata recite—each awoke in me a momentary ego-death. The first quotation is from Emily Dickinson, the greatest poet that America has ever produced, who got scant recognition in her own lifetime:

I'm Nobody! Who are you?
Are you—Nobody—too?
Then there's a pair of us!
Don't tell! they'd advertise—you know!

How dreary—to be—Somebody!
How public—like a Frog—
To tell one's name—the livelong day—
To an admiring Bog! [46]

The second quotation is from the Thomas Merton, the Trappist monk who, after immersing himself in Eastern thought, gave this summary of the thinking of Chuang Tzu, the Taoist philosopher who lived in the 4th century BC:

The man of Tao remains unknown.
Perfect virtue produces nothing.
"No Self" is "True Self".
And the greatest man is Nobody. [47]

The third quotation oft recited by Sunyata was written by Percy Bysshe Shelley when his good friend John Keats died from tuberculosis in 1821. Less than 17 months after these lines were written,, Shelley himself was to drown. When Sunyata would recite the poem, he would change the word "Life" (that appeared in the third line of the original poem composed by Shelley) to "Ego-Life":

The One remains, the many change and pass;
Heaven's light forever shines, Earth's shadows fly;
Ego-Life, like a dome of many-colour'd glass,
Stains the white radiance of Eternity,
Until Death tramples it to fragments.—Die,
If thou wouldst be with that which thou dost seek!
Follow where all is fled! [48]

Fourthly, these are the last words that Sunyata wrote and that he
handed out to us just weeks before leaving his body; I can still hear
him reciting these lines in his own voice:

> You are the whole: the Ghostly Whole.
> Just wake up from the dream of separateness
> of being merely a human, mortal egoji.
> You are the Self—the Eternal Life—
> beyond birth and death and all opposites.
> Thou art thy Self the object of thy search.
> Ego-oblivion is Self-awareness.
> Wake up—into the Ghostly Whole:
> Being—Awareness—Grace: *Tat twam asi*.[49]

8

Can my mind unhook from its stories?

I defined myself for six decades by stories that had their source in the struggles and suffering in the Holocaust. The effect of these stories was to make me a victim—and as a victim, I was filled with fear and anger. How could I find inner peace? How could I find freedom from the weight of this heritage? I have the teacher known as Byron Katie (or just plain Katie) to thank for giving me the tools to free myself from this 'story'.

O *the mind,*
mind has mountains,
cliffs of fall
frightful,
sheer,
no-man-fathomed.

—Gerard Manley Hopkins
'No worst, there is none' (1885)[50]

Faust: *What is thy name?*
Mephistopheles: *I am that force which forever tries to do evil,*
but yet forever works the good.

—Johann Wolfgang von Goethe
Faust (1808) Part One, Scene III [51]

A Fish Gets Hooked by its Desire...

WHILE MOST ROMAN POETS WROTE ABOUT ancient heroes and immortal gods, Catullus's poems were about his personal life and in particular his love affairs. This is Catullus' 85th poem presented in the original Latin:

> Ōdī et amō, quārē id faciam, fortasse requīris.
> Nesciŏ, sed fierī sentiō et excrucior.

An exact English translation might be:

> *I hate and I love. Why might I do this, perhaps you ask.*
> *I know not, but that's how I feel and it torments me.*[52]

Catullus is describing the experience of anyone who has had an unrequited love or cannot let go of an attachment that brings them no peace of mind. Here is a less literal and more imaginative translation by a modern American poet:

> I hate *and* love. Ignorant fish, who even
> wants the fly while writhing.

> —Frank Bidart
> *Half-Light: Collected Poems* (1965-2016)[53]

What Happens to the Monkey who Holds on to the Nut . . .

Another analogy is the age-old parable of the monkey with the paw in the jar. This parable comes from the fact that there are monkeys in India who are captured by villagers who put a nut in a bottle and tie the bottle to a tree. Because the neck of the bottle is too narrow for the monkey to withdraw its paw if he is determined to hold on to the nut, the unlucky monkey is often captured.

My Mind Gets Hooked by the Holocaust

Throughout my early years I was hooked on the story of the Holocaust. When I was around six years old, my mother told me that I was a Jew and she explained that there were evil people in the world who wanted to kill the Jews. These evil people were called Nazis and they were evil because human life was sacred and the Nazis had no respect for human life.

My mother's father made this more specific by talking about what happened in Urech'e (Uretsche), the village in Belarus where he grew up, located between Minsk and Kyiv. My grandfather left the village for America in 1902, but kept in touch by post with friends and family there. Four decades after he left, a Nazi group called the *Einsatzgruppen* came to the village. I later learned *Einsatz* is German for 'task' and *gruppen* is German for 'force', and the purpose of this particular 'task force' was to exterminate the Jews of Eastern Europe.

My grandfather told me that the *Einsatzgruppen* rounded up all the Jews of Urech'e and had taken them to a nearby forest. The men had been made to dig a big pit, and then the *Einsatzgruppen* shot everyone—men, women, and children—and buried them all in that selfsame pit. After that day, my grandfather never received another letter from his friends and relatives in Urech'e.

After hearing my grandfather's story, I felt that I might one day become a helpless and powerless victim. And I was convinced that evil was real.

I had read about the Warsaw Ghetto and the Jews there who had fought heroically—but in vain—against the Nazis. Their fight was in vain because the Ghetto had been levelled and every Jewish fighter had either been sent to a concentration camp—or just murdered outright. In my child's mind, even if the cause was hopeless, I wanted to be a heroic defender of my people. I wanted to prove to myself that no Nazi could make me a victim.

When I was about nine years old, I would often put myself to sleep at night with a story of how I could become a hero in the Warsaw Ghetto. These were not dreams but fantasies. Each night I would place myself on the roof of a tenement in the Ghetto. I was armed with a six-shooter. (I had been watching lots of Westerns on TV and that was the only type of gun that I knew.) The main action in the dream would be that from my vantage point on the roof, I would see a whole group of Nazis below me on the street. As soon as I saw them, I would immediately raise my gun and with the aim of a skilled marksman shoot five bullets and kill five Nazis.

Then each night I would create a dilemma for myself. If I killed another Nazi, I would have no bullets left and all the remaining Nazis would charge up the staircase and torture me for my act of rebellion. I would feel the pain of the torture, but what I felt more strongly was the gratification that I had done what was right to protect my people. But on some nights, I would remember the excruciating pain of having been tortured the previous night (it had only been in my fantasy) and on that night I would use my sixth and last remaining bullet to shoot myself in the head. And then lying in my warm bed in a home where I felt loved by my family, I would feel great shame because I would reason that I had been a coward because I had not been willing to face the torture that would ensue if I had done what was really right—to get justice done by firing my sixth bullet at a Nazi.

In my youth, I saw the purpose and meaning of my life as resisting evil. In my mind what made any action evil was that it was intentionally caused by humans who were in direct conflict with the values that I held as sacred. I would never have viewed a destructive event that just happened—like an asteroid coming from outer space—as evil. My opposition was to other humans who had no respect for human life. The story about how the Nazis had murdered my family was central in my motivation when I was involved in the civil rights movement in the South and later organizing protests against the war in Vietnam. Even though my biological family in Belarus had been powerless victims, I felt empowered when I told myself the story that I was fighting the forces of evil. My identity was to be an angry young man, and I was going to do my damnedest to change the world.

During this time, I was holding onto my convictions for dear life. I would often try to figure out who were the true fighters for freedom and justice. I would sometimes dump an angry outburst upon those who didn't share my views. I would be upset when I thought a fellow freedom fighter was 'selling out' or possibly even 'betraying the cause'.

There is a saying attributed to the Buddha that his core teachings can only be understood by those "with little dust in their eyes". Although I now have no regrets that I had once kicked up a dust storm with my activism, I began to feel that I was being blinded by that same dust. When I felt my cause was losing, I would become anxious and depressed. And then I would blame myself or others. My mind was forever firing up in anger for another war. Sometimes the fire of fury was so hot in my heart that I would become a metaphorical dragon with steam bursting forth from my nostrils.

Making a Shift Doing The Work of Byron Katie

In October of 2004, I got relief from this emotional upset when I did a ten-day School for *The Work* given by a teacher named Byron Katie. (She did not use her first name and everyone just called her 'Katie'.) Katie had had an awakening in which she learned to question all her beliefs. At this School we learned to question any belief or judgment with these four questions:

- Is it true?
- Can you absolutely know that it's true?
- How do you react, what happens, when you believe that thought?

- Who would you be without that thought?

After we finished asking ourselves these questions about any belief, we would be instructed to do what she called *turnarounds*. In a *turnaround*, we look at the opposite of the original thought to consider whether the opposite of our belief or judgment might be as true—or even more true—than the original thought. There are always at least two possible types of turnarounds: one is to consider letting go of the judgment completely by adding the word 'not' and another is by questioning if the judgment might be more true if it were directed against oneself (rather than outwardly).

We had to pick a primary story in which some person or group made us sad or angry. This was my story:

I am angry at the Nazis for murdering my family.

For a portion of each day, I would challenge my story with the four questions and then look to find the turnarounds. On the tenth and last day, a turnaround shifted my attention from my judgment about the Nazis into a prescription for happiness of what I needed to do with my life:

I am angry at myself for murdering the present moment by holding onto an anger about events that happened so long ago.

It seemed miraculous when the emotional charge around the story became so much less. And it was that emotional charge that was the source of my suffering. I did not doubt that my family was murdered nor did I become a Holocaust-denier. What I saw was that my anger at the Nazis was not going to prevent them from having done the murders that had already happened long ago. And my anger at them was not going to prevent future cruelties and horrors. If my anger was like the water in a tank, somehow a hole had been punctured even further down in the tank than had happened during my meditation course in Bodh Gaya. I marvelled as a river of steaming hot fury just came gushing out.

I saw that my work was no longer to live in my past. Changing the past was an argument with reality. To quote another Katie-ism:

When you argue with reality, you lose (and suffer)
—but only 100% of the time.

I recognized that my attachment to a judgment about the Nazis had taken me away from living in the moment. I came to see that it was not what had happened to my family that was making me suffer, but rather it was the way I was holding onto a story in my own thinking that was making me a victim—and rendering me helpless and powerless.

Who would you be without your story?

I often thought of a Katie saying: "Who would you be without your story?" Let me say a word about the way Katie used the word *story* during the School. Essentially a story is any thought or belief that is taken to be true. Katie at times said that in her own experience that no story is true because no thought or belief is true. She then went on to say that if a story works for you, you may choose to keep it. But she does distinguish between two types of stories. There are simple descriptions or narratives that there is really no reason to question—like 'woman sitting on chair reading a book'. Obviously even here the mind could doubt everything and could argue that the woman was really a girl and the chair was really a couch and the book was actually a magazine. But essentially this type of story attempts to give an accurate description or a reliable map of a consensual reality.

The more relevant meaning of *story* is where a person has Velcro-ed to a judgment about what has happened in the past with the *should* thought. This means a person in their thinking has assumed the role of a judge. This is the ditty that was on our worksheets at the course:

Judge your neighbor, write it down.
Ask four questions, turn it around.

When a person holds a judgment about what is right, this thought is linked to an emotional investment in the truth of their story. And when this judgment is applied to a particular person who they perceive has wronged them, the emotion is often anger. Katie would often say to a person sitting in front of her who was caught up in an upsetting story who appeared to be unwilling to investigate its truth: "Sweetheart, do you want to be right or do you want to be peaceful?" I can imagine Katie appearing before our poor tormented deluded chimp in the forest who cannot let go of his nut in the jar and teaching him to inquire: O *sweetheart of a monkey, do you want to be right or do you want to let go of your nut?*

Is Suffering a Story?

What I most wanted was to become unhooked from any story that created suffering. My guideline was this old Buddhist saying:

Pain is inevitable,
suffering is optional.

I had discovered early in my meditation practice that if I remained mindful of pain and did not resist it, the pain would become more bearable and I would suffer less. Now I learned from the School a new meaning of this statement in relation to my emotional pain. If suffering is created by a thought or belief that is taken to be true, I saw that I could stop taking stories to be true that would create emotional pain. I began learning to discern the stories that were creating my emotional pain and I found that I could let go of my attachment to any story that included guilt or shame, blame or resentment, or even regret. And I would feel anxiety when I believed a thought that included worry. Whenever I found myself worrying, I would say to myself: *Elliott, you are now praying for what you don't want.* I enjoyed weakening the binding power of negative thoughts.

My Motto

My motto during this time was . . .

> *As you thinketh in your heart, so will you become.*

This phrase was inspired by the King James Version (KJV) of the Bible, specifically Proverbs 23:7, which states: *"For as he thinketh in his heart, so is he."*

I encouraged myself to embrace my life with this thought: *"The winds of grace are blowing, and it is only with positive thoughts that I will raise the sails."*

My Ego Gets Busted

Once in a gathering of around 50 people at a private home in San Francisco, Katie asked the group if anyone wanted to speak. I had spent the morning reading the teachings of Ramana Maharshi. After Katie acknowledged my raised hand, I stood up and started sharing what I had just been reading. After I spoke for around a minute, Katie interrupted me and turned to the entire group and asked this question: "Who is interested in hearing the rest of what Elliott has to say?" Because I was so fascinated by the ideas that I was expressing, I wondered why Katie was asking this question and I expected everyone's hand to go up. To my complete amazement, not one person raised their hand. After staring at the group for a moment expecting at least one hand to squeak up a little bit, I gave up the ghost, and just sat down and I noticed that I had a bright red blush on my face.

As I was sitting there as bright red as a fire engine, I was grateful to Katie for showing me how much I had not attuned to my audience. I felt like I was on a roller coaster ride wherein the ride was called 'BUSTING THE EGO'.

Becoming a Dharma Bum

In the 1950s, I saw myself as jiving to a different rhythm than the tired repetitions of a materialistic society. As an adolescent, after reading *Catcher in the Rye*, I identified with the rebellious 17 year old Holden Caulfield who viewed most adults as 'phonies'. I viewed myself as a wannabe member of the Beat Generation and looked for heightened—even ecstatic—experience. My goal was to become a *dharma bum*. I was attracted to Eastern philosophy and Zen. I resonated with the rhythms of Ginsberg's *Howl*:[54]

I saw the best minds of my generation destroyed by madness,
starving hysterical naked,
dragging themselves through the negro streets at dawn looking for
an angry fix,
angelheaded hipsters burning for the ancient heavenly connection
to the starry dynamo in the machinery of night . . .
. . . who passed through universities with radiant cool eyes
hallucinating Arkansas and Blake-light tragedy . . .
who studied Plotinus Poe St. John of the Cross telepathy and
bop kabbalah because the cosmos instinctively vibrated at their
feet in Kansas . . .
. . . who threw their watches off the roof to cast their ballot for
Eternity outside of Time . . .

A year later Ginsberg wrote a Footnote to his poem Howl:

The world is holy! The soul is holy! The skin is holy! The nose is

holy! The tongue and cock and hand and asshole holy!
Everything is holy! everybody's holy! everywhere is holy! everyday
is in eternity! Everyman's an angel!
The bum's as holy as the seraphim! the madman is holy as you my
soul are holy! [55]

My favorite beatnik was Jack Kerouac, the author of *On the Road,*
who described his beatific experiences:

> I have lots of things to teach you now, in case we ever meet,
> concerning the message that was transmitted to me under a
> pine tree in North Carolina on a cold winter moonlit night.
> It said that Nothing Ever Happened, so don't worry.

> It's all like a dream. Everything is ecstasy, inside. We just
> don't know it because of our thinking-minds. But in our
> true blissful essence of mind is known that everything is
> alright forever and forever and forever.

> Close your eyes, let your hands and nerve-ends drop, stop
> breathing for 3 seconds, listen to the silence inside the
> illusion of the world, and you will remember the lesson you
> forgot, which was taught in immense milky way soft cloud
> innumerable worlds long ago and not even at all.

> It is all one vast awakened thing. I call it the golden eternity.
> It is perfect. We were never really born, we will never really
> die. It has nothing to do with the imaginary idea of a per-
> sonal self, other selves, many selves everywhere: self is only
> an idea, a mortal idea.

> That which passes into everything is one thing. It's a dream
> already ended. There's nothing to be afraid of and nothing

to be glad about. I know this from staring at mountains months on end. They never show any expression, they are like empty space. Do you think the emptiness of space will ever crumble away? Mountains will crumble, but the emptiness of space, which is the one universal essence of mind, the vast awakenerhood, empty and awake, will never crumble away because it was never born. [56]

Rebel Without a Pause

Throughout my life I have had an aversion to playing by the rules of the game. I experience myself as rebellious and others have labelled me as an instigator, a rascal, or perhaps a trickster. This devilishness does get me into trouble, but luckily most of my transgressions have been sublimated to the heavenly realm of art.

Many people have suggested to me that it was time to grow up and consider becoming a more responsible adult. Actually, it is true that I want to become more responsible, but yet I am still grappling with how I can become dutifully transgressive and responsibly blasphemous. If I imagine myself as that frustrated monkey who has his paw in the jar and cannot let go of his attachment to the nut, I would ask him to inquire if there is a way to destroy the jar without injuring or even hurting his hand.

To give a twist on the same Catullus poem, I would give this advice to our grasping monkey:

"O grasping monkey,
if your desires bind you as tightly as your grip
(and I understand your attachment to what you crave,
and yes, your craving for what you are attached),
remember this:
there are only two ways to escape before you are enslaved:—
the first is not through holding on,
*but by **letting go**;*
however, if you know yourself too bound by the habits of grasping

to LET GO,
then only one option remains to preserve your freedom—
shatter the jar that holds you captive."

How I Applied the Wisdom of My Doctoral Dissertation

When I wrote my doctoral dissertation on evil, my main discovery was that evil and the sacred depended on each other for their existence since they are actually one interpenetrating dynamic whole. This was the conclusion in my doctoral dissertation about the essential elements of evil:

The experience of evil from the subjective viewpoint of the experiencer is a real experience of that which is radically opposed to what the experiencer views as sacred.

The experiencer may later explain or interpret what happened, but accepts that despite whatever analysis may be made, the experience remains beyond rational or mental comprehension.

The relationship between evil and the sacred is quite similar to the way an experience of joy depends on its existence for another experience called sorrow; or that the concept of pleasure does not even have any meaning without the existence of another opposite concept called pain. There was no doubt that my mind liked to make an opposition between these opposites, but I could see that each depended on the other.

Why did so many interviewees, convinced they had encountered true evil, ultimately find their experiences beyond the grasp of reason or understanding? Each wrestled with their own confusion, but I believe they were facing the ancient and unresolved dilemma of *theodicy.* Derived from the Greek words for 'God' and 'justice,' theodicy is the attempt to justify God's ways to man in a world where evil exists; such a justification struggles with the contradiction between a supposedly all-powerful, all-knowing, and entirely benevolent God and the realities of suffering, malevolence, and evil. The classic question is: "If God is both good and omnipotent, how can there be so much evil?" Philosophers have provided countless explanations, yet each—in my opinion— requires a leap of faith that defies both reason and logic.

My own response to the challenge of *theodicy* is equally unprovable, but here's what I see: *the divine isn't something external, but resides solely within.* In reading stories of how various people experienced the divine accident called enlightenment, I was surprised how many had this invitation during a moment of great personal suffering.

As a reward for enduring the inevitable evils of the human condition—what Hamlet calls 'the slings and arrows of outrageous fortune'—we each are capable of discovering a *perfect brilliant stillness* that lies forever waiting within our true nature. Terms like 'the Self' or 'I AM'—or even the term '*that*'—have been used to describe this essence, but really the label does not matter. What I want in my own life is to cultivate the conditions necessary for a direct experience of that inner stillness.

In my own quest for *that*, I realized that what I needed was to undo the stories that were inhibiting my freedom. I knew the difference between ease and dis-ease, and it became clear to me that the path to ease lay in self-acceptance. Since my body was healthy, I recognized that much of my dis-ease came from my own critical self-judgments. I noticed that these judgments, shaped by societal teachings about what is good and worthy, were tied to my desire to identify with the pure white (positive) side of the yin-yang symbol. I came to see that what was keeping me in bondage was my refusal to accept the dark black (negative) shadow side within myself.

Then I had a realization: if I truly wanted to perceive the unity in the apparent opposites represented by the yin-yang symbol, I needed to accept equally both the negative and the positive. I asked myself, *"What if I stopped adhering to society's ethical guidelines and arbitrary judgments about what is good and worthy? What if I simply follow my heart?"*

I must admit that I have my doubts about sharing this experiment with you, the reader. Even though I know that this was a crucial element in my own movement into a mature adulthood, I also see that—with just a little less luck—this experiment could have really gone awry and created much suffering. All I can say is that I was lucky.

This is the Experiment

The experiment was to bring into my awareness everything I had denied or repressed. I found encouragement in a passage from the Gospel of Thomas:

> *If you bring forth what is within you,*
> *what you bring forth will save you.*
> *If you do not bring forth what is within you,*
> *what you do not bring forth will destroy you.* [57]

Part of the reason I was willing to do this experiment is that although I can be unkind, I assessed that I had minimal amounts of greed and hatred. I did not see it as a possibility that I was a Dr. Jekyll who had lurking deep in my unconscious a Mr. Hyde who might want to begin murdering people.

What follows is the story of one incident that occurred after I had taken this vow to bring forth all that was denied and repressed:

Why do I want to tell you this incident, perhaps you ask.

I know not, but the devil makes me do it.

Did I Grow Horns?

When I showed my friend John Threlfall who resides in Hawaii a rough draft of this chapter, he was surprised that I hadn't included an experience that he remembered vividly from three decades previously. John had accidentally arrived just as I had begun my experiment. He had visited me once a year for the last 15 years each summer as he traveled from his home in Hawaii to visit his parents in Wisconsin. He had been at my home for a few days and one day I went out for a few hours and as I returned stepping into the entryway of my living room, he was sitting on my sofa and I soon noticed a look of astonishment on his face. He kept doing a double-take, squinting, and looking at the very top of my head.

Now I will let John tell in his own words what happened that day:

"I was lounging on his sofa when Elliott returned to his apartment. After opening the door, he stood for a while near the entry. Very shortly, I noticed two horns were on his head. They were slightly curved, less than two inches long, and perfectly positioned just as horns ought to be on a head. The horns did not seem volitional on Elliott's part, though the subtle changes in his visage, demeanor, and speech were all congruent with the horns. It was all part of one package, so to speak.

"I tried squinting, and shaking my head, but the horns did not change in any way. My first thought was that I was witnessing the devil, but rather oddly there was no sense of malevolence or evil. It was actually more of a sacred feeling tone. I finally exclaimed in amazement:'Elliott, you have horns! You look like the devil!'

"He responded with an unusually clear and resonant voice with these words: 'I am all that has been repressed and denied.' The horns lingered for a while, not more than a few minutes in total, and all returned to normal though leaving an indelible impression, even to this day. On reflection I would not characterize this as a hallucination, although I suppose it might fit that definition. My best explanation is that it was an emergence of an archetype related to a trickster or a pre-Christian Pan."

What I find most intriguing about this story is that the appearance of a particular archetypal quality of beingness—that John initially mistook for the devil—turned out on reflection to be in its essence closer to a trickster or a pre-Christian Pan—and then the entire experience gained "a sacred feeling tone". My thought is that my experiment brought me closer to transcending the dualities that create so much dis-ease in most humans. John's experience of the horns growing on my head was unique in his life and over three decades later, he still considers what happened beyond his mental or rational comprehension. And like the songwriter Iris Dement, John is willing to "let the mystery be":

> *Some say they're going to a place called glory*
> *And I ain't saying it ain't a fact*
> *But I've heard that I'm on the road to purgatory*
> *And I don't like the sound of that*
> *I believe in love and I live my life accordingly*
> *But I choose to let the mystery be*
>
> *Everybody is wondering what and where they all came from*
> *Everybody is worrying 'bout*
> *Where they're gonna go when the whole thing's done*
> *But no one knows for certain and so it's all the same to me*
> *I think I'll just let the mystery be* [58]

This experiment of bringing forth what was denied and repressed had many good aspects, and I learned much both about my shadow sides and how to embrace those shadow sides. However, I am now back to living by ethical guidelines as this is so much simpler. It is not only work to keep growing horns, but I discovered that it took more effort than I wanted to give to keep them well oiled and maintained.

Can I Ever Unhook from my Stories?

I realize that I still have much work to do if I am ever to be a free man. I apperceive that the way toward freedom is to question my beliefs rather than to find evidence that any stories in my head are true. And now let us segue to the next chapter which describes my attempts to unhook from the most conditioned belief of all: my automatic and habitual identification with the story of a 'me'.

9

The wake-up call: waking up out of the dream of me

I've been fortunate to encounter teachings that truly resonated with me—guiding me beyond identification with the small self. I once had a profound experience of Oneness on Mount Shasta, the Holy Mountain of America. But that luminous encounter led to what I now recognize as a **false awakening**. Many years later, I entered a different kind of passage—what I've come to call **the gray night of the soul**. Not as black as St. John's dark night, but still unsettling . . . and deeply humbling. Emerging from these experiences, I realized that what I most truly know can be summed up in just two (or is it three?) words: **Don't know.**

> We shall not cease from exploration
> And the end of all our exploring
> Will be to arrive where we started
> And know the place for the first time.
>
> —T.S. Eliot
> *Four Quartets* [59]

> If the doors of perception were cleansed,
> then everything would appear to man as it is, Infinite.
> For man has closed himself up,
> till he sees all things through narrow chinks of his cavern.
>
> —William Blake
> *The Marriage of Heaven and Hell* [60]

The Infinite a sudden Guest
Has been assumed to be–
But how can that stupendous come
Which never went away?

—Emily Dickinson
Poem 1344 [61]

Man sacrifices his health in order to make money,
*   then he sacrifices his money to recuperate his health.*
Then he is so anxious about the future that he does not enjoy the present,
*   the result being that he never actually lives in the here and now.*
Even as man lives as if he is never going to die,
*   he dies never having really lived.*

Anonymous wisdom, often wrongly attributed to the Dalai Lama [62]

And the princess and the prince
Discuss what's real and what is not
It doesn't matter inside the Gates of Eden . . .

Leaving men wholly, totally free
To do anything they wish to do but die
And there are no trials inside the Gates of Eden . . .

At times I think there are no words
But these to tell what's true
And there are no truths outside the Gates of Eden.

—Bob Dylan
"Gates of Eden"
Bringing It All Back Home [63]

The truth is out there—the void, the abyss, no-self—and our fragile little bubbles are what let us float around in the infinite, able to enjoy the experience of somethingness when only nothingness exists. The illusion of opposites—good and bad, love and hate, joy and sorrow—these aren't available out in infinite reality, but only in the artificial micro-environment of ego.

—Jed McKenna [64]

My Father and his Dream

IN 2003 I FLEW FROM SAN FRANCISCO TO MY childhood home where my father was now living alone. Even though he was in his late nineties, he was almost independent, managing with only a little help. Two years previously and after a marriage of 57 years, his wife (my mother) had died. In the aftermath of my mother's funeral, my father had said to me for the first time in my 56 years: "I love you." I always felt loved by my father, but I was still more than shocked to hear him express this sentiment in words.

My father was now quite open to the spiritual path as he had good experiences in meeting my Hindu and Buddhist teachers when he had come to San Francisco after his wife's death. Earlier that year in New York City he had met Ammachi, the Indian saint, who had actually left her seat to give my father a hug when she saw my father with his cane ever so slowly approaching her—and my father had started crying as she was hugging him.

My father and I had tickets to go to a theatre in Manhattan to see the Dalai Lama and hear his teachings. The night before this, I was awakened by screams coming from my father's room in the wee hours of the morning. When I opened the door to his bedroom, he was tossing and turning in the bed. I sat close to him and, once he was awake, he sat up and told me a recurring nightmare had just come back again. I told him that we had all the time in the world and I jokingly reminded him that we had the advantage that he had once taught a course on how to interpret dreams at the Karen Horney Clinic. I asked him to tell me the dream in as much detail as possible and this is what he said:

I was falling and I remember this luminous bright blue turquoise sky . . . and then I was falling . . . and then I was falling . . . and that was all that ever happened. The sky never changed its turquoise blue color and all that changed was that I became more and more scared because the thought arose: "When will this ever end?" And then I was falling some more and then some more and that's when I must have screamed . . .

We sat in silence for a few moments. I wanted him to talk first, but since he did not speak, I eventually gave my interpretation: "What is obvious to both of us is that you must be closer to your death than to your birth. I feel that your dream is about how you can no longer hold on to life. As you see, nothing bad ever happened in your dream except falling, and what makes it a nightmare is because you want the falling to end. Might it not be possible for you to let go and just enjoy the ride?"

My father remained quiet and then I noticed that we were both getting sleepy and we had to get up early to see the Dalai Lama, so I said: "Let's get a good night's sleep." The dream did not recur for the rest of my stay at my father's home, but as you will see there was synchronicity at work later that very same day.

The Teachings of the Dalai Lama on Emptiness

I had gotten $100 seats for us to sit together at the Beacon Theatre in Manhattan—this meant that we were quite close to the stage (with a good view of Richard Gere). The Dalai Lama spoke English to start with, but for the main teachings he spoke in Tibetan with an excellent translator. He began by saying that the nature of experience in the world is constant and never-ending change and there was not now, nor could there ever be, any secure place where one might stand rooted and immovable. Both my father and I realized that this spoke directly to his dream of the night before and we exchanged a knowing glance.

The rest of his talk was devoted to a particular teaching called *In Praise of Dependent Arising* by a 14th century Tibetan Buddhist monk named Je Tsongkhapa. The Dalai Lama said that this teaching could be summed up in one phrase:

> *Whatever depends on conditions*
> *Is devoid of intrinsic existence.*[65]

The Dalai Lama explained this by telling us that since all phenomena are dependent on the law of cause and effect, they are "empty" of any self-nature. When one can eliminate the "mis-knowing" that sees any thought or object—including one's small self or ego —as real and permanent, it becomes possible to abide in clarity, luminosity, and unboundedness.

I was familiar with the Buddhist notion of *sunyata,* so this felt like a direct transmission of the meaning of 'full solid emptiness'. In the original language of Je Tsongkhapa's teaching, he concludes that everything that depends on conditions is devoid of *svabhava*— which can be translated as 'self-nature' or 'own-being'. Objects are devoid of a permanent and eternal essence (*svabhava*) because, like a dream, they are mere projections of human consciousness. I perceived that the Dalai Lama was not arguing for his own conceptual model, but rather his concepts were being used to point to a true experience of awakening that was potentially available to all human beings.

Afterwards

I stayed with my father for another week after our visit to the Dalai Lama. This was when he told me the full story of what had happened to him as a medical student in Nazi Germany. My father died one month later at the age of 97 years and four months. In our last phone conversation—which was the morning of his death—I asked him how he was doing and he responded, "I'm doing fine. I don't have the energy I once had . . . and I have no complaints."

Am I Awake or Asleep?

I am using both of these terms *asleep* and *awake* in a spiritual sense. To be fully asleep is to be ignorant of our true nature. In Buddhist philosophy, this means to be caught up in greed, hatred, and delusion—and suffering. This brings to mind my favorite scene from *The Matrix*.[66] In the movie, Neo is a hacker recruited by a rebellion to aid humans in the fight against machines. These machines have taken over the world and placed humanity inside a simulated reality called *"the Matrix"*. Morpheus—the leader of the rebellion—asks Neo if he is feeling a bit like Alice "tumbling down the rabbit hole". Eventually he tells Neo that he must choose between a blue pill and a red pill. The blue pill means to stay asleep in the dream while the red pill is the wake-up call. This is part of their dialogue:

Morpheus (to Neo, as he walks into the room): At last. Welcome, Neo. As you no doubt have guessed, I am Morpheus.

Neo: It's an honor to meet you...

Morpheus: No, the honor is mine. Please, come. Sit. I imagine that right now, you're feeling a bit like Alice. Hmm? Tumbling down the rabbit hole?

Neo: You could say that.

Morpheus: I can see it in your eyes. You have the look of a man who accepts what he sees because he is expecting to wake up. Ironically, this is not far from the truth.

Let me tell you why you're here. You're here because you know something. What you know you can't explain, but you feel it. You've felt it your entire life—that there's something wrong with the world. You don't know what it is, but it's there, like a splinter in your mind, driving you mad. It is this feeling that has brought you to me. Do you know what I'm talking about?

Neo: ... the Matrix.

Morpheus: Do you want to know what it is?

Neo: (*nods yes*)

Morpheus: The Matrix is everywhere. It is all around us. Even now, in this very room. You can see it when you look out your window or when you turn on your television. You can feel it when you go to work ... when you go to church . . . when you pay your taxes. It is the world that has been pulled over your eyes to blind you from the truth.

Neo: What truth?

Morpheus: That you are a slave, Neo. Like everyone else, you were born into bondage. Born into a prison that you cannot smell or taste or touch. A prison for your mind. (*takes a deep breath*) Unfortunately, no one can be told what the Matrix is. You have to see it for yourself. (*Morpheus then takes out two pills, one is blue, the other red*) This is your last chance. After this, there is no turning back. You take the blue pill, the story ends, you wake up in your bed and believe whatever you want to believe. You take the red pill, you stay in Wonderland, and I show you how deep the rabbit hole goes. Remember, all I'm offering is the truth, nothing more.

Neo: (*takes the red pill*)

Morpheus: Follow me.

The concept of *The Matrix* is remarkably similar to the fundamental Hindu concept of *māyā*. This is usually translated as *illusion* in the sense that what may appear to be true is not the deeper truth. In Hindu philosophy, *māyā* has beoame associated with the sleep of ignorance that mistakenly takes what is transitory as being what is real.

Fifty years ago, when I first learned about *maya* in India, I wanted to find *That Which Is Real*. As I have fallen deeper and deeper into my own personal rabbit hole, the matrix still seems real and is ever presenting me with new apparent obstacles.

To be fully awake is to be at one with our true nature. In Buddhism this means the end of suffering. I am lucky to have met many beings in my life who I believe are free of suffering. To the extent that I have a goal, it would be to end suffering both for myself and for others. But there is the rub.

In India, I learned that the path to ending suffering is to let go of the mistaken belief that our true self is separate from the ultimate reality. The idea of a 'me' represents this false identity. To end suffering, we simply need to wake up from the illusion of a 'me.' Here, 'me' refers to the self-image of someone who identifies with their individual personhood.

In humans, a muddle arises when we mistake ourselves for the roles we play. We need not confuse the roles we play with reality. Shakespeare knew this when he wrote:

> All the world's a stage,
> And all the men and women merely players;
> They have their exits and their entrances;
> And one man in his time plays many parts . . .

> *As You Like It*, II, vii, 139-142

Over the course of a lifetime, we may be children, parents, and then grandparents, but we don't need to be trapped by any of these roles. Similarly, throughout life, we take on various occupations, but none of these jobs defines our true essence. We might also label different stages of consciousness, but none of these labels capture the unchanging nature of our beingness.

While we can embody roles, we don't need to become them.

When we identify with roles, the mind mistakes these roles for our true self. This objectification causes us to lose touch with our eternal nature, the ever-present, awake awareness. By loosening our attachment to what is temporary and fleeting, we create space to become aware of that which never dies.

I do have a belief that at the moment of the physical death of my body, I will lose the possibility of identifying with a 'me'. In this belief, I will still be awareness, but that which is aware will see a corpse and what used to be my brain will have lost the capability to be aware of a thought. In this thought experiment, assuming that there will still be awareness, I believe I will have a moment of clarity that who I am is neither my body nor my mind. *The Tibetan Book of the Dead* describes *bardos as* 'environments' where the energy of a particular person may abide after death before taking another birth. Many of my spiritual friends want this to be their last birth, but I notice that I don't have this desire. However, I do have the desire to wake up this lifetime. The goal of my spiritual path is to break out of the identification with the 'me' thought before that inevitable moment when I will leave my body.

Me?

Although I still live my life with the feeling that there is a 'me', when I slow down enough to become quiet and introspective, all I discover is a stream of thoughts observing an ever-changing reality. I never do find a 'me'. Moreover, as a trained psychologist, all of my fellow theoreticians who study the nature of consciousness agree that the concept of a 'me' cannot be found either as part of the brain or as a meaningful description of an individual's experience. A 'me' has the same reality as a unicorn. The felt sense of a 'me' is an experience created by an emotional attachment to what has been conditioned into individuals, yet the feeling that the 'me' exists does not prove that it really does exist.

If you are interested in learning more about this point of view from a psychologist, I would recommend the book by Thomas Metzinger titled *The Ego Tunnel: The Science of the Mind and the Myth of the Self.* The book begins with this **Introduction**:

> In this book, I will try to convince you that there is no such thing as a self. Contrary to what most people believe, nobody has ever *been* or *had* a self. But it is not just that the modern philosophy of mind and cognitive neuroscience together are about to shatter the myth of the self. It has now become clear that we will never solve the philosophical puzzle of consciousness—that is, how it can arise in the brain, which is a purely physical object—if we don't come to terms with this simple proposition: that to the best of our current knowledge there is no thing, no indivisible entity, that is us, neither in the brain nor in some metaphysical realm beyond this world.[67]

If we take it as true that the way we represent ourselves with the words 'I', 'me', and 'mine' are merely conditioned, we will see that these words do not describe an actual entity but are merely a strange loop where the concept proves its own existence. The separate self, not being an entity, is merely an activity that appears in Consciousness. This does not deny the reality of consciousness—what is being questioned is the common belief that there is a separate entity called a subject that is separate from the objects that appear in consciousness. It is this common belief that creates the mistaken identity.

The fact that that there is no 'me' does not deny that there must be skills needed by the apparently separate individual to both survive and thrive in the world. Examples of such skills might include performing manual tasks, reasoning, problem solving, focusing attention, learning to be responsive rather than reactive, and taming one's animal instincts. Just because these skills would be helpful to any body-mind mechanism does not prove that the person who can learn these skills is really a separate self.

The Ocean and the Wave

A story that has been with me as long as I can remember is the need to be 'special' and have 'special days'.

I remember being in the 2nd grade of elementary school—my age was around 7 years—when my mother promised to come on a class trip with me to the Queens Botanical Garden, and I was excited that I was going to have my first ever school day with my mother. But the moment after my mother and I had left our apartment to go on the class trip and the door of the apartment had already been shut, we heard the telephone ring—and my mother decided she had to go back to answer the telephone. She found out that her father's brother—her Uncle Samuel—had died in the middle of the night and as he was an Orthodox Jew, the burial was going to be on that very day in just a few hours. My mother apologized profusely, and when I realized she would not be coming with me, I could not stop crying. I still have a distinct memory of not leaving the bus to see the Queens Botanical Gardens while sobbing and sobbing—and my 2nd grade teacher trying to convince me that I should leave the bus to see the trees and flowers of the garden. But I could not let go of the story of how 'my special day' had been so suddenly ruined and spoiled.

This is how my higher self Eliyahu might speak to the ego of my lower self Elliott who holds the story that he needs to be 'special' and have 'special days':

> Elliott, you are no more than just a wave in an ocean of consciousness. Just like each snowflake is unique, so you are a unique wave. But in essence you are made of the same stuff as every other wave. If you maintain your identity as a separate wave, you will waste so much time trying to prove that you are special. Even if all the other waves ever

agreed that you were indeed a special wave, it would just be a blink of the cosmic eye before there arose a whole new batch of ocean waves.

As an alternative, if this story of 'special' ever lets go of you, you may know yourself as alone—but you will never again be lonely. You will become one with the ocean. Even if there is a storm or—God forbid—tsunamis do happen, you can sink to the depths of the ocean and still be at peace. In an ocean of love, there are no separate waves, but only the ocean 'waving'.

And from the highest perspective, one could follow the advice of Ram Dass in **Be Here Now**:

Emotions are like waves.
  Watch them disappear in the distance on the vast
calm ocean.

Will I wake up?

I once believed that like the Alice character in *Alice in Wonderland*, I might fall through a rabbit hole—and awaken into a reality where I no longer identified with the dream of a 'me'. In this fantasy, having died to my separateness, I would be watching the wheels go round and round, the lights would still be on, but there would be no one home to suffer. I would finally free my thinking from the desire to be a special person, thereby "draining the swamp" of my thinking from the wrong belief that I am separate from the whole.

My self-joke is that on that day I would wake up with my 'magic W'. What I mean by this phrase is that since I believe that there is a 'hole' created by my belief that I am a separate self, I would finally discover a 'magic W' to put before my 'HOLE' to be made 'WHOLE'.

A False Awakening

In my quest for wholeness, I had a false awakening. This happened after I became a student of Karl Renz, the author of **The Myth of Enlightenment**. In my experience, he was beyond brilliant and I organized dialogues with him in October of 2007 in a home of a friend in San Francisco. I must confess that part of my attraction to Karl was that his father had been a soldier in Hitler's army fighting on the Nazi side.

On the last day of the gathering, he told me that he wanted to visit Mt. Shasta (in northern California). He said that Mt. Shasta was known in India as "the holy mountain" of North America and that he wanted to see this mountain for the first time for himself. This majestic peak rises to an elevation of 14,179 feet (4,322 meters). What makes Mt. Shasta unique is its solitary grandeur. Unlike most high mountains that are part of larger mountain ranges, Mt. Shasta stands alone, dominating the landscape with its snowy cap and rugged slopes. In this way, it is quite similar to Mount Kilimanjaro. But Mt. Shasta—unlike Mt Kilimanjaro—is a potentially active volcano, with its last eruption spewing forth lava and ash in 1786.

On October 9th of 2007[68], Karl and I ended up going together (along with three other people who he had invited) to the spring that is known in the creation story of the local Winnemem Wintu tribe as "The Source" or "The Mouth of God". This spring lies in Upper Panther Meadow in a delicate alpine environment just below where the timberline ends at 7500 feet and just a few hundred feet walk from the one double-laned paved roadway that ascends snake-like to the hiking trailhead at 7,900 feet (2,408 meters).

There we found a small pool in the middle of a flat meadow being fed by a spring gushing forth from nothingness. (Scientists explain that this is possible because here lies the opening of an underground lava tube that descends from the glacier on the top of the mountain.)

After spending five minutes in the meadow, Karl (and also the three other people he invited) left me alone to meditate on a morning that was both cold and winterish. While gently looking at the peak of the mountain, all time disappeared. And then instantaneously, all space disappeared. The mountain to my astonishment catapulted inside of me. Once there was no longer any time or any space, it seemed that the house of my ego lost its supports and began collapsing—and I thought I found myself staring at THAT—the ineffable eternal sun of the Self.

Absorbed and drenched in a vast sense of IS-ness, I felt a peace beyond comprehension. It felt like my mind had stopped and I was no longer trapped by either my fears or my desires. Being directly illuminated by the light of consciousness felt simultaneously both a strangely familiar place and beyond my wildest imagination. The source of awareness, once so securely arising from inside my own mind, was now seemingly coming from nowhere — and simultaneously from everywhere.

An Agent of Kali?

That moment on the slopes of Mt. Shasta, I felt more peaceful than I had ever felt before. However, I immediately understood that my chaotic scattered states of mind could not maintain such a peaceful state. Even though I had an experience of not being a separate self, I felt I needed a power greater than my own ego to keep aligned with this peace. When in India, I had developed a devotion to Kali, the consort of Shiva, and I was enamored by her fiery energy that was able to destroy that which was unreal. Since at that moment it felt like any experience other than this peace was unreal, my thought was that I could make a deal with Kali. If I surrendered to Her, I could focus my energies on becoming Her Agent. In my delusional mind, I saw this as a way of preserving the peace. Little did I realize that this seemingly innocent desire "to become the agent of Kali" was an opening to ego's desire to be special. Had I truly understood the implications of identifying with a 'me' trying to become a self-appointed agent of a Goddess, I would have awared that this was a child-like form of narcissistic self-love. Giving myself over to a Goddess is all about staying asleep, not waking up. But that seeing did not occur to me at that time. What actually did happen is that this experience of oneness gave me a whole new identity.

That evening when I told Karl I wanted to become a spiritual teacher, he spontaneously shook his head and looked at me with astonished skepticism. Since I thought I had experienced an awakening, I began telling everyone what had happened to me at "the Source". The universal response was this question: "What drug were you on that day?" After assuring my listeners that I was quite sober and had been free of all drugs for several years, I was told that I didn't look or feel like a spiritual teacher and that I was only a normal person who had happened to have seen the emptiness of my true nature. Because I wanted to believe that I had a mission to become an agent of Kali, my ego usurped this moment of clarity and created an identity that was now in a missionary position.

Undermined by the Supermind

Sri Aurobindo talks in his book *The Life Divine* [69] about a *supermind* that is the highest level of consciousness that one can achieve. This is a plane of unity and harmony, where all contradictions are resolved and all divergent forces are reconciled. What had happened to me is that my own lifelong attachment to being special had led me to create a new identity out of a glimpse of unity and harmony—and the inevitable result was that I was *undermined* by the *supermind*.

Nisargadatta's Teachings

Realizing that I had fooled myself into believing that 'I' had awakened, I humbly dedicated myself to a new spiritual practice whose purpose was to assist me in letting go of the belief that I have a separate self. The practice comes from Nisargadatta Maharaj (1897-1981), an Indian spiritual teacher. Several of my friends spent time with him in India, the country he never left. His spiritual lineage was of teachers who were householders. For many years, he supported himself and his family through selling *beedis* (small, strong Indian cigarettes) in a booth outside his tenement in a hectic highly urbanized area of Bombay (now Mumbai). My friends described meeting Nisargadatta in a crowded mezzanine loft that he had fixed up to receive disciples and visitors. Never was there a charge to enter into the room, where every day of the week in the afternoon there would be a dialogue. Anyone who did not speak the local language of Marathi was free to ask questions through a translator. Even though my friends were not able to understand him in his original language, they could feel the earnestness in his way of addressing them. When he answered questions, he never quoted scriptures, but only spoke from his own direct experience.

Nisargadatta was also a *bhakta*. *Bhakti* is the Sanskrit word for devotion, and a *bhakta* is one who follows a devotional path. A bhakta experiences an intense emotional love toward an aspect of the divine. There is no word in English that gives the sense of devotion combined with active participation in this devotion through chanting the name of God. Through this path, the *bhakta* surrenders to the divine. Every day when devotional songs called *bhajans* were sung in his apartment, Nisargadatta would enthusiastically clash his cymbals while singing the names of Krishna and other divine beings. He also gave mantra initiation with the underlying point that the mantra was the Absolute Itself which could reverberate throughout life in all circumstances. Although these initiation mantras were a secret between Nisargadatta and the devotee, I did discover that one common mantra in his lineage was *Aham Brahmasmi*—translated as '*I am Brahman*' or less literally as '*I am Divine*'.

Nisarga is the Sanskrit word for the natural state. Nisargadatta means 'the giver of the natural state'. The yoga is straight-forward and simple: the mind, which is always becoming, must recognize and penetrate its own being, not as being this or that, here or there, then or now, but just timeless being. The knowledge of 'I Am' is the timeless form of being. Any attachments or identifications are seen as misdirecting us to live in a world that is symbolic and unreal. To break out from this prison of the conceptual mind, Nisargadatta suggests that the way is to shift our attention away from the stories in our mind and towards an awareness of that which is always present—*beingness*. In this awareness, there is no longer any difference between becoming and being.

To connect with this timeless *beingness*, the work is to keep bringing the attention to the sense of *I Am* or the sense of *Presence*. This means pointing the arrow of attention away from any outside phenomena—whether they are thoughts, objects, or experiences—and toward what is always present. This method is described in his book *I Am That,* a series of dialogues between Nisargadatta and the visitors who had come to his loft. In these dialogues, Nisargadatta is clear that the world is only an appearance and the way to perceive *That Which Is Real* is through abiding in the sense of *I Am* or the sense of *Presence*. The aim of meditation on one's sense of *I Am* is to reach its ultimate source, which Nisargadatta called the Self. For Nisargadatta, this is what is necessary if we are to relax into our natural state. For him, even the words *I Am* or *Presence* are but pointers to the truth that is ineffable and must ever remain ungraspable through any conceptual understanding. When we discover that we no longer need to identify with the body or the mind, we realize that who/what we are is unborn and does not die.

Nisargadatta describes his own practice in these words (*I Am That,* Dialogue 48):

> My teacher told me to hold on to the sense 'I am' tenaciously and not to swerve from it even for a moment. I did my best to follow his advice and in a comparatively short time I realized within myself the truth of his teaching. All I did was to remember his teaching, his face, his words constantly. This brought an end to the mind; in the stillness of mind, I saw myself as I am—unbound.[70]

And in that state of being 'unbound', there was a peace that passes any mental understanding (*I Am That,* Dialogue 51):

> I am now 74 years old. And yet I feel that I am an infant. I feel that in spite of all the changes, I am a child. My Guru told me: "That child, which is you even now, is your real self (*svarupa*). Go back to that state of pure being, where the 'I am' is still in its purity before it got contaminated with 'this I am' or 'that I am.' Your burden is of false self-identifications—abandon them all." My guru told me: "Trust me, I tell you: you are Divine. Take it as the absolute truth. Your joy is divine, your suffering is divine too. All comes from God. Remember it always. You are God, your will alone is done."
>
> I did believe him and soon realized how wonderfully true and accurate were his words. I did not condition my mind by thinking, "I am God, I am wonderful, I am beyond." I simply followed his instruction, which was to focus the mind on pure being, "I am," and stay in it. I used to sit for hours together, with nothing but the "I am" in my mind and soon the peace and joy and deep all-embracing love became my normal state. In it, all disappeared—myself,

my guru, the life I lived, the world around me. Only peace remained, and unfathomable silence".[71]

In pointing toward *beingness*, Nisargadatta implies that whatever we can perceive is not what we are—since we are the subjective experience of knowing rather than the objects that are known. In ignorance, the see-er identifies their separate self with what is seen, and in wisdom the separate self is seen as a meaningless projection: all that is left is the seeing. The ego is not capable of seeing beyond the duality of subject and object. We could say that this is a possibility only for the super-conscious mind. According to Nisargadatta, our true nature is infinite subjectivity, and this means abiding in a reality where there is no other.

Cogito, Ergo Sum?—or Sum, Ergo Cogito?

It may be evident to the reader that Nisargadatta's way of seeing the world contrasts sharply with Western philosophical traditions, which generally prioritize thinking over feeling or being. René Descartes' famous assertion, *Cogito ergo sum* ("I think, therefore I am") exemplifies a Western perspective wherein *beingness* is dependent on the faculty of thought. Were Nisargadatta to articulate his philosophy with similar conciseness, it might rather be stated as: "Before thinking arises, I AM."

For Nisargadatta, being is not derived from thought; instead, thought arises within being itself. Thoughts can be compared to ripples on the vast, still ocean of pure awareness. Thus, the Western belief in the mind as central to one's identity is inverted; for Nisargadatta, the mind has no autonomy apart from the Self. Objects do not have *consciousness*; *consciousness* can take on the appearance of being an object.

Descartes' *cogito* originates from systematic doubt, seeking a secure foundation by isolating beliefs that withstand skepticism. Conversely, Nisargadatta identifies with a *beingness* that is self-evident, self-luminous, beyond proof or doubt, and antecedent to thought. Since thought emerges within *beingness*, Nisargadatta does not rely upon thinking to affirm his existence.

While perception typically refers to becoming aware of objects through the five senses and the mind, Nisargadatta introduces the concept of *apperception*, an intuitive knowing centered in one's true nature as awareness itself. Apperception is immediate, direct, non-conceptual, and non-dual—recognizing reality without labeling, identifying, or dividing subject and object. One might say that while Nisargadatta perceives others, he apperceives the underlying truth that there is no separate "other". Apperception is thus not perception in the usual sense; rather, it is awareness recognizing itself directly as prior to thought.

What is apperceived is not a separate self, but the Self manifesting both as the world of objects and also as Silence. Such apperception remains untouched by doubt, as it is possible to effortlessly abide in Presence.

A key insight of Nisargadatta is that thought cannot grasp ultimate reality—it can only point toward it. One cannot know *beingness* as an external object; one can only BE it. And, crucially, one always already IS it.

Nisargadatta presents *beingness* as the singular experience that is not affected by thought or sensory perception. While the mind and senses reveal only ever-changing appearances, the apperception of the "I AM" directly discloses a changeless, enduring reality.

Asked how it is possible that he does not perceive himself as either the subject or object of his experience, Nisargadatta answered:[72]

> *"Love tells me I am everything.*
> *Wisdom tells me I am nothing.*
> *Between the two my life flows."*

Rupert Spira to the Rescue

I wanted a conceptual representation in more Western terms to better grasp what Nisargadatta was saying. And Rupert Spira came to the rescue when I attended one of his Webinars. He presented this model to understand what is meant by the Self; in his conceptualization, the Self is the vertical dimension:

> Thinking and perceiving are faculties of the mind. Mind is experienced when there is a movement in consciousness. We can imagine two dimensions to classify all that is experienced: a horizontal dimension of time and a vertical dimension of presence. On the horizontal dimension, the mind moves in duration from the past to the future through a stream of ever-changing *conceptions* and *perceptions*.
>
> The *conceptions* are the images and thoughts in our thinking; the *perceptions* are what comes in through the five senses: seeing, hearing, tasting, smelling, and touching. Together thinking and perceiving present us with the contents of experience.
>
> But if we shift our attention away from these contents toward a vertical dimension (that might also be called a context or a field) in which all this content arises, we can experience the Self. Thinking is made up of knowing, and the Self is beingness. The mind can never know the Self, but only be it. On this vertical dimension is "I AM"—a beingness that does not change—and this reality of awareness is always shining. While many names have been given to this vertical dimension, all these names come from the horizontal dimension.
>
> While that which arises on the horizontal dimension is ever-changing and never ever-lasting, in contrast that which awares all experience on the vertical dimension

never changes, as its nature is both ever-present and eternal. Meeting at the intersection of the two dimensions, the NOW partakes of both a moment in time and timelessness. The HERE is both a particular place from a localized perspective and boundless space on the vertical dimension. The world is not what we see, but the way we see. We cannot grasp the vertical dimension with our minds. Both time and space can only appear when infinite consciousness localizes itself into an apparently separate self through the mind.

Self-realization, then, is not the gaining of a new experience, but the recognition of the changeless presence within every experience. When the mind is entangled in the ever-changing contents of what arises in time and space, the vertical dimension is veiled. Mind might be viewed as the activity of consciousness through which consciousness seems to veil itself from the vertical dimension of its own infinite beingness. In Vedantic tradition, this is called *maya*.

When the mind learns to rest and then to abide in the awaring of the vertical dimension, a portal opens to an all-embracing peace that is beyond words—innate, subtle, silent, ineffable, and always right HERE NOW. That background of peace can pervade the present moment. Within that beingness is the happiness that you seek.

God Tells Moses His Name

While I was reading about the importance of paying attention to the sense of I AM in Nisargadatta, I realized that in Hebrew school I had learned that God's name was I AM THAT I AM. In the only verse of EXODUS that has the most common numerical approximation of the geometrical number called π (pi), God gives Moses an answer when Moses questions him about his name:

And God said unto Moses, **I Am That I Am**:
and he said, Thus shalt thou say unto the children of Israel,
I Am hath sent me unto you.

Exodus 3:14

(King James Version)

This is God's name in *Exodus 3:14* verse in its original Hebrew
before it was translated:

אֶהְיֶה אֲשֶׁר אֶהְיֶה

(Ehyeh-Asher-Ehyeh)

Here Ehyeh can mean either 'I AM', 'I WILL BE' or even 'I AM
BECOMING'; and Asher is a relative pronoun in Hebrew that can
be translated (depending on the context) as "that," "who," or even
"that which". Exodus 3:14 could also be translated as . . .

I WILL BE that which I WILL BE
I AM that which I AM
I-AM-who-I-AM
I AM is BEING
I AM is BEINGNESS
I am that which being BECOMES
I am that which becomes BEING
I am the one who is always ARRIVING
I am the one who is always LEAVING
I am that which neither comes nor goes but always IS.
I AM that which does not change.
I AM is not a thing.
I AM is love.
I AM is no body.
I AM nobody.
I AM is no thing.
I AM nothing.

The phrase "Ehyeh Asher Ehyeh" suggests a state of consciousness that is self-defined, self-sustaining, and transcendent, yet immanently present in every conscious being at every moment.

Jesus Tells It Like It Is

When Jesus tells a group of Jewish religious leaders that he is glorified by God the father, they question his authority to make such a claim, and Jesus responds:

> Verily, verily, I say unto you,
> Before Abraham was, *I AM*.

John 8:58
(King James Version)

This can be read as a statement from timeless awareness—not a chronological boast, but a pointer to the unconditioned presence of **I AM**. In this sense, Jesus is speaking from what Rupert Spira would call "the vertical dimension". He's not asserting egoic identity—"I, Jesus of Nazareth, existed earlier"—but rather expressing his direct realization of a unity with a boundless *beingness* that transcends both birth and death.

Is the Spirit Forever?

The quotation in English that most reminds me of the eternal presence of I AM is also the one most recited by Sunyata:[73]

> *Never the spirit was born;*
> *the spirit shall cease to be never;*
> *Never was the time it was not;*
> *End and Beginning are dreams!*
> *Birthless and deathless and changeless remaineth the*
> *spirit forever;*
> *Death hath not touched it at all,*
> *dead though the house of it seems!*

Search-ing or Be-ing?

One of my pastimes is going to operas. Because I cannot understand most operas in their original languages, I make use of the
English supertitles that appear above the stage translating the
words being sung. When the characters in the opera get hooked
into stories that lead to their destruction, I feel for their suffering.
As I found that I enjoy the operas more when I can see the faces of
the singers, I recently indulged myself by buying a pair of binoculars that had image stabilization. I still experience a moment of
joy when I push the image stabilization button and find that even
though my hands cannot be totally still, the image is both stable
and luminous.

This is the dream that I had during the night after I watched
an opera with my new binoculars: (I should mention that coming
back home on the San Francisco underground, the thought arose
that I should take good care of my binoculars to make sure that
they got home.)

> When I am in the passenger seat of a car coming home at
> night, I hear a crash and I know that somehow my binocu-
> lars have just fallen out of the car. I have a thought that I am
> losing a treasured possession and I notice fear emanating
> from my solar plexus.

And then I gained a moment of *lucidity*. What *lucidity* means to
me is that while I am still dreaming, I absolutely know for sure that
everything that is happening is *really* only happening in a dream.
For those moments, I may have been *in* the dream, but I was no
longer *of* the dream. I told myself in my lucidity that I am safely
in my bed and in that lucidity I knew for sure that my binoculars
were still securely in my possession. Then I lost my lucidity and
was again sure that the dream was really happening as I dreamed
on and the same dream continued:

...it is morning and since there is more light, I think it might now be possible to find my lost binoculars. I walk down the street around the corner from my home and—to my amazement—sitting under a parked car, I see my lost binoculars. On examining them, I realize that they are dusty and dented, but when I test them out and know that they are still working, I experience a moment of joyful exuberance.

Dreams quite similar to this had been recurring throughout this past year. Always I am lost or have lost an object—and then I gain lucidity—and yet a moment later I am back believing in the story of the same dream and searching for what has only been lost in the dream. I always question myself upon really waking up why I continue searching in my dream when I already have known for a moment that it is all a dream. After one of these recurring dreams, I wrote in my dream journal: "I am embarrassed that I spent most of the dream search-ing while I could have just been peacefully enjoying be-ing."

Neem Karoli Baba Visits Me in a Dream

Many years ago while I was writing my doctoral dissertation I had this dream:

My guru Neem Karoli Baba suddenly appears. He tells me that he is now going to show me the book that I would write one day. (When this dream happened, I didn't even know then that I was ever going to write a book and I get really excited.) He takes me to a room to show me the book and there in the center of the room is a huge book that is similar to a giant English dictionary that I had once seen in the British Museum in London. Each page of this book is around two feet by three feet and the book is sitting on a wooden stand with opened pages. I peer at the opened double set of pages and each page is totally blank. I turn several of the pages and each is still equally blank. I quizzically look at Neem Karoli Baba and with a nod he tells me to look at the spine on the book cover to see the title of the book. It is an effort to move such a big book, but I eventually see that the title of the book on the spine is just one word in big capital letters: PROJECTION.

To me that dream was about how something can exist in nothing. Mind can always project 'this and that', but I saw that ultimately it's all just made up by our thinking. The Self is free from all 'this and that'.

How Emptiness Scared Me

I began the practice of meditating on my sense of *I Am*—and I noticed right away I was able to let the reality of impermanence into my awareness more deeply than I ever had before. The way I expressed this is that *the only constant is change*—or, more poetically, *everything comes to go—not to stay.*

Unfortunately for me, it seemed that this growing clarity from abiding in this sense of *I Am* was like a medicine that had a side effect. Every medicine has a warning label that there may be unwanted side effects for people with pre-existing conditions. For me, the pre-existing condition that created the unwanted side effect was a (mostly unconscious) expectation that doing my spiritual practices would get me a more pleasurable experience of life.

I realized that my secret wish had always been to find the octopus's garden far beneath the waves, of which The Beatles sang:

I'd like to be
Under the sea
In an octopus's garden
In the shade

I'd ask my friends
To come and see
An octopus's garden
With me
We would sing and dance around
Because we know we can't be found [74]

Like my imaginary octopus, I had been travelling along the ocean floor picking up stones and shiny objects to make a garden. I realized that my dwelling was made up of impossibility.

To put it metaphorically: I had been wandering a scorching desert yearning for water when the shimmering lake I thought would quench my thirst revealed itself as a mirage. And as my blistered (or is it bliss-teared?) feet throbbed—not with ecstasy, but with pain—the fantasy of bliss dissolved into the very suffering I had been trying to escape.

Being Caught in Nothingness

The problem was that I hadn't yet developed a new way of running my life that would give meaning to what was routine and ordinary. I had wrongly assumed that in my process of awakening, I would be given a sense of an 'especially pleasurable state' that would exist in a transcendental realm. No perpetual bliss had happened. And I had lost the solid ground of believing in the identities that had been given to me by society.

Let me use a few metaphors to describe my confusion. It was similar to being in a dark hallway where I had just shut one door and I knew there was a doorway at the other end of the hall, but I could not find this new doorway. And some days it was like a tunnel with no light coming from either end where I lost my orientation and I could no longer figure out which way was forward and which way was backward.

Even though nothing bad had happened, I experienced myself

as a particularly insubstantial and ephemeral nothingness. My last metaphor to describe my state is oceanic—I felt like the misty froth of a wave with no direction home to any shore. If we make me a human being again, it was like being on a raft in the middle of the ocean where I not only could not see any visible land—but even more challenging—I had no oars.

A Gray Night of the Soul

In the middle of this mood, I read a book by Robert Wolfe called **Emptiness**. It said what I had known for many decades—that there is no inherent meaning in the world and that everything is all made up. However, this time I let the message enter my emotional body. This was the straw that broke the camel's back. My mood turned gray and somber. My friends reported that when standing, I was slumped over; and when sitting, I was slouched over.

For decades I had been searching for *śūnyatā*—the emptiness of the void—and now that I was emptying out conceptually, I was crying out in pain. I wished that I could go back to my old secure identity where I could believe the 'made-up' story that my spiritual path would lead to unimaginable pleasures in both the mundane and transmundane realms. At one time I had been so excited by the directive "to dance with the void", but now that I had a glimpse of its true nature as no-thing-ness and no-body-ness, my mind told itself a story that generated fear.

My Self-inquiry Group

In the midst of this self-doubt, I joined a group dedicated to pursuing the 'wake-up call'—this was defined as a journey toward what is real, meaning toward that which never changes. Other ways of expressing this purpose might be ideas like nonduality, Self-remembering, Self-realization, or—most commonly—enlightenment. We explored the teachings of Ramana Maharshi, Nisargadatta Maharaji, George Gurdjieff, Lester Levenson, and A. Hameed Ali (aka A. H.

Almaas). Many of these teachers are practitioners of *jnana* yoga, a path of Self-knowledge through self-inquiry. The group also explored various models that derived from recent discoveries in quantum physics. The most advanced practitioner in the group was a chiropractor named Steve Forrest. Steve's central message was simple yet profound: once an individual wakes up out of 'the dream of me', their suffering comes to an end. Steve named us the *Ultimate Medicine Group*—he took this phrase from Nisargadatta Maharaj who coined the term 'ultimate medicine' because his own non-medical prescription had the potential to end the 'dis-ease' of the human condition. According to him, an individual would have to follow their beingness—the I AM—beyond the utmost bounds of human thought to find their true nature. That which is aware of the mind is still, unchanging, and always ever-present. Once we identify with the content of the mind, the result is experiencing ever recurring excitement—eventually to be followed by anxiety. To experience the stillness of the time-free silent intelligent awake aware presence that is witnessing the mind, one must release one's attachment to and identification with the ceaseless flux of what will always be the mind's perpetual motion mechanisms.

Steve saw that the fastest path to expedite such an awakening was through self-inquiry about the nature of the self. He said that the mind works so much better when we ask it questions rather tell its answers. He suggested that the members of the group open-heartedly and earnestly ask ourselves such questions as:

* Where is the 'I' that thinks my thoughts?
* Where exactly can that 'I' be found?
* Do 'I' want to wake up out of the dream that there is a 'me'?
* Might that 'I' already be awake unbeknownst to me?
* When was the very first moment in my life that I was aware of a 'me'?
* Who was born at that very moment when my 'me' was born?

The Three Directives

Since most of the members of the group including myself thought of ourselves as being separate selves, Steve gave us directives to make us happier before we woke up out of the dream of the 'me'.

He explained that these directives were not about the *wake-up*, but merely about a *clean-up*. He added, however, that such a *clean-up* might have the effect of freeing up energy to pursue the call of the *wake-up*. Steve suggested that if we wanted to *clean-up* our lives, we master these three directives:

Manage the mind
Release the emotions
Tame the instincts

Each member of the group may have interpreted what Steve said in their own unique way, and this is my interpretation. To me the goal of *managing the mind* meant to let go of believing thoughts of guilt, shame, blame, resentment, regret, or worry. The goal of *taming the instincts* would require keeping in the forefront of awareness the intent not to be controlled by fear and desire. Just like the first and third directives were for me obvious, my way of living in the world was challenged by the middle directive: *Release the emotions*.

Although I could grok that I would be much happier if I released negative emotional states of *mad, sad,* and *scared,* I did not see why it might be in my interest to release the positive emotional state of *glad*. I enjoyed desiring objects that promised satisfaction upon their attainment. I would say to Steve, "What is wrong with enjoying being glad or joyful . . . or an occasional LSD trip?" (I knew that Steve had taken more than the usual amount of psychedelics, particularly LSD, psilocybin, DMT, ayahuasca, and more recently he had been exploring the dissociative states induced when using a nasal spray of ketamine prescribed by his doctor.) Steve's response was that the craving for any state, even joy, is a form of attachment. He would continue by saying that there was nothing wrong with any emotional state, sexual experience, or any drug trip, but the obstacle was in my craving for the dopamine fix of gladness. If I was serious about the wake-up call, Steve believed that it was necessary for me to give up my craving for pleasurable experiences.

Steve suggested that by pursuing pleasure, I was creating an unstable foundation for my life. He saw my desire for *gladness* as part of a quest to make the moment different than it was, and such an argument with reality would inevitably bring about suffering. His command to me was: "Drain the swamp of your mind from satisfying those wants that are not necessary." He explained that if I were willing to replace my quest for pleasure with a quest for Being, I could be much more peaceful.

When I heard these words from Steve, what came to mind were these lines from T.S. Eliot:

You say I am repeating
Something I have said before. I shall say it again.
Shall I say it again? In order to arrive there,
To arrive where you are, to get from where you are not,
*   You must go by a way wherein there is no ecstasy.*
In order to arrive at what you do not know
*   You must go by a way which is the way of ignorance.*
In order to possess what you do not possess
*   You must go by the way of dispossession.*
In order to arrive at what you are not
*   You must go through the way in which you are not.*
And what you do not know is the only thing you know
And what you own is what you do not own
And where you are is where you are not.[76]

A Teaching from Steve

In September of 2023. Steve was diagnosed with cancer. He gathered all of us together right after his cancer diagnosis and he told us he wanted to present a succinct summary of his way of thinking:

> "As all of you know, I was given a cancer diagnosis. The doctors have told me that I will be dead by Christmas. What I thought might be most important today is to share with you what I see as clearly true. I would like to make an attempt to systemize my thoughts. I want to give you training wheels that you can keep after I am gone. You will each have to be your own guru.
>
> "Let me ask each of you to go inside for a moment and ask yourself this question: 'Are you in some ways a captured bird staring out through the bars of your cage?' If that is the case, then you are a slave to your conditioning and your conditioning owns you. If you truly want to break free out of your cage, you've got to start really questioning all the stories you cling to, especially the ones about there being a 'real me'. True spiritual growth means letting that imaginary person die. The death of the ego is the beginning of a greater freedom than you have ever known.
>
> "Waking up hinges on two principles: non-attachment and dis-identification. Non-attachment means letting go of your cravings and addictions, leaving you with nothing but preferences. Identification is nothing but a belief. The most superficial belief is that I have a sex and a country, more deep are positions and values, deepest are usually identities that are unconscious until the moment of your death. Dis-identification means letting go of all your identities, leaving you with nothing but the bare thought 'I AM'. When you

stop attaching and stop identifying, there's no one left behind to be a separate self.

"Ego is nothing more than the belief that you have an identity as a separate self. This identity is entered around a simulation called 'me'. This is based on sensations and memories, and people live their entire lives in this simulation as if it is true. I call this a *mindscape*. In most humans, this simulation called 'me' wants to maximize pleasure and minimize pain. For those on the spiritual path, the maximum pleasure is enlightenment. But the fundamental conflict of the spiritual quest is that although the ego desires enlightenment, what enlightenment means is the end of believing that you are a separate self or a 'me'. Self can never achieve no-self. Ego wants the goodies, but the price of the goodies is to see and actually know that you are a nobody. Ego can never be free *of* ego. The ego can never know what it really means to let go of 'me' and 'mine' on every level of the emotional body.

"You have not yet realized that whatever you are searching for exists only in the reality of an absence. You are an *awake aware Beingness* who has been conditioned to identify with a particular body-mind mechanism. Once you stop thinking of yourself as a person, your memories will still be there, but they won't belong to you anymore. The illusion of a separate identity falls away. Even though a character still shows up in the grand drama of life, the character knows that there is nobody home. The character sees that their seemingly separate self is merely playing a dream character in a dream play. With no one any longer pretending to be a person, what's left in the absence of ego is simply Beingness, fully awake and aware.

"Nature has designed all sentient beings for survival and experiencing. A human being in this way is no different from an insect, a fish, a bird, or an animal. We all share fundamental biological instincts rooted in survival and reproduction—like seeking food, water, and sex.

"Among all sentient beings, humans are now the apex predator. Most humans are not only predatory, but also have the potential to be narcissistic and greedy. However, a few humans are becoming aware that there is a backdoor. That backdoor opens when experience becomes aware of itself. You could call this backdoor mindfulness or self-reflection, but I follow George Gurdjieff in calling this backdoor 'self-remembering'. This backdoor requires a backwards step where we become the witness of our thoughts and actions. It requires taming our instincts.

"Anyone who practices mindfulness will move up the pyramid of consciousness. There will be a gain in balance and ease, and, most important, greater clarity. More energy is produced to both expand and brighten consciousness. And as consciousness expands, it becomes possible to let go of attachments.

"I have been given a death sentence. However, because I've spent decades breaking my identifications and attachments, I am at peace. I have no aversion to dying. I am ready to move on. Every day I'm still doing my Chi Kung and exercising. And I'm not going to self-pity.

"When the doctors told me that I had a terminal case of cancer, I went: 'I'm OK.' I did then get sad and tear up, and that lasted literally about 30 seconds, and then I went again: 'I'm OK.' And that's pretty much how it's been. 'I'm OK.' It's not my preference, mind you. Nothing wrong with having preferences, but I'm not attached to my preferences. It's like, so OK. It's OK. I'm OK."

Self-Forgetting

In the weeks following his cancer diagnosis, Steve became assertive in demanding that I become more attentive to the wake-up call and pay less attention to my desire for pleasure. My ego found his insistence quite irritating and when he escalated by exclaiming: "Elliott, the spiritual path is not about you—STOP IT!", I was so shocked by his demand that I didn't even pause to consider what I was supposed to stop. All I heard was "STOP IT!" and I immediately took it as a criticism and an attack. My knee-jerk reaction startled even me—I shouted back at him: "I won't shed a single tear for you after you're gone!"

The moment after I said that I would not shed a single tear when he was dead, I was not happy with what I had said. It was a "WOW" moment. I saw that I was triggered because I was defending my ego's desire for comfort and pleasure. I had not tamed my instincts. In that instant, I had failed to step back and watch my own defenses from a more spacious, witnessing perspective. If I'd managed to take a backward step right then—staying grounded in my body while calmly pausing to observe my heated reaction—I might have given myself the time to wait until a kinder, more thoughtful response had come to mind.

Wanting to learn to take advantage of that brief window between stimulus and response, I grokked that I would need to cultivate self-discipline. The desire arose to use my free will to cultivate *free won't*. I thought of *free won't* as the ability to exercise a veto power the moment right after I wanted to react to a trigger. *Free won't* would prevent me from reacting like a cornered animal. Even if I wanted to lash out, I would choose to hold back until I was calm again.

Later, I realized this backward step is a key part of what Steve called "self-remembering". What I'd done by blowing up at Steve was its very core the opposite: "self-forgetting". Instead of observing, I got lost in my reactivity. Instead of hitting pause, I hit fast-forward. Instead of being curious, I had become furious. In the end, that jarring encounter taught me a crucial lesson: if I want to practice kindness—even in the midst of a trigger—I needed to remember to slow down and breathe deeply.

Last Words with Steve

Steve's pancreatic cancer had metastasized to many other parts of his body. He was in a lot of pain, but he still managed to function with the opiates supplied by hospice. And his mind was as sharp as ever.

I did call him up a few days before he died and told him how much I appreciated the work that we'd done together. I admitted that I finally got that he hadn't been trying to criticize me when he yelled "STOP IT!" I told him that I now saw that his intention had never been to attack me, but rather to snap me out of a self-centered haze so that I would become focused on what truly mattered.

I mentioned a saying that I had heard credited to Chögyam Trungpa where he supposedly once said: [77]

Enlightenment is the ego's ultimate disappointment.

Steve said that was the exact point he was trying to make to me. He continued: "Elliott, don't fill your life with trying to fulfill unnecessary desires. Quit chasing the next pleasant moment. You love your ego because you have the delusion that pleasure will give you what you want. Be ruthless about this—no attachment, no aversion. You don't need to clutter up your life with new experiences and new possessions. What you really need is to focus on the wake-up call. That will be so much more lightening and enlightening than all your games and toys—and give you even more light than your best light show during an LSD trip."

He continued: "Nothing is personal in any body-mind

mechanism. The true blasphemy is not in declaring that you are God, but it is indeed blasphemous to miss-take yourself to be a person. Enlightenment isn't something you achieve by effort—it's what remains when you have completed the effort to undo all your beliefs. And no one is forcing you to believe that you are a person. What is here now is only your awareness of Beingness. Being is just Being—it's not something more—in truth, it's so much less. Do you want the truth more than the life that you were taught to call your own?"

And to my surprise, these were his gentle final words to me: "I know this may shock you, but your life is not about YOU."

When he died a few days later early in December, I did shed a tear.

In my own words, Steve's message to me was that awaring Being is the gateless gate to peace, and I should make that 'IS-ness' my primary business. I could be either "busy" or "IS-sy", but not both. Since in his view I will only "run out of time once"—it will either be on the day of my physical death or alternatively on the day that I drop my identification with what I now believe to be 'my' separate self—he did his best to make it more possible for me "to die before I die".

As I experience myself being on the razor's edge of a spiritual path, I feel it might be relevant to mention the words of an ancient sage:[78]

"The sharp edge of a razor is difficult to pass over;
thus, the wise say the path to Salvation is hard."

EPILOGUE

Better... is the day of one's death than the day of one's birth.

—*Ecclesiates* 7:1

The kind of art closest to my heart is precisely a regression,
childhood revisited.
If it were possible to reverse development,
to grasp some road back around to childhood again,
to have its abundance and limitlessness once more
then that "age of genius,"
those "messianic times"
promised and sworn to us by all mythologies,
would come to pass.
My ideal goal is to "mature" into childhood.
That would be genuine maturity.

—Bruno Schulz [79]

In Xanadu did Kubla Khan
A stately pleasure-dome decree:
Where Alph, the sacred river, ran
Through caverns measureless to man . . .

A savage place! as holy and enchanted
As e'er beneath a waning moon was haunted
By woman wailing for her demon-lover! . . .

Weave a circle round him thrice,
And close your eyes with holy dread
For he on honey-dew hath fed,
And drunk the milk of Paradise.

—Samuel Taylor Coleridge, *Kubla Khan* [80]

Perfect happiness is the absence of striving for happiness.
Out of the great struggle comes the great stillness.
To a mind that is still, the whole universe surrenders.

–Taoist proverbs[81]

BEFORE GOING TO SLEEP LAST NIGHT, I WAS noticing how I have had a lifelong pattern of collecting memories, quotations, poems, ideas, imaginings, and all types of other stories. I was wondering whether this pattern might be getting in the way of my freedom. I thought of Steve Forrest's directive to me: "Drain the swamp." I had this dream:

In a sunny southern climate, I am at a retreat center where I choose to do a workshop called 'Letting Go'. All the participants introduce themselves and when I stand up, I surprise myself by exclaiming in a loud and definitive voice:

"I am a hoarder."

From the faces in the room, I see that everyone else is just as shocked as I am by my declaration.

After the workshop ends for the day, I venture out by myself into a field behind the retreat center. I walk for a while and I am continually awed by how really awesome nature is just by being Herself.

Suddenly, I come onto a large patch of psilocybin mushrooms. As I have never before seen them growing in the wild in a natural setting, I have a desire to ingest them. But then I go to my mind and say to myself, "I wonder if there is a look-alike to a psilocybin mushroom that is a deadly poison?"

I sit down amidst the mushrooms and I break off one and I start chewing it very slowly and I say to myself: "It sure does taste like psilocybin . . ."

There are so many mushrooms that I begin imagining that tomorrow I would like to invite the other participants at the workshop to come and meet me at this field.

Not knowing whether I will die or have a really good trip, I lay back in the grass and put a second mushroom into my mouth and begin slowing chewing when...

I awake...

Or did I die?

BIBLIOGRAPHY

Adamson, Sailor Bob. **What's Wrong with Right Now? If You Don't Think About It** (Composed by Gilbert Schulz). Self-published by Kat Adamson, 2022.

Adyashanti. **Emptiness Dancing: Selected Dharma Talks.** Los Gatos, California: Open Gate Publishing, 2004.

Adyashanti. **The Way of Liberation: A Practical Guide to Spiritual Enlightenment.** San Jose, CA: Open Gate Sangha, 2012.

Almaas, A.H. **The Point of Existence: Transformations of Narcissism in Self-Realization.** Boulder, CO: Shambhala Publications, 1996.

Arnold, Sir Edwin. **Bhagavad Gita: The Song Celestial**, Large Print Edition (originally written in 1885). Independently published: December 26th, 2020.

Attar, Farīd ud-Dīn. **The Conference of the Birds** (written in 1177 CE). Translated by Sholeh Wolpé. New York: W.W. Norton & Company, 2017.

Aurobindo, Sri. **Arya Edition with Sri Aurobindo's Revisions.** Haryana, India: Savitri Foundation, 2022.

Balsekar, Ramesh S. **Your Head in the Tiger's Mouth.** Redondo Beach, CA: Advaita Press, 1998 (published in the Chinese Year of the Tiger).

Blake, William. **William Blake: The Complete Poems**, edited by Alicia Ostriker. New York: Penguin Books, 1977.

Bregman, Rutger. **Humankind: A Hopeful History** (translated from the Dutch by Elizabeth Manton and Erica Moore). New York: Little, Brown and Company, 2020.

Carse, David. **Perfect Brilliant Stillness: beyond the individual self.** Shelburne, Vermont: Paragate Publishing, 2006.

Catullus. **The Poems of Catullus: A Bilingual Edition** (first published in Latin in 54 BCE). Translated by Peter Green. Berkeley, CA: University of California Press, 1987.

Catullus: **Selected Poems.** Translated by Stephen Mitchell. New Haven: Yale University Press, 2024.

Chestnut, Beatrice. **The Complete Enneagram: 27 Paths to Greater Self-Knowledge.** Berkeley, CA: She Writes Press, 2013.

Conrad, Joseph. **Heart of Darkness** (first published in 1902). Everyman's Library Edition, 1993.

Conway, Timothy. **Women of Power and Grace: Nine Astonishing, Inspiring Luminaries of Our Time.** Clarkdale, AZ: The Wake Up Press, 1994.

Dante, Alighieri. **The Divine Comedy: The Inferno, The Purgatorio, and The Paradiso** (completed in 1321). Translated by John Ciardi. New York: New American Library, 2003.

Dickinson, Emily. **The Poems of Emily Dickinson.** Compiled by R.W. Franklin. Cambridge, MA: The Belknap Press of Harvard University Press, 1999.

Dickinson, Emily. **The Complete Poems of Emily Dickinson.** Compiled by Thomas H. Johnson. Boston, MA: Little, Brown and Company, 1960.

Dwoskin, Hale. **The Sedona Method: Your Key to Lasting Happiness, Success, Peace and Emotional Well-Being.** Sedona, AZ: Sedona Press, 2003.

Eliot, T.S. **The Poems of T.S. Eliot, The Annotated Text.** Baltimore: John Hopkins University Press, 2015.

Farley, James (author) and Nicolas C. Grey (illustrator). **This Dog Barking: The Strange Story of U.G. Krishnamurti.** New York: Harper/Element, 2017. This is an artist's rendering in comic book form of the teachings of U.G. Krishnamurti.

Frankel, BeQui (RamsaLove). **The Power of Dreamland.** San Francisco, CA: self-published, 2016. A children's bedtime story that invites us to explore the power and magic of Belief. Copies can be ordered at: BeckyFrankel@gmail.com

Frankl, Victor. **Man's Search for Meaning** (first published in German in 1946). Boston: Beacon Press, 2006.

Frost, Robert. **The Collected Poems, Complete and Unabridged,** edited by Edward Connery Lathem. New York: Henry Holt and Company, 1979.

Gibran, Kahlil. **The Prophet** (first published in 1923). New York: Alfred A. Knopf, 1951.

Ginsberg, Allen. **Howl and Other Poems** (City Lights Pocket Poets, No. 4). San Francisco: City Lights, 1956.

Ginsberg, Allen **"Footnote to Howl"** in **Collected Poems** 1947-1997. New York: Harper & Row, 1984.

Goldstein, Joseph. **One Dharma: The Emerging Western Buddhism.** New York: HarperCollins, 2002.

Goldstein, Joseph and Kornfield, Jack. **Seeking the Heart of Wisdom: The Path of Insight Meditation** (Shambhala Classics). Boulder, Colorado: Shambhala Publications, 2001.

Hafez. **Hafiz's Little Book of Life** (originally published in the 14th century CE). Translated by Erfan Mojib and Gary Gach. Newburyport, MA: Hampton Roads, 2023.

Haldane, J.B.S. **Possible Worlds and Other Essays** (originally written in 1927). London, United Kingdom: Routledge, 2001.

Hawkins, David MD, PhD. **Letting Go: The Pathway of Surrender**, Carlsbad, CA: Hay House, 2012.

Heinlein, Robert. **Strangers in a Strange Land** (first published in 1961). An Ace Premium edition of Penguin Random House, 2018.

Hunt, Dorothy S. **Only This!: Poems and Reflections.** San Francisco, CA: Center for Meditation and Psychotherapy, 2004.

Ibn Al 'Arabi. **The Bezels of Wisdom** (first written in 1232 CE). Translated and introduced by R.W.J. Austin. Paulist Press, **The Classics of Western Spirituality**, 1980.

Isenberg, Elliott. **The Experience of Evil: A Phenomological Approach.** Unpublished doctoral dissertation completed in 1983. Permanently embedded at this website: eliyahu108.com

Kastrup, Bernardo. **The Daimon and the Soul of the West: Finding identity, meaning, and purpose in a sacrificial life.** Hampshire, United Kingdom: John Hunt Publishing, 2025.

Katie, Byron with Stephen Mitchell. **A Mind at Home with Itself.** New York: HarperCollins, 2017. Here Katie illuminates the *Diamond Sutra*, one of the most profound ancient Buddhist texts.

Katie, Byron. **Losing the Moon: Byron Katie Dialogues on Non-Duality, Truth, and Other Illusions**, edited by Ellen Mack. Manhattan Beach, CA: The Work Foundation, Inc., 1998.

Kerouac, Jack. **On the Road: The Original Scroll** (the actual original scroll was written in 1951). New York: Penguin Classics Deluxe Edition, 2007.

Khosla, Monica. **The First and Last Belief: A theory of Liberation in the age of neuroscience.** Salisbury, United Kingdom: New Sarum Press, 2025. This book describes what it is like to no longer have the experience of a separate self.

Kornfield, Jack. **A Path with Heart: A Guide Through the Perils and Promises of Spiritual Life.** New York: Bantam Books, 1993.

Krishnamurti, U.G. **The Mystique of Enlightenment.** As this book was never copyrighted, there are many inexpensive print editions and it can also be read for free online.

Levenson, Lester. **No Attachments, No Aversions: The Autobiography of a Master.** Sherman Oaks, CA: Lawrence Crane Enterprises, 2003.

Maharshi, Ramana. **Talks with Sri Ramana Maharshi: On Realizing Abiding Peace and Happiness** (first published in India in 1955). San Diego, CA: Inner Directions, 2000.

Maharshi, Ramana. **The Spiritual Teaching of Ramana Maharshi** (foreward by C.G.Jung). Boston, Massachusetts: Shambhala Pocket Library, 2004.

Marshall, Bart. **The Perennial Way: New English Versions of Yoga Sutras, Dhammapada, Heart Sutra, Ashtavakra Gita, Faith Mind Sutra, and Tao te Ching.** Wheeling, West Virginia: TAT Foundation Press, 2009.

Maugham, W. Somerset. **The Razor's Edge** (first published in 1944). New York: Random House, 1973.

McGilchrist, Iain. **The Matter With Things: Our Brains, Our Delusions, and the Unmaking of the World** (2 Volume Set). London, England: Perspectiva Press, 2021.

McKenna, Jed. **Spiritual Enlightenment: The Damnedest Thing.** Wisefool Press, 2010 edition. (First published in 2001).

McKenna, Jed. **Spiritual Warfare.** Wisefool Press, 2010 edition. (First published in 2007).

McLuhan, Marshall and Fiore, Quentin. **The Medium is the Massage: An Inventory of Effects.** New York: Bantam Books, 1967. (A double page spread with a photograph of the walk-out at my Amherst graduation is on pp.102-103.)

Merrell-Wolff, Franklin. **Pathways through to Space: A Personal Record of Transformation in Consciousness** (first published in 1944). This book is now more accessible inside **Franklin Merrell-Wolff's Experience and Philosophy.** Albany, New York: State University of New York Press, 1994. (This book recounts Merrell-Wolff's deeply personal inward journey toward Self-realization that culminated in August 1936 when he transitioned from identification with the egoic personal mind to the recognition of the impersonal transcendent Self.)

Merton, Thomas. **The Way of Chuang Tzu.** New York: New Directions, 1969.

Metzinger, Thomas. **The Ego Tunnel: The Science of the Mind and the Myth of the Self.** New York: Basic Books, 2009.

Nisargaddatta Maharaj. **I Am That.** Translated from the Maharathi tape recordings by Maurice Frydman in 1973. Durham, North Carolina: Acorn Press, 2012 (second American edition, revised).

Omar Khayyam. **The Rubáiyát of Omar Khayyám: Illustrated Collector's Edition** (first published in the 12th century CE). Translated by Edward Fitzgerald in 1869. CreateSpace, 2017.

Patanjali. **The Yoga Sutras of Patanjali.** Translated by Sri Swami Satchidananda. Yogaville, Virginia: Integral Yoga Publications, 1978.

Prendergast, John. **In Touch: How to Tune in to the Inner Guidance of Your Body and Trust Yourself.** Boulder, CO: Sounds True, 2015.

Prendergast, John. **The Deep Heart: Our Portal to Presence.** Boulder, CO: Sounds True, 2019.

Rajneesh, Bhagwan Shree (Osho). **Beyond Enlightenment**. Boulder, CO: Chidvilas Foundation, Inc., 1986.

Ram Dass. **Be Here Now.** San Cristobal, New Mexico: Lama Foundation, 1971.

Renz, Karl. **The Myth of Enlightenment: Seeing through the Illusion of Separation**. Carlsbad, CA: Inner Directions, 2005.

Sa'di. **Golestan (The Rose Garden)**, written in 1258 CE. Translated by Mahmoud Rezvani. Shiraz, Iran: University of Shiraz Press, 2018. (This is the most poetic and also faithful to original spirit of the writings by Sa'di, but can only be bought from the University of Shiraz Press.)

Sah, Krishna Kumar (K.K.). **Deva Bhumi: The Abode of the Gods in India.** Los Angeles, CA; Love Serve Remember Foundation, 2016.

Salinger, J.D. **The Catcher in the Rye.** Boston, MA: Little, Brown and Company, July 1951.

Sapolsky, Robert M. **Determined: A Science of Life Without Free Will.** New York: Penguin Press, 2023. (This book denies the existence of both *free will* and *free won't*.)

Schulz, Bruno. **Letter and Drawings of Bruno Schulz with Selected Prose**, edited by Jerzy Ficowski. New York: Harper & Row, 1988.

Seltzer, Henry. **The Tenth Planet: Revelations from the Astrological Eris.** Bournemouth, England: The Wessex Astrologer, 2015.

Shah, Idries. **The Way of the Sufi.** New York: E.F. Dutton & Company, 1970.

Shukman, Henry. **One Blade of Grass: Finding the Old Road of the Heart, a Zen Memoir.** Berkeley, CA: Counterpoint, 2019.

Spira, Rupert. **Being Aware of Being Aware.** Oakland, CA: New

Harbinger, 2017. (This is a collection of guided meditations.)

Spira, Rupert. **The Shining of Being**. Oxford, United Kingdom: Sahaja Publications, 2025. (This is his most recent book and a succinct summary of his wisdom.)

Spira, Rupert. **You Are the Happiness You Seek: Uncovering the Awareness of Being**. Oakland, CA: New Harbinger, 2022. (This book evolved from an online retreat and includes a question and answer format.)

Sri Ramakrishna. **The Gospel of Sri Ramakrishna** (translated into English with an Introduction by Swami Nikhilananda and a Foreward by Aldous Huxley). New York: Ramakrishna-Vivekananda Center, 1942.

Sunyata. **The Life & Sayings of a Rare-born Mystic**, edited by Betty Camhi and Elliott Isenberg (first published in 1990). San Francisco, CA: Nobody's Home Press, 2024.

Sunyata. **Dancing with the Void,** edited by Betty Camhi and Gurubaksh Rai (first published in 2001). Salisbury, Great Britain: New Sarum Press, 2024.

Talbot, Michael. **The Holographic Universe: The Revolutionary Theory of Reality.** New York: HarperCollins, 1993. He presents an intriguing scientific theory to explain how the yogis of India are able to have supernormal powers called siddhis.

Tao Te Ching: A New English Version, edited by Stephen Mitchell. New York: Harper Collins, 1988.

Tarnas, Richard. **Prometheus the Awakener: An Essay on the Archetypal Meaning of the Planet Uranus.** Woodstock, CT: Spring Publications, 1995.

10,000 Jokes, Toasts & Stories, edited by Lewis and Faye Copeland. Garden City, NY: Garden City Books, 1940.

Tollifson, Joan. **Awake in the Heartland** (1st ed. 2003). Salisbury, Great Britain: New Sarum Press, 2022.

Tollifson, Joan. **Nothing to Grasp** (first published in 2012). Salibury, Great Britain: New Sarum Press, 2025.

Trungpa, Chögyam. **The Myth of Freedom.** Boston, MA: Shambhala, 1976.

Truss, Lynne. **Eats, Shoots & Leaves: The Zero Tolerance Approach to Punctuation**, Foreword by Frank McCourt. New York, NY: Gotham Books, 2004. (In this humorous and witty guide to punctuation, this very British lady makes fun—on p. 153—of the way Americans illogically insist on placing the terminal punctuation of a sentence inside the quotation marks "even when this doesn't seem to make sense".)

The Upanishads. Translated by Eknath Easwaran. Tomales, California: Nilgiri Press, 2007.

Vaughan, Judy Beil. **Strawberry Roan: A True New Mexico Coming of Age Story.** Santa Fe, New Mexico: Irie Books, 1970. Judy was another participant in my Quaker Voter Registration project in Warrenton, North Carolina during the summer of 1963. She describes what happened in Warrenton on pp. 151-54.

Watts, Alan Wilson. **The Book: On the Taboo Against Knowing Who You Are.** New York: Pantheon Books, 1966.

Wolfe, Robert. **Emptiness.** Ojai, California: Karina Library Press, 2020.

Xenophon. **Memories of Socrates: Memorabilia and Apology** (originally written in 371 BCE). Translated by Martin Hammond. Oxford, England: Oxford University Press, 2023.

Wei Wu Wei. **Open Secret.** Hong Kong: Hong Kong University Press, 1970.

Recommended DVD Videos:

A Complete Unknown. Directed by James Mangold, 2024. This biographical musical drama shows how in 1961 a penniless 20-year old Bob Dylan arrives in Greenwich Village with a guitar on his back and revolutionizes the world of popular music by 1965. (Runtime: 2 hours, 21 minutes)

Fierce Grace with Ram Dass. Directed by Mickey Lemle, 2001. The documentary shows how Ram Dass discovers 'fierce grace' after a he experienced a major stroke in 1997. (Runtime: 1 hour, 33 minutes)

Kundun. Directed by Martin Scorsese, 1997. This docudrama tells the story of the life of the 14th Dalai Lama from his recognition as a child to his dramatic escape from Tibet following the Communist Chinese invasion of 1959. Philip Glass composed a hauntingly beautiful score. (Runtime: 2 hours, 14 minutes)

Rashomon. Directed by Akira Kurosawa, 1950. Set in 12th-century Japan, this film revolves around an incident in which a samurai is killed and his wife is assaulted; presenting four contradictory versions of what might have actually happened, this film depicts how reality is shaped by pre-existing biases. (Runtime: 1 hour, 28 minutes)

Siddhartha. Directed by Conrad Rooks, photographed by Sven Nykvist, 1972. Set along the Ganges in Northern India, this is an interpretation of Hermann Hesse's 1922 novel *Siddhartha*. The film features the songs of wandering sadhus from Rishikesh and the chants of Buddhist monks from Tibet, all accompanied by the flutes of Bengali melodies. With only Indian actors, the story follows Siddhartha's search for enlightenment as his journey takes him through austere asceticism, indulgence in sensual pleasures, the pursuit of material wealth, and moments of self-hatred. (Runtime: 1 hour, 24 minutes)

GLOSSARY

Advaita
Vedanta
(pp.253-
261)

Advaita literally means "**not two**" (*a* = not; *dvaita* = dual). The *Vedanta* means the end of the Vedas. These teachings assert that the ultimate reality is non-dual, infinite, and indivisible. The term *Advaita Vedanta* translates as the "non-dual end of the Vedas". The **Upanishads** are the books that are the last writings in the Vedas, the holy scriptures of Hinduism.

akasha
(p.169)

Akasha has different connotations within Hinduism and later Western adoptions of the term. In ancient Hinduism, it is the first element that is all-pervading, but is also seen as the ether, the upper space, sky. Sound is a special quality of *akasha*. Theosophy and other Western esoteric models perceive *akasha* as a cosmic field that records every thought, action, and word for all time.

anatta
(p.164)

Often translated as "non-self" or "not-self", this concept challenges the common assumption that there is a permanent, unchanging essence or self (ātman) underlying our existence. *Anatta* asserts that there is no fixed, eternal, or independent self within the individual. Instead, what we think of as "self" is a collection of impermanent, interdependent processes. In Buddhism, the belief in a permanent "I" or "self" is seen as an illusion caused by ignorance and attachment. In realizing there's no self, one doesn't become "nothing". One becomes **everything**—or, more precisely, one recognizes that **everything is arising within and as awareness**, without center or boundary.

anahata
chakra
(p.135)

Anahata in Sanskrit means 'unhurt, unstruck, unbeaten, and unwounded', and symbolizes a pure place where suffering is met with compassion. Located at the center of the chest, near the heart, this chakra is the bridge connecting the lower three chakras, which are associated with material existence, to the upper three chakras, which are related to creativity, intuition, and Silence.

anicca
(p.164)

The term *anicca* comes from the Pali language, where "*a*" means "not" and "*nicca*" means "permanent". This is a fundamental concept in Buddhism, usually translated as "impermanence". It represents the idea that all conditioned phenomena—everything that arises from causes and conditions—are in a constant state of flux. Recognizing and understanding *anicca* is crucial in Buddhist practice because it leads to insight into the true nature of reality, helping to alleviate attachment, suffering, and ultimately leading toward liberation.

asanas
(p.83)

Postures. In yoga philosophy, the body is seen as a temple of the spirit, and *asanas* are a way of honoring and maintaining this temple. The practice of *asanas* is deeply connected to the breath through *pranayama* (breath control practices), which enhances the ability to move energy throughout the body, leading to increased vitality and a sense of inner peace.

avatar
(p.120)

The word *avatar* comes from the Sanskrit for 'descent'. It implies the crossing over from the divine realms to the human realm, a deliberate descent or incarnation of a supreme being onto the earth. The purpose of an *avatar* is to restore dharma (cosmic order and righteousness). In Hinduism, this is the form taken on earth by Vishnu in different epochs. The most well-known avatars are Rama and Krishna. Some Hindus celebrate such great beings as Buddha and Jesus as *avatars* too. The coming *avatar* is said to be Kalki who will come to destroy *adharma* or the unrighteous way of life.

awareness
(p.254)

The experiential space in which both conscious and unconscious contents arise.

awaring
(p.199)

The active, continuous practice of becoming more aware that involves a deliberate, mindful attention to the present moment in the here and now. *"Awaring"* is relevant to the journey of self-realization as it suggests an active, ongoing exploration and understanding of the self beyond the surface level of personality and ego. Through continuous *'awaring'*, one might peel back the layers of identity, reaching closer to the core of one's original nature.

bardos
(p.116)
(p.246)

In Tibetan Buddhism, the realms following death and before the next rebirth. A *bardo* is an intermediate state where consciousness finds itself in between death and birth. *The Tibetan Book of the Dead* (*Bardo Thodol*) is a guide for the dying and the dead, offering instructions on how to navigate this intermediate state to achieve a favorable rebirth or even liberation. For those still in a body, *bardos* are a reminder of the impermanence of existence and the importance of living a virtuous life, preparing oneself for the moment of death.

bhakta (p.253).	A *bhakta* is someone who practices *bhakti*, which is devotion toward the Divine. A *bhakta* practices one-pointed devotion to an aspect of the divine (often a form taken by an avatar, such as Krishna). A *bhakta* moves beyond ritual and dogma to reach the truth by means of love and comes to what in the West we might call a mystical union with the Absolute, where subject and the object, the knower and the known, the lover and the object of that love, become one.
bhakti (p.253)	The *yoga of devotion*. This comes from the Sanskrit root *bhaj*, meaning "to share" or "to partake". It implies a relationship where the devotee and the Divine are deeply interconnected. It is the yoga designed to channel emotion into spiritual practice, centering on love as the path to liberation (*moksha*). This love is not possessive or self-serving; it is selfless and transcendent. One of the forms of *bhakti* is *shravana*, which means the telling of stories about the Divine.
bodhi (p.165) (p.176)	Deep, experiential realization of the true nature of reality: *nirvana* in Buddhism, *samadhi* in Hinduism, *fanaa* in Islam, and the mystic union in Christianity. In ancient China, *bodhi* was translated as the *Tao*.
daemon (p.321) (p.360)	This concept (δαίμων in Greek) suggests that each of us has an internal voice that can guide our life. For the Romans, *genius* was merely their Latin word for *daemon*. Just like Socrates acknowledged his *daemon* both for preventing him from making mistakes and also as the source of his wisdom, the *daemon* is an impersonal and ingenious guide who can lead the apparently separate ego-ji to self-actualization and then to Self-realization.

dakini
(p.79)

Dakini is a Sanskrit word which can be translated to mean 'sky dancer' or 'space-goer', suggesting a being who traverses the expanse of the sky or the vastness of consciousness. They are guardians and protectors associated with wisdom, insight, and the dynamic, transformative aspects of the mind. They embody qualities like insight, freedom from attachment, and the ability to cut through illusion. Most are depicted as being feminine, some are wrathfully ferocious, most are playfully blissful.

darsan
(p.112)

Darsan (sometimes spelled *darshan*) stems from the Sanskrit word dṛś, which means 'to see'. In its devotional quality, it's way deeper than just looking at something. When devotees go for *darsan*, they're seeking a moment of direct visual and emotional contact with the divine. What is divine can be a guru or a high spiritual being or possibly the statue of a deity in a temple. An individual who has *darsan* experiences a blessing by being momentarily united with a reality that is experienced as being divine.

dasa
(p.156)

This term means 'servant' and is connected to the yogic path of *bhakti*. The total surrender by the servant to what is divine means the transformation of the servant-master relationship into what will ultimately be a union between the servant and the master. This path requires that the servant cultivate and energize a faith that there is a divine energy that truly can be experienced. The surrendering of the ego out of love towards the divine can lead to ego-transcendence and ultimately Self-realization.

dharma (p.176)	This has no exact translation in English because it has three meanings: first, what is true; second, the path towards what is true; and, lastly, an individual's own unique path towards what is really true. To explicate further, the first definition is about universal laws that govern the cosmic order; the second includes human virtues and ethical principles that righteously respect these cosmic laws; and, lastly, one's *dharma* is about an individual's own vocational and life callings that assist that individual to live in accord with these universal laws.
dukkha (pp.163- 164)	The term *dukkha* is derived from the Pali/Sanskrit words *duh* (bad, difficult) and *kha* (space, axle-hole of a wheel). Literally, it can mean "a wheel out of alignment", symbolizing the inherent discomfort and imperfection of life. Often translated as "suffering" or "unsatisfactoriness", it is intimately connected to *anicca*, the impermanence of all phenomena that are conditioned by cause and effect.
ego (p.34) (p.148) (pp.202- 204) (pp.271- 273)	The Latin root ego simply means "I" or "self". These are some of its main uses, all connected to the belief in the reality of a separate self: 1) Everyday usage: On the negative side, someone with "a big ego" often comes across as overbearing or full of themselves, unable to see beyond their own spotlight. On the positive side, there is the notion of a balanced ego acting like an inner shock absorber—enough self-worth to weather setbacks without tipping into arrogance.

2) Freud's *ego*: In psychoanalysis, Freud cast the ego as the referee between our raw instinctual drives for sex and aggression (the id) and society's moral standards (the superego). This is where rational planning lives—guided by what Freud called the reality principle—to find the balance between inner drives and external rules.

3) Philosophical *ego*: Philosophers often identify the ego with the "I" doing the thinking. Descartes' famous *cogito, ergo sum* ("*I think, therefore I am*") places the ego at the center of self-awareness. Here the ego is the part of the individual who is the agent through his or her thinking.

4) Eastern perspective: In Buddhism and Hinduism, the *ego* is seen as an illusion—a flimsy boundary that is the source of both attachment and suffering. This perspective suggests that once we drop this false sense of separateness. we are on the fast track to enlightenment or Self-realization. The *ego* isn't evil—it's just a tool that has become a tyrant.

ego death (pp. 274-275) In spiritual contexts, '*ego death*' refers to the dissolution of the ego's boundaries. The awareness of one's identity with a 'cosmic consciousness' that is boundless and eternal may lead to a profound sense of peace. It involves the transcendence and release of one's limited sense of self, often resulting in a radical shift in perception wherein dualities such as 'self' and 'other' dissolve. As the familiar self fades away, what emerges is a direct realization of unity with a greater whole. Common metaphors include:

"A wave realizing that it is not separate from its ocean."

"A caterpillar entering a cocoon and emerging as a butterfly."

"A phoenix dying and then arising reborn from its ashes."

Ego-death isn't about permanently destroying the ego, since a healthy ego is necessary for functioning in everyday life. Rather, the goal is integration, where the ego serves as a helpful tool, but no longer dominates as tyrannical master.

ego-ji
(pp.202-204)

Sunyata's made-up word that combines the suffix -ji with the notion of the ego to indicate a respect for the necessity of the ego's place in the cosmic order. *Ego-ji* embodies an approach where one works with the ego in a way that supports growth, self-awareness, and enlightenment. This involves practices like mindfulness, which helps observe the ego's patterns without attachment, and compassion, which softens the ego's harsh edges. Sunyata would tell people to never engage in any practice that would try to destroy or kill the ego, but rather to recognize that the ego truly has its (time-bound) place in both the natural and societal order.

Enneagram
(p.34)

The *Enneagram* maps out nine fundamental personality types. Each of the nine types has a distinct worldview and strategy for coping with the existential realities of life. It is a dynamic tool for understanding our core motivations, fears, desires, and the mechanisms we use to navigate our relationship with ourselves and others. The *Enneagram* doesn't just expose our limitations; it offers a pathway to transcend them, encouraging us to evolve beyond the confines of our type towards a more balanced and holistic understanding of the self.

free won't
(p.273)

While *free will* implies the ability to choose and initiate action, *free won't* highlights the capacity to veto impulses, delay gratification, or say "no" to a course of action. It's the flip side of agency—a quiet but vital restraint that prevents the self from being hijacked by fleeting desires, automatic reactions, or external pressures. If a person does not have *free won't*, it could be argued that they lose their *free will*. *Free won't* embodies the mindful moment between stimulus and response—the inner pause that allows reflection, discernment, and self-restraint to take precedence over instinct and habit:

Free Will says: "I have the agency to choose what to do."

Free Won't replies: "Do you have the agency to choose what *not* to do?"

Gopis
(p.120)

The Gopis of Vrindavan hold a central place in the *bhakti* tradition. These cowherd girls are depicted as having unconditional love for Krishna, an *avatar* of the supreme god Vishnu in his form as a prepubescent boy. The Gopis' love for Krishna is depicted as selfless and pure devotion. As this love is not bound by societal norms or marital statuses, it embodies the idea that the soul's love for the divine transcends all earthly obligations.

grok
(pp.214-
215)

Originally coined by Robert A. Heinlein in his
science fiction novel **Stranger in a Strange Land**,
grokking involves a complete merger of the observer
and what is observed. This unity of knowledge goes
beyond mere intellectual comprehension to include
absorption into an object so completely that the subject and the object become one.

Hanuman
(p.120)

The monkey God who is the supreme devotee
(*bhakta*) and selfless helper of Rama, an incarnation
of Vishnu. Celebrated in the epic **Ramayana**, he is the
epitome of devotion, strength, courage, wisdom, and
selfless service. *Hanuman* performed extraordinary
feats and had unwavering dedication to righteousness. His life teaches that true devotion is not passive,
but is an active, dynamic force that empowers one to
overcome great obstacles and serve the divine with
pure love and devotion.

hatha yoga
(p.83)

The term *hatha* itself is often interpreted as the
union of the sun (*ha*) and moon (*tha*), representing
the balance of masculine and feminine aspects within
us, as well as the balance of effort and surrender in
our practice. *Hatha Yoga* is a path that integrates
physical postures (*asanas*), breathing techniques
(*pranayama*), and meditation (*dhyana*) to achieve a
harmonious balance between body, mind, and spirit.
Hatha Yoga is both a spiritual practice and a form
of physical exercise that prepares the body for the
awakening of the *kundalini* energy.

headucation
(p.201)

This is Sunyata's made-up term that emphasizes the
way conditioned learning may lead to the abandoning

of one's own heart. It mocks a model of education that overly prioritizes intellectual development, rationality, and the accumulation of knowledge (the 'head') at the expense of emotional intelligence, intuition, devotion, and creativity (the 'heart').

innerstance (p.200)

Innerstance is a term coined by Sunyata that emphasizes how one's attitude may be more important than circumstances in determining one's fate. By merging the concept of 'inner' with 'stance', what is being suggested is that our internal posture—our mindset, beliefs, and attitudes—holds significant power over our external circumstances. It aligns with the notion that while we may not always have control over the external events or challenges we face, we have the ability to choose our reactions and attitudes toward those circumstances. A resilient *innerstance* enables individuals to view challenges as opportunities for growth rather than insurmountable obstacles.

innerstand (p.199).

Comprehending through intuitive awareness. A term coined by Sunyata, it is about trusting those intuitions that arise from within, which often guide us more faithfully than the analytical mind. The suggestion is that attuning to the wisdom of the heart may be a better way to comprehend reality than the understanding of the head.

jnana (p.267)

Jnana yoga is called the "path of Self-knowledge". Its practice emphasizes self-inquiry to uncover the true nature of the self and reality. While it seems cerebral, *jnana yoga* ultimately leads to experiential realization, not just intellectual understanding. Central to *jnana yoga* is the recognition that the individual self (*Atman*) is not separate from the universal consciousness (*Brahman*). The core teaching is *"Tat Tvam Asi"*—translated as *"That Thou Art"*. What is required is the ability to distinguish the eternal (the Self) from the transient (the body, the emotions, the mind, and the world). The illusion of separateness (*maya*) veils this unity and leads to suffering. By negating all that is not the true self (*Neti, Neti* – "not this, not that"), the seeker comes to recognize their true nature as pure consciousness.

karm-uppance (p.xvi)	'Karmuppance' is an evocative term that encapsulates the idea of *karma* manifesting in the here and now. The term suggests an immediate consequence for the intentions in one's acts according to the laws of *karma*. By blending the concept of *karma* with the notion of something coming upon one both suddenly and deservedly ('comeuppance'), it highlights how our choices create our reality.
Krishna (p.120) (p. 253)	An *avatar* of Vishnu, worshipped today in different forms—as a charming child who stole butter from his mother, a prepubescent lad sporting with the Gopis or cowherdesses, a wise and mighty prince, and the epitome of wisdom giving advice to Arjuna on the eve of a battle as recorded in the **Bhagavad Gita**.
kundalini (p.83)	This refers to a form of primal energy said to be located at the base of the spine. When awakened, it travels up through the chakras, leading to heightened awareness, mystical experiences, and eventually enlightenment. As the embodiment of *Shakti* (*Shiva's*

feminine consort), *kundalini* represents the energetic and creative power of consciousness.

Maha-
bharata
(p.121)
Hindu epic, recounting life, loves, battles and spiritual experiences in the time of Krishna and containing the **Bhagavad Gita**, one of the most influential writings in Hinduism.

maha-
samadhi
(p. 155)
Mahasamadhi is the conscious departure from the physical body of a realized or enlightened being. It is not seen as death in the ordinary sense, as that particular flavor of beingness is now merging with the absolute or divine consciousness. This is considered the ultimate act of spiritual achievement, where the apparent separate self of a mind-body mechanism merges with the absolute reality, thus transcending the cycle of death and rebirth.

mahasiddha
(p.129)
In Sanskrit, while *maha* is the word for great, the term *sidh*, means to accomplish, to attain, or to succeed. Thus, a *mahasiddha* refers to one who has achieved or attained something great in spiritual terms. This achievement often relates to spiritual powers (*siddhis*), but it can also indicate a profound and lasting level of spiritual mastery without such supernormal powers.

manipura
chakra
(p.135)
The energy center in the third chakra that is associated with power. Positioned around the area of the solar plexus, which is just above the navel and below the chest, it is traditionally represented as a bright yellow lotus with ten petals. It is associated with the element of fire and is considered the center of self-esteem, confidence, and empowerment. The term *manipura*

itself can be broken down into two Sanskrit words: *mani*, meaning gem, and *pura*, meaning city—thus, it is often interpreted as the *"City of Jewels"*.

maya
(pp.140)
(p.148)
(pp.245-
246)
(p.259)

Maya drapes an illusion in a cloak of substantiality, making the unreal appear as real. Seen as consciousness momentarily obscuring its own infinite nature, it's the mind playing a game of hide-and-seek. For anyone walking the spiritual path, this notion can lead to an awareness that our beliefs can become obstacles to experiencing beingness.

mindscape
(p.271)

A *mindscape* is a self-generated mental simulation —an immersive landscape of thoughts, beliefs, memories, emotions, and narratives—within which the illusion of a separate self appears to exist. It is the virtual reality created by the mind, projected as a world in which "I" am the central character. In this context, a *mindscape* is not reality itself but a **story-space**, a stage constructed by the ego to organize experience round the fictional identity of a "me". Each person's mindscape carries a unique story of what matters—what is good or bad, desirable or to be avoided, meaningful or meaningless—but these mindscapes are just made up. They are **dreams mistaken for truth.** Most people live within a *mindscape* that is structured around the pursuit of pleasure and the avoidance of pain. For spiritual seekers, the *mindscape* may evolve—substituting ordinary pleasures with higher ones (like enlightenment), but still clinging to the illusion of a seeker, a self who can "attain" no-self. In this sense, the ego adopts a more refined costume, but remains intact. There are **no true mindscapes**, because what they represent—a self within a world—is a virtual reality. The *mindscape* called "me" is just a simulation. Enlightenment, then, is not an improved or perfected *mindscape*, but the collapse of the illusion that any mindscape centered on a "me" is real.

moksha
(p.113)

Liberation from suffering. It is freedom from the cycle of birth, death, and rebirth (*samsara*). In *Advaita Vedanta*, moksha is the experience of the ultimate, non-dual reality. It involves dissolving the illusion of separateness and ego. It is not merely an escape or a state, but a realization of one's true nature, which is infinite, unchanging, and beyond dualities. *Moksha* is the recognition of what always was—the inherent freedom in existence. In the Sikh religion, there is a similar notion called *mukti*.

murti
(p.127)

A *murti* in Hinduism refers to an image, statue, or idol of a deity or figure that is worshipped. These *murtis* are seen as physical embodiments of the divine, making the divine accessible to human senses and providing a focal point for devotion and prayer. This tangible representation of the divine or spiritual principles allows for a form of connection with the unmanifest Absolute through something that can be seen, touched, and experienced within the rituals of daily life.

nonduality
(pp.253-
261)
(pp.266-
267)

The insight that reality is ultimately undivided and cannot be adequately described or understood in terms of separate or distinct entities. This challenges the conventional way we perceive reality and ourselves by pointing to the fundamental unity underlying all

(pp.270-
272)
(pp.274-
275)
(pp.354-
360)

apparent dualities. At its core, non-duality asserts that the separation we experience between "self" and "other," subject and object, or the material and spiritual, is ultimately an illusion. Reality, it posits, is indivisible—a single, undivided whole. Duality arises from the mind's tendency to categorize and fragment experience, but in truth, these divisions are merely an appearance. As an appearance, they will undergo a disappearance when the ego dies or, if not then, the moment the physical body dies when the lungs stop breathing and the brain stops thinking.

pranayama
(p.83)

Breath Control: *Pranayama* involves controlling the breath to influence the flow of *prana* (energy) in the body. This can calm the mind and prepare it for meditation. *Pranayama* techniques vary from simple breath awareness to advanced practices involving specific rhythms and patterns of breathing. Anything other than simple *pranayama* should not be practised without guidance, as there is a danger of premature movement of the *kundalini* energy with unpleasant psychological and physical consequences.

prasad
(p.112)

Prasad is sometimes translated as 'a gift of grace'. In Hinduism and Buddhism, *prasad* is considered a divine gift or offering that has been blessed. It may be food that is offered to a deity who is treated like an honored guest or food that is eaten that has been blessed by a guru, and then distributed to devotees. The act of consuming *prasad* is seen as receiving a blessing directly from the divine.

rakshasa

In Hindu and Buddhist mythology, *rakshasas* are

(p.132)   fierce and war-like spirits with supernatural powers,
who are capable of shape-shifting and creating illusions. *Rakshasas* are often (but not always) evil. For
instance, the ruler of the kingdom of Lanka (now
associated with Sri Lanka), who abducted Rama's
wife Sita was a *raskshasa* called Ravana. He is not evil.
After being mortally wounded by Rama in a fierce
battle, later traditions suggest that as Ravana lay
dying, he let go of his pride, turning his mind toward
Rama—and so, even in defeat, he won freedom.

Rama   An avatar of Vishnu. As the protagonist of the ancient
(p.132)   Indian epic *Ramayana*, Rama's unwavering adherence
to *dharma* in the face of many obstacles offers insights
into the nature of righteousness and duty and the
sacrifices involved in adhering to one's principles. His
exile, the abduction of his wife Sita by the rakshasa
king, Ravana, and the ensuing battle to rescue her,
all symbolize the external and internal struggles
that individuals face in their quest for integrity and
Self-realization.

rudraksha The word *'rudraksha'* itself is derived from Sanskrit,
beads   where *'Rudra'* is a name for Lord Shiva, and *'aksha'*
(p.144)   means eye or tear. According to mythology, the
first Rudraksha tree grew where Shiva's tears fell on
earth, imbuing these beads with profound spiritual
power. Made from the seeds of the Rudraksha tree
(*Elaeocarpus ganitrus*), each seed is covered by a blue
outer husk when fully ripe. The seeds inside are used
to make malas or rosaries, often with 108 beads.

samadhi   In the yogic tradition, *samadhi* is the final limb of

(See bodhi on p.293)	the Ashtanga (eight-limbed) yoga system outlined by Patanjali in the Yoga Sutras. It represents a state of complete absorption in the object of meditation, where the meditator and the object meditated upon become one. This is often seen as the culmination of practice, where all sense of individuality and separation falls away, revealing a state of pure consciousness where all that remains is undivided presence.
sangha (p.176)	The community of people seeking to wake up to their true nature. It represents a spiritual fellowship united by their commitment to this awakening and the desire to support each other in achieving this goal. It underscores the idea that the wake-up call is not a solitary endeavor but is enriched by shared experiences and mutual support.
sattvic (p.83)	The concept of *sattvic* originates from the ancient Indian system of Ayurveda that offers insights into a way of living that promotes harmony and balance. It is one of the three *gunas* (qualities or tendencies) that describe the essential characteristics of all things in the universe. The other two *gunas* are *rajas* (passion, activity, restlessness) and *tamas* (inertia, darkness, ignorance). *Sattva* embodies purity, wisdom, and harmony, and is considered the most conducive to health, happiness, and spiritual well-being.
self (pp.200-204)	More than any other word in the English language, this term has a diversity of philosophical implications for each of its meanings:

The individual person: *"I found myself in trouble."*

Subjectivity: *"The self perceives the world."*

Essence: *"Know thyself."*

Identity: "I am me." This is the experience that one is a separate entity with an identity.

In addition, there are other layers of meaning in religious and spiritual contexts:

Christianity: The ultimate goal is to transcend selfish desires and align the *self* with divine will. Views the *self* as a creation of God, imbued with a soul. The idea of sin often involves the *self* in conflict with God's will because of pride, highlighting the tension between ego and humility.

Western humanistic traditions Leans toward defining and celebrating the *self*, seeing it as central to individuality, autonomy, and nurturing personal values and goals. In Abraham Maslow's *Hierarchy of Needs*, the *self* represents the unique potential within each inner-directed individual, and *self-actualization* is the process of realizing and expressing that potential.

Eastern traditions question the very existence of the *self*, framing it as an illusion to be transcended for spiritual awakening. In Hinduism, the belief in a separate *self* (ego) is seen as a result of *maya* (illusion), causing suffering and preventing liberation (*moksha*). Buddhism radically denies the existence of a permanent, independent *self*: the emphasis is on transcendence and emptiness.

siddha (p.126)	A person with great spiritual attainment, often including supernormal powers. The term *siddha* is deeply rooted in the Indian spiritual traditions of Hinduism, Buddhism, and Jainism. This state of perfection is not just about supernormal powers, but

also about achieving Self-realization.

siddhis (pp.131 -137)	This is the Sanskrit word for accomplishment or perfection, but in common usage it often used to refer to supernormal powers. In the **Yoga Sutras of Patanjali**, *siddhis* are treated with cautious reverence. Patanjali warns that while *siddhis* can be signs of progress in the spiritual journey, they can also be distractions, leading the practitioner away from the ultimate goal of liberation (*moksha*) if pursued for their own sake.
supernormal powers (pp.135-137)	These powers range from clairvoyance, levitation, and telepathy to more startling abilities such as changing one's size or bilocation.
sunyata (p.197)	Full solid emptiness. The concept of *sunyata* suggests that all phenomena are devoid of an intrinsic, independent essence. This means that things do not exist in isolation, but are interdependent, coming into being through a web of causes and conditions. Although the objects that appear in consciousness may appear to be real and substantial, they are in reality ephemeral and insubstantial.
Tao (p.218) (p.299)	The *Tao* (or *Dao*) is often translated as *the Way*. It is unmanifest—the eternal unseen source beyond all causes and conditions. The hidden essence that is the *Tao* is also the 'ten thousand things', the impermanent, conditional manifestation. The *Tao* is the natural order of the universe in which everything ('heaven and earth') is interconnected. Life flows within this natural order with effortless ease—a

concept known as *Wu Wei*. *Wu Wei* is about acting in accordance with the *Tao*, which means moving with spontaneity and surrender, without force or resistance, allowing happenings to unfold with their own natural rhythms and harmonies.

tilak
(p.150)

The *tilak* is a mark or pattern placed in the middle of the forehead, significant in Hindu tradition not merely as ornamentation but as a bearer of deep symbolic meanings. Its form, color, and manner of application vary across sects and practices. The site of the *tilak* corresponds to the *ajna* chakra, or third eye, which is regarded in both Hindu and yogic thought as the locus of wisdom, consciousness, and spiritual perception. To apply the *tilak* here is to consecrate this subtle center, strengthening concentration and protecting the inner life of the devotee.

vibhuti
(p.150)

Vibhuti is made from the grey ash of ceremonially burnt cow dung, sometimes mixed with other substances. This sacred ash is a symbol of purity and reminds the wearer of the temporary nature of physical life. *Vibhuti* is commonly associated with Lord Shiva, the destroyer.

Vamana
(p.155)

An avatar of Vishnu who came in the form of a dwarf. He represents the potential for immense power and divinity within what appears to be small or insignificant. This serves as a metaphor for the spirit's boundless nature, regardless of apparent physical limitations. It implies that within every being resides the infinite, waiting to be recognized and honored. Born to Kasyapa (Vision) and Aditi (primordial-vastness), the tiny dwarf came to preserve cosmic harmony.

vipassana (p.132) (pp.160-173)	*Vipassana*, which means insight or clear seeing in Pali, is a traditional Buddhist meditation practice rooted in the Theravadin tradition of Buddhism. Through direct observation of one's own experiences, *vipassana* aims to foster insight into the three marks of existence: impermanence (*anicca*), suffering (*dukkha*), and non-self (*anatta*).
Vishnu (p.132)	*Vishnu* is the timeless preserver, guarding the universe, while Brahma breathes creation and Shiva releases its end. In each age or yuga, Vishnu descends as an Avatar (examples are Vamana, Rama, and Krishna). He is often envisioned lying on a serpent floating upon the cosmic sea, embodying stillness and radiant harmony, sustaining the eternal rhythm flowing through creation, preservation, and destruction.
yoga (p.80) (p.83) (p.124) (pp.135-137) (pp.253-259)	Union of the individual self with the Absolute. In current common usage, the term yoga often refers only to physical postures. However, this is only one of the 'eight limbs' of Ashtanga Yoga. A wider perspective would see yoga as moving the energy (*prana*) through subtle pathways (*nadis*) and the seven centers (*chakras*) to awaken the *kundalini*. When the individual mind reaches the *anahata* or heart chakra, it is said that there is no going back to ignorance, greed, and anger. The goal of yoga is Self-realization: this happens when an apparently separate self realizes they have always been united with an infinite consciousness that is both boundless and eternal.

IN DEFENCE OF LOGICAL PUNCTUATION

I am writing this Defense because many of my American editors thought that I did not know how to punctuate properly. Actually, I am well-schooled in syntax and I prefer what is known as "logical punctuation". In this very last sentence, please notice that the period is after the final quotation mark. Whenever my American editors saw a comma or a period outside of the quotation mark, I would be reprimanded for my grammatical ignorance.

When I lived in England for 3 years in my early twenties, I noticed that the British people were much more "logical" and put their commas and periods and question marks where it felt to me they belonged: right after the quotation mark. Here is a concise statement of the two different stylistic customs:

> In America, the custom is to place the period and the comma within the closing quotation mark, even when they do not form a part of the quoted matter. The English, more logically, put them outside unless they actually belong to the quotation.

Doing some historical research, I discovered that there was a reason that the writing stylists of the USA diverged from the way that their English counterparts had done their punctuation for centuries. It turns out that the typographers in the USA in the late 18th century and early 19th century developed a "typesetter's rule". At that time, as all printing was done with movable type, the small punctuation marks like periods and commas were prone to break off when placed outside the quotation marks. To make their typesetting easier, American printers promulgated this "typesetter's rule" that would (with a few exceptions) require punctuation marks to be placed inside the quotation mark.

Eventually in the mid-20th century with the rise of photo-typesetting, the necessity to set type physically came to an end. And then with the digital revolution in the late 20th century, computers rendered traditional typesetting obsolete for all but highly niche applications. Today, there is no practical reason to obey the "typesetter's rule".

I would argue that logical punctuation is not only more logical, but is also more aesthetic. Even now in much non-literary printing, logical punctuation is gradually making a come back. I predict that by the end of the 21st century, we Americans will join the British in punctuating more logically. Let the British win this revolution!!!

Let me give examples of two sentences to present my point of view. In this next sentence, it is INDEED logical to follow the American way to have the period before the quotation mark:

I am sending this message to the typesetters of the world: "Your Rule has come to an end!!!"

However, here is a sentence where I feel it is both logical and aesthetic to have the period outside the quotation mark and thereby flount the "typesetter's rule":

An American editor reprimanded me for what he labelled a "disobedience to the typesetter's rule".

Since the times they are a-changin', here is a neo-Marxist battle-cry relevant for the 21st century:

> *Editors and Writers of America, Arise!*
> *Join your British Sisters and Brothers!!*
> *Destroy the Chains of a Tyrannical Rule!!!*
> *You have nothing to lose but your Conformity to an*
> *Out-Dated Convention!!!!*

ACKNOWLEDGMENTS

THERE IS A FAMOUS AFRICAN PROVERB THAT says that "it takes a village to raise a child". Less well-known is the complementary proverb:

The child who is not embraced by the village . . .
may well burn down that f*ckern village to feel
its warmth

These acknowledgments are a recognition that it took a village to write this book—and it is also true that this book is a story of an Elliott who once wanted to burn down his village to get inwardly warm. Luckily, I had many friends and teachers who showed me how to take full responsibility for my own life—once I grokked that I was not a victim, I lost the ability to believe all those stories that generated such a reactive anger.

The spark that started this project was a movie called *The Bucket List*. Starring Jack Nicholson and Morgan Freeman, this is the story of two elderly men who live out their wishes before they each "kick the bucket". After seeing the movie, I decided to spend my 70th birthday seeing if anything might pop up to be on my 'bucket list'. During a meditation, only one wish came to mind and the wish was accompanied by this directive: "Write a memoir".

This book had a life of its own. It took more than ten years to travel from that birthday meditation to the finished manuscript. I experience this book as a group effort and I felt that everyone who helped me deserved at least a little bit of credit. In any case, that is my excuse for the length of these *Acknowledgments*.

Consider what follows similar to the acknowledgments at the end of a movie—obviously the credits must roll for a while, but I would understand if you, my reader, might walk out before the names of all the contributors have been duly displayed on the screen.

I do feel gratitude toward each person who appears in the pages of this book. It always felt important to me to write a true memoir, and I accordingly gave all the people who are mentioned their real names. The one exception is the real person called Jack Fate—as I have lost touch with him and if he is indeed still alive over 52 years later after we met in an Iranian prison (as described in Chapter 3), I thought it would be kinder to keep his 'drug trafficking' hidden from the glare of publicity.

Writing these *Acknowledgments* has been a joyful experience for me. I enjoy being in the grateful flow. Two of the people for whom I have the greatest gratitude have left their body:

Neem Karoli Baba	(c. 1900– 11 September 1973)
Ram Dass	(1931– 22 December 2019)

I notice a parentheses after their death date that seems to imply an ending. However, I know that their contributions have not died in my heart. So rather than put a parenthesis after their names, I am knocking over the end parenthesis that appears after their death date with enough force so this end parenthesis has become a smile:

Neem Karoli Baba	(c. 1900 –11 September 1973 ⌣
Ram Dass	(1931–22 December 2019 ⌣

Another person who I am including in these *Acknowledgments* who no longer has a physical body is Steve Forrest:

Steve Forrest	(1953–5 December 2023 ⌣

Steve led a weekly Self-inquiry which he called *The Ultimate Medicine Group* (discussed in Chapter 9 of this book) that I

315

attended for the last 7 years. Many of the insights in Chapter NINE of this book arose in these gatherings that combined various strains of teachings to create a vehicle for what Steve named 'the wake-up call'. Other members of this group who influenced my thinking were Chris Haase, David Matchett, Jeff Turner, Joanie McGovern, Sarah Threlfall, Tilla Torrens, Tina Tran, and Victor Amezcua. I want to thank Peter Scarsdale, co-leader of this group, whose steady support assisted me in blossoming like a tulip stirred by the first warmth of spring; his inner presence gradually guided a tightly budded Elliott into flowering like an Eliyahu.

I want to acknowledge David Matchett for correctly perceiving that my personality has the archetypal quality of a magpie that is "irresistibly drawn to objects that are bright and shiny". I was disappointed to learn that real magpies in nature neither collect nor hoard shiny objects, but nonetheless David is correct that my emotional body is habitually attracted to objects that shimmer, glow, and levitate.

A friend who first suggested that I write this autobiography is Stephen Mitchell, a fellow graduate of Amherst College, a translator of such books as Lao Tzu's *Tao Te Ching*, and also the husband of Byron Katie. In the year of 2001 (shortly after Stephen and Katie met), I told Katie that I wanted to write a book about her life and teachings. I thought this book could be dramatic because I would emphasize how Katie's awakening occurred at a moment of intense longing for an end to her extreme emotional suffering. During the lunch break in a hotel where Katie was doing *The Work*, Stephen and Katie asked to talk with me privately in a closed conference room. Stephen spoke (while Katie listened) and he said that it would be much better if I wrote a book about mySelf. A seed was planted that took 24 years to manifest as this book.

Byron Katie is my most important living teacher and her way of doing *self-inquiry* permeates this book. There is rarely a day that goes by without me asking myself this question: "Who would I be without *THAT* story?" By consistently asking 4 questions and finding the turnarounds, I have come to be less Velcro-ed to the stories to which I experienced an attachment. Although 'the great un-doing' has not (yet) ended my suffering, it does give me a way to do self-inquiry when my mind is not at home with itself. Katie taught me that there is no final state called 'enlightenment', but only the lightening that occurs when *self-inquiry* is awake and aware in the present moment. This process was greatly aided by Celeste Gabriele who kindly did *The Work* with me whenever I realized that I was (again) believing my thoughts.

I also want to thank my spiritual teacher Karl Renz for taking me to Upper Panther Meadow on Mount Shasta. By doing so, he set up the preconditions for a moment of clarity. Even if I deluded myself that I had a Self-realization, my motive was not fraudulent; it was my self-evaluation that was indeed grandiose. When I wrote Karl to tell him that I had discovered that I was not *awake* in the sense of being enlightened, this message came back:

> *"The one who discovers that he is NOT awake*
> *will NEVER be awake, but the discovery of*
> *seeing is done by that which is always awake,*
> *so you CANNOT NOT BE AWAKE when*
> *discovering that."*

Even though I was comforted by Karl's words, there is nothing so humbling to the ego as the humiliation of claiming a spiritual achievement that was obviously bogus to everyone except me and one disciple.

I want to thank Michael Colombo for being that one disciple who remained loyal to me even after it was apparent to everyone including myself that 'my' awakening was flawed. I treasure the many spiritual experiences that Michael and I had together while we were governed by a *folie à deux*, the mutually shared delusion that I might be awake. Michael now says he knows that I have not 'woken up', but believes that our relationship continuously gives him meaningful gifts in his own lifelong process which he calls 'waking down'.

I met Alicia Ephraim when we were both rooming at *Mrs. Mahwah's Rooming House* right near Connaught Circle in New Delhi in what was to be for both of us our last week in India (in December of 1973). We became lovers 26 years later when she moved to San Francisco. Once I told her I was writing a memoir, she encouraged me to make this project a priority.

To assist me emotionally when my thinking included the delusion that I was awake, she referred me to the homeopathic doctor named Nancy Herrick in Richmond, California. Nancy first gave me (entirely homeopathic) LSD, then arsenic, and lastly polonium. She told me that the polonium was made from actual polonium that was stolen from a nuclear power plant by a homeopath in Eastern Europe. Doing the math to take into account the very high level of homeopathic dilution, I figured that in the entire bottle of tiny pills for each of these remedies, I might have taken as much as 1 molecule of LSD, 1 atom of arsenic, but only a whiff of polonium. Amazingly, I felt her medicines had a real effect in calming what was clearly a manic state.

Alicia also referred me to a doctor at Kaiser Permanente named Thoby Lawrence MD. He was a Harvard graduate and had expertise in diagnosing mental illness. In the middle of my supposed awakening, he gave me a diagnosis that he said was so rare that he had never seen anything like this before — and this diagnosis does not even appear in the *Diagnostic and Statistical Manual* (DSM) of mental ailments. He diagnosed me as having a *Unipolar* Mania. In the DSM, this is not possible as all mania is classified as being *Bipolar*; from the perspective of the DSM, any mania must be followed by a depressed mood. Dr. Lawrence said that since he observed me being truly *Unipolarly* manic for years on end, I had hit "the sweet spot" of mental diagnoses by manifesting a continuous 'high'.

My doctor for alternative medicine was Paul Lynn MD. To my surprise, I eventually discovered he was born on the same day and the same year as my other healer named Byron Katie: the 6th of December of 1942. During my manic episode, he recommended that I find out about a true awakening by reading the teachings of a provocative iconoclast called U.G. Krishnamurti. I admired U.G. for emphasizing the uncommodifiable nature of truth; he writes at the beginning of all his books in big letters these exact words:

"You are free to reproduce, distribute,
interpret, misinterpret,
distort, garble,
do what you like,
even claim authorship without my consent
or the permission
of anybody."

I was also assisted by Arny and Amy Mindell whose workshops I attended both in San Francisco and in Yachats on the coast of Oregon. (Arny died while writing these *Acknowledgments*.) They are committed to *Process Work*, a method of therapy that embodies the insight that through amplifying any symptom, one can find the cure to that ailment. Their work helped me to find an inner peace—and ease—in the midst of mental dis-ease.

I feel that it is unfair of me to give credit to my one teacher who descends from a Nazi father—meaning Karl Renz—without giving due credit to my one teacher of non-duality who descends from two Jewish parents. By evoking from me the deep undercurrents of anger and rage that I felt toward my very own Jewish father, Stuart Schwartz helped me to confront the deep conditioning that long existed buried in my unconscious.

I often reflect on the wisdom of a psychic named Hank Friedman. During his very first reading, he told me: "You are an old soul. Your mother was toxic for you in that she was transactional, but she fooled herself (and you) into thinking that her love for you was unconditional. You knew that breaking free from this mutual delusion was going to be your life challenge before you were born. If there are 1000 levels of defenses, you had 999 before you left your mother's womb. Defenses are as natural to you as a forehand to a tennis player."

I offer heartfelt thanks to my teacher, Adyashanti, whose Zen-rooted yet original teaching helped me recognize awareness as the essential nature of my being. His insight about time when I was upset about the destruction of the Bamiyan statues profoundly shaped my innerstanding of impermanence.

My two friends who have decided to permanently reside in Thailand—Stephen Lyons (who goes by the nickname of Avi) and Robert Pfefferle (who worked for over a decade as my carpenter designing my San Francisco apartment)—got me out of the groove of my life in San Francisco by offering to host me in Chiang Mai (where the Himalayas come to their end). Living 9 months in a small very quiet room next to a monastery looking out at a Bodhi tree was my home while composing the first half of this book.

The rest of the book was composed in my home in San Francisco during the COVID-19 epidemic. I would like to thank Azucena Lemus Hugel and Robert Hugel for making the house we share a genuinely inviting quiet environment where I could complete this work.

Joanie McGovern (Neti Neti) immediately recognized the cinematic power in the story of my older brother's escape from Nazi Germany, envisioning its potential as a film. Through every year of writing this book, her steadfast friendship and unwavering encouragement were a sure and dependable source of support.

Marvin Ratner assisted me in clarifying what happened when we were together at the Neem Karoli Baba ashram in Vrindavan (in Chapter 4). Heather Thompson (Sita) is the one person with whom

I am still in contact who was at not only at the Vrindavan ashram, but also at the Kainchi ashram of Neem Karoli Baba when I was there. I thank both of them for assisting me in describing more accurately what it was like to be in the presence of a *mahasiddhi*.

I want to thank Elizabeth A. Behnke PhD for clarifying my thoughts about evil (that appear in Chapter 8). She is the only member of my 4-person doctoral dissertation committee who is still alive. She taught me enough phenomenology to make a real discovery in my doctoral dissertation called *The Experience of Evil: A Phenomenological Approach*. Betsy guided me into many of the free-phantasy variations (applying the exact instructions of Edmund Husserl) on our mutual quest to discover the essential nature of evil. In the twelfth chapter of my doctoral dissertation—named *The Essential Elements of Evil*—I illustrate how we jointly determined that *'evil'* and *'the sacred'* are so intimately linked that it is not possible to have one conceptualization without the other. The entire doctoral dissertation can be found at: eliyahu108.com

Makenzie Darling introduced me to the notion of "row and release" that appears in Endnote #40. She is planning to do a book on this topic. To both of us, this phrase points to a dynamic inter-play between efforting and surrender. Her website can be found at: www.globalmovementmaker.com

Dylan Kelleher is writing the great American novel. I appre-ciate that he questioned me on whether it was *hubris* when I once told him that I believe that the writing of my own book may have been guided by a *daemon*.

Dr. Carolyn Stroebe, a fellow Licensed Psychologist, and I have a mutual love of an Emily Dickinson poem where all three para-graphs begin with the same phrase: *"Nature" is what we . . .* :
"Nature" is what we see—
The Hill—the Afternoon—
Squirrel—Eclipse—the Bumble bee—
Nay—Nature is Heaven—

"Nature" is what we hear—
The Bobolink—the Sea—
Thunder—the Cricket—
Nay—Nature is Harmony—

"Nature" is what we know—
Yet have no art to say—
So impotent Our Wisdom is
To her Simplicity.

Emily wrote two versions of this poem, one ending as above with the word "Simplicity" (Poem 668—Johnson) and another ending in "Sincerity" (Poem 721—Franklin). Carolyn and I have long debated which was the better version—until she discovered that, unlike today, back in the 19th century, the two words actually had much more similar meanings. Dr. Stroebe, whose Ph.D. is in Personality Psychology, has helped me to see that context is an important consideration in the search for truth. (She also assisted me in verifying that my enneatype is a *counterphobic Six* on the Enneagram.)

My relationship with a dog (who has the heart of a wolf) named Bodhi—owned by my long-lasting friend Dhyana Justl—inspired me to contemplate the truth suggested by Henry David Thoreau in his essay "Walking":

We can never have enough of Nature....
In Wildness is the preservation of the World.

During long nature walks. I would discuss my ideas about this book with my dear friend Anu Mahajan. After meeting Anu at Burning Man in 2017 (on a particularly hot and windy day in the Nevada desert), a few minutes into our conversation we both were surprised to learn that we shared a birthday—and even more surprisingly, soon after she was born, I had hitchhiked right past her home where she was residing in Jalandhar City (50 miles south of

Amritsar on the main road to New Delhi).

An artist in Sonoma named Prasanna engaged me in many challenging dialogues about how I might break my identification with my body, my emotions, and—most importantly—my mind. He suggested that I might study Ramana's answer to a question that occurred on the 29th of September in 1935 (that appears in the bibliography as *Talks with Sri Ramana Maharshi: On Realizing Abiding Peace and Happiness*):

> {The mind's} destruction is the non-recognition of it as being separate from the Self. Even now the mind is not. Recognize it. How can you do it if not in everyday activities? They go on automatically. Know that the mind promoting them is not real but a phantom proceeding from the Self. That is how the mind is destroyed.

In the1990's, Prasanna created a series of 15 paintings that each in its own way captured the ineffable nature of the VOID. Although he has never permitted any photographs or copies of these 15 paintings, he has given me kind permission to include in this book his portrait of Albert Einstein (that appears at the end of these *Acknowledgments*).

As it was hard for me to grok the double negative in what Ramana was saying, I formulated with Prasanna an alternative way of expressing the same idea:

> *Apperceiving*
> *that the mind does not exist*
> *(as an autonomous independent object)*
> *separate from the Self,*
> *that is the destruction of the mind.*

During a weekend course with Rupert Spira, I got the tools to better innerstand what Prasanna was saying. I learned that *consciousness* is that with which everything is known, it is that which

323

in which everything appears, and out of which everything is made—and all that happens is its impersonal activity. If the mind is a limited expression of this unlimited infinite consciousness, then suffering stems from an identification with these limitations. According to what I heard Rupert say, since consciousness is all that matters and thought creates all that is real, Self-realization arises when it is deeply recognized that our true nature is this boundless consciousness.

Charles Troob gave me emotional support by always picking up the telephone when I called. I have known him since 5th grade when I was 9 years old. He read various chapters of an earlier edition of this book and he managed for a moment to let down his critical mindset by acknowledging to his surprise that this book might even have some redeeming (and possibly even enduring) social value. He asked me why there was so few of my personal feelings in the book and I responded that I was more interested in 'the Eliyahu' than 'the tales told by an Elliott'.

I found Richard (Rick or Rashidi) Zimmerman—a fellow graduate of Forest Hills High School whom I had met only once before—sitting outside on the grass at the Khartoum Youth Hostel smoking a joint. He offered me a toke and our relationship took off from there. We became traveling companions through the Sudan, Ethiopia, Kenya, Tanzania. We then lived for a week at a communal apartment in Salisbury (now re-named Harare) in what was then a White-ruled colonial state then known as Rhodesia (now re-named Zimbabwe). A little later, we lived together for 9 months in a communal household in Ann Arbor, Michigan. It was in this setting that I conceived of the idea of a pilgrimage to India to look for Neem Karoli Baba. In our shared adventures in both Africa and Ann Arbor, Rick opened up to me a whole new world of ideas and a series of experiences that nobody else could ever quite understand. In 2023, after 52 years of sporadic and mostly superficial contact, we found ourselves once again actively sharing aspects of our lives, albeit from a distance, as Rick was residing on Guam in the Western Pacific while I remained in San Francisco. In the interim, Rick had, among other things, worked for years as a teacher of English composition. He became a tremendous help in making the writing in this book not only more grammatically correct, but also clearer and more engaging.

John Prendergast and I entered the counseling program of our graduate school at the same moment in September of 1978. He has been an ever loyal friend in dialoguing with me in a mutual attempt to successfully integrate the teachings of non-duality with the challenges of daily living.

Sandy Kepler has been a true friend to me since me met in September of 1978 in a class at the California Institute of Asian Studies called *"The Helping Relationship"*. She is the only close woman-friend with whom I have never had even the slightest whiff of a conflict.

I thank Simcha Raphael, Ph.D. for being my long-suffering rebbe. Throughout this book-writing process, he made an effort to make me more conscious of my narcissistic tendencies. He pointed out that in the Greek legend of Narcissus, the fate of this boy is to fall to his death in a pool of water once he becomes absorbed in the desire to merge with his own reflection. By encouraging me to become a more sensitive listener and also a kinder friend, he may have even succeeded in making me a finer human being.

Another rabbinical presence in my life has been Jah Levi (called Doctor Yes by his friends), an ethnomusicologist and a creator of divine musical melodies. By insisting that I clearly state to him what I want and what I need —and helping me to discern that what I think I want may not be what I really in truth need—he has assisted me in simplifying my life.

Ramón Sender, son of the Spanish novelist Ramón J. Sender, is known in San Francisco as *His Imperial Nothingness, Zero the Clown*. He has instructed me on how to cultivate the spiritual practices that will be required if I am to remain a true hippy 'til death do me part.

Danny Castro of Santa Fe, New Mexico told me this joke in an attempt to wean me from my desire to be *'special'*:

> *A wife tells her husband: "In a contest of schmucks,*
> *you would come in second."*
> *The husband is indignant and wants to be special and says:*
> *"Why wouldn't I come in first?"*
> *The wife responds, shaking her head:*
> *"Because you really are a schmuck!"*

Just in case you don't get the joke, the wife's point is that if even if you might seem to win because you really are the greatest schmuck, you are not even special in that department—because the greatest schmuck still is a second-rate human being.

BeQui (RamsaLove) Frankel—who worked as my secretary during the first years of writing this manuscript—assisted me in much of the obligatory mundane interfacing with the world.

Jami Grich inspired me with her psychological acumen. Although we live a frisbee throw from each other in the Mission District of San Francisco, we met on the shuttle bus at Burning Man in the Nevada desert. We have shared clients and explored the peaks and valleys of various healing modalities.

Rod Hogan—Jami's husband—has encouraged me to balance my playfulness with a commitment to being scrupulous in keeping my agreements. He has pointed out to me that once you are the captain of a ship, unless you are responsibly attentive to all your duties, there is a real potential for a shipwreck.

Kelsey Blumrich—Jami's sister—kept my house in order by being my assistant while the book was being fine-tuned for its publication. By not letting me get away with my rationalization that my home was "a perfect mess" and that "creative people all have messy homes", she kept my home (barely) livable.

Kelsey's husband—Danny Blumrich—has been a guardian of my integrity. We made mutual vows in a Lavender Temple in Thailand to always follow the path of telling the truth.

Tatiana Ginzburg and Polina Krasikova are two courageous Russians who inspired me by their creativity in starting a restaurant called Russian House on the very spot where the Russian River meets the Pacific Ocean. Within their experiment, labor was voluntary and no money was exchanged. If we are ever to have peace on this planet, we will need to be disciplined about respecting people who come from different cultural orientations. I admire Polina for her cultivating the virtue of letting go of her preferences. I admire Tatiana for advocating a post-classical science that she views as a tool for seeking enlightenment.

Polina introduced me to Sasha Vasilyuk, a lass from Belarus. (*Did you notice that two of these last three words almost rhyme?*) She and her husband William Kelly became a crucial part of my support system. They minded my home while I was in Thailand writing this book and their daughter Iris had her first home in my attic. Their son Alexander Elliott was given my first name as his second name. When Sasha and William were visiting Sasha's family in Belarus, they made an extra day trip as a favor to me—they searched for and then found a stone monument deep in the forest on the outskirts of Urech'e (Uretsche); under this monument was a mass grave where lay buried the remains of my mother's family. The monument commemorates (in Russian) the 830 Jews shot on that spot by the *Einsatzgruppen* on the 8th day of May in 1942.

I picked Michael Steeb to be my Assistant Financial Aid Officer when in 1980 I was the FAO of the California Institute of Asian Studies (now CIIS). We have remained friends and he keeps on reminding me of the truth of this saying from Oscar Wilde (said by Lord Darlington in Act One of his 1892 play called *Lady Windermere's Fan*):

In this world there are only two tragedies:
one is not getting what one wants—
and the second is getting it.

Henry Seltzer has been my astrological consultant. He is my most long-standing friend in California as I have known him since adolescence. I first met him at Halsey Junior High in the Rego Park section of Queens when I was 11 years old. He told me that my birth chart is ruled by Pluto (less than 3 degrees before my Ascendant in the 12th House) and that my book will have its heyday during these 20 years (beginning in November of 2024) wherein Pluto will again abide in my moon sign of Aquarius. He informed me that the last time Pluto was in Aquarius (Pluto's orbit is 248 Earth years), there were such happenings as the American and French revolutions. Henry discovered the meaning and invented the glyph that is commonly used for Eris, a new dwarf planet that is further out than Pluto. Here is the glyph for this new planet that was created by Henry:

⚲

Henry says that in everyone Eris represents the energy of a feminine warrior in support of their deepest intentions. He tells me that it is particularly active in my birth chart because in the 6th degree of Aries, it is in opposition to Chiron conjunct the almost exact Jupiter-Neptune conjunction in a tight T-square to Mars conjunct the North Node. I go along with Rick Tarnas that the planet Uranus should be renamed Prometheus; whatever the name, Henry tells me that I will have my Uranian—or is it possibly Promethean—return in the year 2029. You can find my birth chart by knowing that I was born in Springfield Missouri at 3:37 AM (Wartime) on Tuesday, September 18th of 1945.

Friends who helped with the editing include Bettina Schneider,

Carolyn Stroebe, Dan Buckler, Charles Troob, Derek Bernard, Jami Grich, Jo Babcock, John Amodeo, John Threlfall, Nachshon Lustig, Rick Zimmerman, Tamara Edwards, and Timothy Conway.

Ken Blady has a special place among my editors for his conscientiousness in requiring both proper grammar and the elimination of jargon; he was punctilious in his attention to detail and he chastised me for indulging in what he considered "psycho-babble".

Lester Yagoda assisted me with the editing in a unique way. He was my "bullshit detector". This means that he would immediately sense whenever there was the slightest bit of 'bullshit' in a sentence—and he would have me correct what was untrue and replace that with a a more exact (but often less spectacular) truth. Lester diagnosed me as a *Drama Queen* with a hysterical grasping for connection, and although he found the motive quite loveable, he wanted me to keep stories in this book without any exaggeration or even slight embellishments.

Gilles Ruppert was masterful in putting all the various rough drafts of this manuscript onto the Internet.

Gary Wolf, an attorney in Tucson Arizona, read a book contract that I once considered signing with a publishing company, and gave me excellent professional advice about how to look out for myself.

The book was almost finished when Ted Rosengarten, a member of my biweekly (meaning every two weeks) meeting of Amherst College graduates on ZOOM, wrote me a polite letter kindly suggesting that the original title of this book—*Circumstances and Innerstances*—was not sufficiently expressive of my nature. When this group of my friends from Amherst devoted an entire hour to finding me a new title, Aryeh (Lennie) Lamm found the current title of the book: *Call me Eliyahu*. Other members of this ZOOM group who had an influence on this memoir are Al Leisinger, Dan Keller, Gordy Jones, Ira Karasick, Ron Berenbeim, and my dear friend and college room-mate John Merson.

I discussed this book with my two friends John Threlfall and

David Matchett in a regularly scheduled 3-way ZOOM. I was the one to introduce them many decades ago because I had taken note of the fact that they were born just a few hours apart on the same day of the same year. I told them that I had the thought that because they had almost identical astrological charts that this might make them predisposed to becoming good friends. John and David both loudly expressed their skepticism for entertaining such a ridiculous idea—and the 3 of us went on to become really good friends. When I told John that the title of the book was to be *Call me Eliyahu*, John told me a much more accurate title would be:

Who the F*ck is Elliott Isenberg
by Elliott Isenberg

My friends vetoed the idea, convincing me that a book with such a title would never sell. Still, we all agreed John's title was funnier and captured the truth that in the eyes of society I was very much a nobody. Even though John failed to get his way about the title, he did succeed in proposing what is now the book's subtitle: *Tales Told by an Elliott.*

My friend Zohar believed in this book from the moment she heard about it when we accidentally met in the Tulum commune called *Holistika* in March of 2018. As a priestess of New Age religion, Zohar has a magical gift in leading ceremonies that use the Mexican form of hot chocolate called *cacao*. She did everything she did to promote the book including eventually introducing me to her partner Vinny Olimpio.

My friend Vinny Olimpio used his immense graphic intelligence to design the book. He was the one who designed the front and back covers, the icons at the end of each chapter, and chose and readied for publication the photos in the middle of the book. I have always been amazed by his ability to discern the right design to entertain the eye. When there was a change in the graphics that required Vinny's assistance to get this book published as a present to mySelf for my 80th birthday, Vinny came through for me.

David Brusa, my tax preparer in San Francisco, was an expert in navigating the various tax laws of the Internal Revenue Service (IRS) to which I had to comply once I formed a publishing company called *Nobody's Home Press, LLC.*

I met Elizabeth Bartmess the week before this book went to press. Together we fashioned what I consider a comprehensive *Index of Names* for this book.

Although I have already dedicated this book to them, I would like to again thank my two brothers—Howard now 77 and Edward now 90—for being there for me as 'family'.

This may be my most peculiar acknowledgment, but I am being genuine when I want to thank CONSCIOUSNESS for letting me know my beingness as I AM. When I wake up in the morning, I often experience a moment when I aware that there really is something happening both inside and outside of me. It seems that it would have been so easy for the consciousness that runs this universe just to have been a little bit lazy and create nothing at all or almost just as easy, a something of frozen matter that had no sentient beings and never changed. My feeling is that God does play dice with the universe and She loaded the dice in the favor of sentient beings. The spelling is not wrong here when I call myself *optimystic.*

I also want to acknowledge the readers of this book—for you are the reason that I bothered to write it. I offer you my favorite wish (as composed by Bob Dylan in his song *"Forever Young"*):

May you have a strong foundation when the winds of changes shift.

(Elliott Isenberg)
Eliyahu

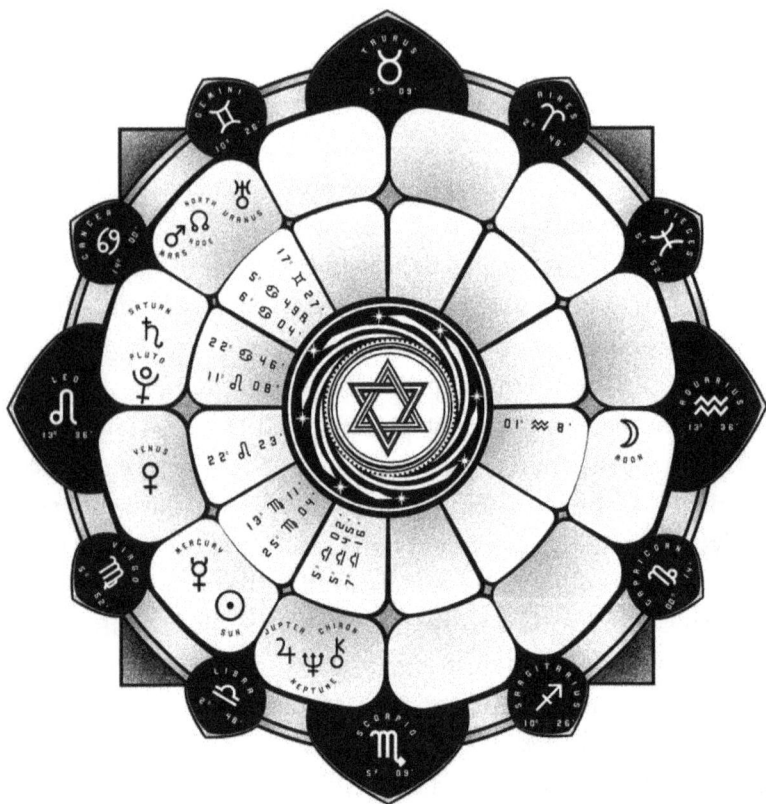

ELIYAHU

18ᵀᴴ OF SEPTEMBER 1945

3:37 AM
(WAR TIME)

SPRINGFIELD · MISSOURI · USA

PLACIDUS
HOUSE SYSTEM

Albert Einstein by ©Prasanna Seth

INDEX OF NAMES

A
Adams, Justin, 51, 56
Adyashanti (teacher), x, 110, 180, 320—see Photograph 20.
Alpert, Richard (see Ram Dass)
Amarnath, 144
Amherst College, X, 39-42, 46, 61, 89, 205, 213, 335, 316, 329
Ammachi, 240
Arnold, Edwin, 196, 285,293, 300
Aurobindo, Sri, 252, 280, 353 (see Endnote 69)

B
Bau, Barbara, viii, x, xiii, 50-51, 57-58, 60-61, 65-67, (Photograph 7)
Beatles, 85, 170-171, 264, 346 (see Endnote 28), 354-355
    (Endnote 74)
Besant, Annie, 210
Bidart, Frank, 221
Bonnie (friend of Barbara), 50–51
Byron Katie, x, xiii-xiv, 80, 220, 224, 226-229, 283, 316-317,
    (Photograph 19)

C
Camhi, Betty, 212-216, 287
Conrad, Joseph, 67, 280, 281
Choegyal Rinpoche, Drugu—See Photograph 17.
Cruz, Michael, 184, 192

D
Dalai Lama, 239-242, 289, 352
Dement, Iris, 236, 350 (Endnote 58)
Descartes, Rene, 256, 316

Dickinson, Emily, 217-218, 239, 281, 321-322, 348 (Endnote 46), 351 (Endnote 61)

Draupadi (disciple of Neem Karoli Baba), x, 120-121, 125-126, 143-144, 146, 282-283, (Photograph 10)

Dylan, Bob, 40, 108-109, 159, 174, 175, 239, 289, 331, 346 (End-notes 27, 30, and 31), 351 (Endnote 63)

E

אֵלִיָּהוּ (Hebrew for Eliyahu), xvi-xvii, 155-157

Eliyahu, *see* Isenberg, Elliott Stephen

Epstein, Frieda. *see* Isenberg, Frieda

Evil, 58, 92, 99, 207, 211, 220, 222-224, 232-234, 283, 321, 349 (Endnote 51)

F

Fate, Jack (the only alias in this book), 97-107, 315

Forrest, Steve, xi, xiv, 267-270, 273-274, 278, 315-316, 355 (Endntote 75)—see Photograph 29.

Freud, Sigmund, 6, 9-10, 32, 296

Friedman, Hank, 319-320

Friedman, Harry and Mae, 22

Friedman, Larry, 22

Frost, Robert, xv, 100, 342 (Endnote 20)

G

Gere, Richard, 241

Ginsberg, Allen, 229, 282, 349 (see Endnotes 54 and 55)

Goenka, Satya Narayan, 160–167

Goldstein, Joseph, 165-170, 180, 282

Goodall, Jane, 54–55

Grey, Alex and Allyson—See Photograph 18.

Grossinger, Richard, 213

H

Hafez (Sufi master), 94-96, 282
Hegel, Georg Wilhelm Friedrich, 78
Heinlein, Robert A., 214-215, 283, 299, 348 (Endnote 43)
Hitler, Adolf, x, 7, 9-11, 15-16, 169
Hoffmann, Abbie, 33
Holmes, Ward (see Yongdu)
Horney, Karen, 32, 240

I

Ibn 'Arabi, 85, 283
Ingram, Rufus Suggs, 44
Isenberg, Edward Leonard (older brother), vii (book's dedication page), x, 4-5, 14-29, 32, 331, (Photographs 2 and 3)
Isenberg, Elliott Stephen (Eliyahu)
    Africa trip, 49-61, 65-71, 73-76
    on the big Self, 253-261
    at California Institute of Asian Studies, 155, 205-207, 211, 232
    childhood, 24-25, 32-39, 78
    civil rights activism, 39–46
    conception, 1
    dreams, xvii-xviii, 155-157, 191, 262-264, 278-279
    false awakening, 238, 250-252
    Fez Morocco successful robbery, 70–71
    Hawaii and tsunami, 174-195
    and Holocaust, xv, 1, 220-228
    in India, 79-83, 119-173, see also Neem Karoli Baba
    in NYC after India, 114–117, 174–175
    San Francisco California thief's unsuccessful robbery attempt, 71-73
    self-inquiry group and Steve Forrest, 266-275, 278
    on the small self, 243-249
    Soviet Union trip, 46–48

on spiritual suffering, 80
Timothy Leary and LSD, 61-65
views on social change, 77–81
Isenberg, Frieda (mother), x, xii, xvi-xvii, 1, 22-23, 27, 32, 34-38, 45-46, 50, 55, 78, 80, 169. 175, 222, 240, 248, (Photographs 1 and 5)
Isenberg, Howard Warren (younger brother), vii (book's dedication page), xii, 23-24, 36, 171, 331, (Photographs 2 and 3)
Isenberg, Margaret (mother of Edward), xii, 11-18, 20-21, 25-28
Isenberg, Morris (Morrie; father), viii, x, xii, 2-15, 17-29, 32-34, 36, 87, 207, 240-242, (Photographs 5, 14, and 15)

J
Jack Fate (the only alias used in this book), 98–108, 334
Jake (Englishman), 74–75

K
Kalu Rinpoche, 176
Katie, Byron (see Byron Katie)
Kerouac, Jack, 230-231, 283, 350 (Endnote 57)
Khanna, Ravi, viii, 152-154
King, Martin Luther (MLK), 39-40, 43-44, 130
KK (see Sah, Krishnna Kumar)
Kornfield, Jack, 162, 302, 303
Krishnamurti, U.G., 282, 284, 319

L
Leary, Timothy, 31, 61-65, 207
Lucidity in dreams, 262-263
LSD (Lysergic acid diethylamide), xiii, 35, 61-67, 81, 124, 144-145. 157, 268, 274, 318

M

Maharaji. *see* Neem Karoli Baba

Maharshi, Ramana, x, 197, 213, 228, 266, 284, 323, 357-358 (Endnote 78)—see also Photograph 22.

Martin (artist in Salisbury Rhodesia), 60-61

Martin Luther King (see King, Martin Luther)

Marx, Leo, 213

McKenna, Jed (the only pseudonym in this book), 240, 304, 352 (Endnote 64), 355 (Endnote 75)

McNamara, Robert Strange, xi, xii, 41-42, (Photograph 31)

Meredith, James, 42-43

Metzinger, Thomas, 247, 285, 352 (Endnote 67)

Metzner, Ralph, xiii, 206-207

Millbrook (psychedelic commune)—See Photograph 34.

Mindell, Arny and Amy, 319

Miss Jones (receptionist), 190

Mitchel, Dr. James, 183, 186, 192

Mobo (Nigerian), 86–87

Moses (from the Bible), 7, 259-60

Munindra, Acharya Anagarika, 164-165

N

Neem Karoli Baba (Maharaji), viii, xiii, 81-82, 119-158, 159, 196, 325, 345 (Endnote 26)—see also Photographs 9 and 10.

Nisargadatta Maharaj, xi, 253-259, 266-267, 285, 347 (Endnote 39), 353-354 (Endnotes 70-72)—see Photograph 23.

O

Omar Khayyam, 96-97, 285, 342 (see Endnote 18)

P

Prasanna, 323, 333

R

Rai, Gurubaksh, 214, 287

Ram Dass (formerly Richard Alpert), xi, 64-65, 81-82, 120, 130-31, 134-135, 153, 207, 249, 286, 289, 315, 344 (Endnote 23)—see Photograph 24.

Ratner, Marvin, 123-125, 143, 157-158, 320

Renz, Karl, x, xiv, 250-252, 260, 286, 317, (Photograph 21)

Rubin, Jerry, 88-89

S

Sa'di (Sufi poet), 93-94, 286, 342 (Endnote 16)

Sah, Krishna Kumar, 146-148, 286, 344 (Endnote 25)

Schulz, Bruno, 277, 286, 359 (see Endnote 79)

Shelley, Percy Bysshe, 90, 188, 348-349 (Endnote 48)

Siddhi Ma, 126, 146, 152

Socrates, 89, 212, 342 (see Endnote 14)

Spira, Rupert, 258-259, 286-287, 323-324

Steinbeck, John, 24

Students for a Democratic Society (SDS), 41, 88

Sunyata (Emmanuel Sorensen), x, xiii, 196-204, 207-219, 261, 287, 297, 299-300, 346-349 (Endnotes 36-38, 40-45, 49)—see Photograph 16.

T

"The Mouth of God", xii, 250

"The Source", xii, 250, 252

Threlfall, John, xiii, 234-236, 316, 329, 330

Toon, Jerry, 119-121, 144-145, 282

Trotsky, Leon, 46-47

Trungpa, Chögyam, 153, 274, 288, 357 (see Endnote 77)

Tsongkhapa, Je, 242, 352 (Endnote 65)

W
Watts, Alan, 38, 198, 207-208, 288
Weaver, Judyth O.—See Photograph 12.
Weber, Max, 48-49
Wessel, Horst, 10-11
Williams, Hosea, 43-44

X
Xanadu, 277
Xuanzang, 109

Y
Yongdu (Ward Holmes), 175-176

ENDNOTES

1. "Purgatorio" is the second part of **The Divine Comedy**. A common theme of the hero's journey is to return to where one began —and with more wisdom.

2. This is often attributed to George Bernard Shaw, but there is no evidence that he ever said or wrote this.

3. *The counter-phobic Six* is well-described in Beatrice Chestnut's book **The Complete Enneagram** on pp. 208-11. Her entire chapter on Sixes is a good general description of how the Six tries to defend against the fear that is ever-present in the mind of this enneatype.

4. **10,000 Jokes, Toasts & Stories**, p.816. This joke is # 8122 and is in the section labelled "Suggested Epitaphs".

5. This anachronism is even more famous than when Cleopatra in Act II, Scene 5 of **Anthony and Cleopatra** suggests playing billiards—which was not invented until the Middle Ages in Europe.

6. MLK's famous "Letter from a Birmingham Jail" was written on April 16th, 1963. His oft-repeated quote about 'justice' and 'righteousness' is from the Bible in the **Book of Amos** 5:24.

7. These lines appear in the first of the four quartets called "Burnt Norton", Part II, lines 16-21.

8. The edition of Joseph Conrad's **Heart of Darkness** was the Everyman's Library Edition of 1993. The sections in quotations come from Part I, p.10; Part II, p.70; Part III, p.81; and Part III, p. 98.

9. This specific expression coined by Karl Marx comes from his work written in 1875 called **The Critique of the Gotha Programme**.

10. The English poet William Ernest Henley wrote **Invictus** in 1875 when he was facing the possible medical necessity of

amputating a second leg.

11. The first edition of **Be Here Now** appeared in 1971.

12. "**Heart of Gold**" is a song by Canadian singer-songwriter Neil Young from his fourth album *Harvest*, first released in 1972.

13. Ibn 'Arabi's **Bezels of Wisdom**, composed during the later period of Ibn 'Arabi's life, has his most important mystical teachings

14. Xenophon was a contemporary of Plato who knew Socrates well. **The Memorabilia** is his own defense of Socrates, offering examples of Socrates' conversations and activities.

15. "Ozymandias" is the Greek name for the pharaoh Ramesses II (1279–1213 BC), the most powerful ruler of ancient Egypt.

16. Sa'di used the metaphor of the rose and the thorn in **The Rose Garden** written in 1257 CE.

17. These sayings can be found in Hafez's book of poetry called **The Divān**.

18. These translations of Omar Khayyam are from a 19th century Englishman named Edward Fitzgerald. Although the translations are not exact, they occasionally have greater poetic expressiveness than the original.

19. The phrase "conference of the birds" is taken directly from the Koran 27:16, where Solomon and David are said to have been taught the language of the birds.

20. "Stopping by Woods on a Snowy Evening" is found in Frost's 1923 collection of poems with the title **New Hampshire**.

21. **The Confessions** is divided into thirteen books and this quotation comes from the middle of a paragraph-long Chapter 1 in Book 1.

22. The Story of a Heroine named Draupadi

When I told my new friend Jerry that I knew nothing about either Draupadi or the *Mahabharata*, he told me this tale about how a virtuous woman avoided a shameful disrobing:

Draupadi was a Bronze Age Indian princess born from fire, famed for her beauty and strength of character. When Prince Arjuna won a contest to have Draupadi as his wife, he went to his mother to tell her the great good news, but before he could tell her the news, Arjuna's mother told him that whatever he won he had to share with his four brothers. It was therefore Draupadi's karma to be the wife of five brothers.

The oldest brother, named Yudhishthira, had a gambling problem. He lost his fortune and then his freedom at a game of dice where the dice had been hexed by the machinations of a Kaurava prince named Durodhyana. In a final desperate effort to win back his freedom and his fortune, Yudhishthira put up his wife Draupadi as the stake. He did so without consulting his brothers, with whom he was now partnering as a common 'owner'. Once Yudhishthira had lost this last desperate gamble, Duryodhana demanded that his newly acquired merchandise—meaning Draupadi—be brought in front of him.

When Draupadi was told about the wager and that she was now to be owned by a new tyrannical male chauvinist, she cried out: "Is a woman her husband's property? Is she an object that can be gambled?" As she refused to come peacefully, she had to be dragged by the hair from the room where she was both menstruating and meditating. When she was eventually pulled into the room full of men, she tried to convince both her new 'owner' and the assembled company of men—including all five of her husbands—that the bet wherein she had become the slave of a new master was illegal because her oldest husband who had made the bet only owned one-fifth of her. When that argument was met with blank stares, she pointed out that her gambling husband had already lost his own freedom a moment before and therefore since he was no longer a free man when he made the final wager, he did not even retain one-fifth of the right to put her up as a stake.

Despite her passionate pleas and impeccable logic, the elders in the room, and her five husbands too, declined to stand up for her. Duryodhana said he wanted his newly acquired merchandise to be completely his possession, and he intended to begin this process of making her vulnerable by stripping off all her clothes until she was naked in front of the assembled men. As soon as he began tearing off her sari, she called out: "KRISHNA, KRISHNA, I want you always, but INDEED now is the moment that I REALLY do need you." Krishna heard her plea and made her sari of endless length —so after an hour when the whole room was filled up to the ceiling with cloth, it was clear that the attempt to disrobe Draupadi would be futile. Draupadi never was disrobed.

Draupadi then derided Yudhishthira for his gambling problem and reprimanded all five of her husbands for not coming to her defense.

23. Ram Dass's mastery in story-telling combined with the unconventional graphics made this book ideal for bringing Eastern spirituality to the Western mind.

24. John Burdon Sanderson Haldane was a British-Indian scientist who studied genetics and evolutionary biology. This quotation can be found in his essay entitled "Possible Worlds".

25. KK Sah's book about the siddhas of the Himalayas appears in the **Bibliography**.

26. The only fact that is certain about Neem Karoli's death is that it occurred in the wee hours of Tuesday morning on the 11th day of September of 1973.

Later on that same day in the same year, the first democratically elected socialist President in the Americas was committing suicide in his own office in Santiago, Chile. The Generals of Chile were using the missiles sent to them by the Central Intelligence Agency of the USA to bombard the presidential palace of Salvador Allende. Due to the coincidence that the successful *coup d'état* by the Generals occurred on the same date as the attack (which occurred 28 years later) on the World Trade Center on September 11th of 2001, this bombing is still known in Chile as "the other 9/11".

And exactly 108 years to the day before the planes flew into the World Trade Center, a Hindu yogi hitch-hiked his way into Chicago to be the first speaker at the globe's first **World Parliament of Religions**. Swami Vivekananda had great charisma and got a several minute standing ovation. Today this **Parliament** is recognized as the birth of the worldwide interfaith movement. Swami Vivekananda on the 9/11 of 1893 declared to thousands of listeners that unless we begin to see all the religions of the world as merely fingers pointing to the same goal, hatred between the religions might well destroy the human race.

But I will let Swami Vivekananda speak for himself in the exact words by which he concluded his speech:

"Sectarianism, bigotry, and its horrible descendant, fanaticism, have long possessed this beautiful Earth. They have filled the earth with violence, drenched it often with human blood, destroyed civilization, and sent whole nations to despair. Had it not been for these horrible demons, human society would be far more advanced than it is now.

"But their time is come; and I fervently hope that the bell that tolled this morning in honor of this convention may be the death-knell of all fanaticism, of all persecutions with the sword or with the pen, and of all uncharitable feelings between persons wending their way to the same goal.

27. Written in 1962 and released on his 1963 album *The Freewheelin'*
Bob Dylan, the song "Blowin' in the Wind" was adopted as an
anthem of the burgeoning civil rights movement.

28. The Beatles song "Here Comes the Sun" was written by George
Harrison and appeared in their 1967 album **Abbey Road**.

29. The man who first said these words did not know it would
become a poem called *Fear*. These italicized lines were spoken
spontaneously by Osho (Bhagwan Shree Rajneesh) in response to a
question on October 18th, 1986 in Pune, India. They appear in his
book **Beyond Enlightenment** in Chapter 16 on page 398. For some
mysterious reason, this quotation often appears on the internet
as a poem called *Fear* and incorrectly attributed to the Lebanese
mystic Kahlil Gibran.

30. These lines begin the third stanza of "A Hard Rain's A-Gonna
Fall". This song was one of his first songs and appeared in 1963 in
his second studio album called **The Freewheelin' Bob Dylan**.

31. Dylan wrote "It's Alright, Ma (I'm Only Bleeding)" in the summer of 1964, and included it his fifth album called **Bringing It All
Back Home**. The lyrics of this grim masterpiece express Dylan's
anger at the perceived immorality and hypocrisy in contemporary
American culture.

32. Shakespeare has Ariel, a spirit servant to the sorceror Prospero,
sing this song in the first Scene of the first Act of **The Tempest**.
The song suggests that within the ocean's power to destroy there is
beauty that is both ethereal and otherworldly.

33. Edwin Arnold's **The Song Celestial** contains Krishna's advice
to Arjuna about ethics, duty, and the nature of reality. This is an
English translation of the **Bhagavad Gita**, a 700-verse Sanskrit
scripture that's part of the Indian epic **Mahabharata**.

34. These words of Sunyata are from my memory and include an

insight that Sunyata got from Sri Anandamayi Ma. On page 4 of **The Life & Sayings of a Rare-born Mystic**, Anandaya Mayi Ma is quoted as saying how 'understanding' which means 'to stand under' can mean that one is "burdened by mental conceptions".

35. Ibid., p. 22.

36. Ibid., combines quotations from p. 20 and p. 6

37. Ibid., p. 8

38. Ibid., p. 6

39. From Dialogue 59 in **I Am That** entitled *"Desire and Fear: Self-Centered States"*.

40. **The Life & Sayings of a Rare-born Mystic**, p. 106. Although Sunyata never categorized using these terms, it is possible to give names to each of the four levels. I would label the first level where the ego is greedy and arrogant as 'egotistical' and the second and the third levels as both being 'egoic'. The evolution between the second and third levels comes as an individual gradual masters the skills and virtues that will make up the components of being 'free *in* ego'. The fourth and last level is what made it accurate to describe Sunyata as 'a rare-born mystic'—while he never considered himself special, his destiny was to prove that it was possible to live 93 years on this planet Earth while being 'free *of* ego'.

I give the name *'row and release'* to this process of gaining mastery over the ego and gradually becoming more ego-free. Three types of 'rowing' required on the second level are to 'manage the mind', 'release the emotions', and 'tame the instincts'. The third level is the beginning of a 'release' of all efforting that reaches its culmination in the fourth level wherein the ego dies.

Even though one purpose of any map is to give guidance in navigating an unknown territory, a useful axiom is that 'the map is not the territory'. In this rudimentary sketch of a map, many more subtleties and gradients could have been categorized and recognized in describing the evolution from being 'free *in* ego' to being 'free *of* ego'.

41. Ibid. Part of this quotation comes from the memory of the author and part of it from page 40 of **The Life & Sayings.**

42. **The Life & Sayings of a Rare-born Mystic**, p. 94.

43. Robert Heinlein first published **Stranger in a Strange Land** in 1961. The idea of spiritual water being the antidote to spiritual thirst also appears in the Bible in John 4:14 (King James Version):

> ... but whosoever drinketh of the water that I shall give him shall never thirst;
>
> but *the water that I shall give him shall be in him a well of water springing up into everlasting life.*

44. **The Life & Sayings of a Rare-born Mystic**, p. 118.

45. Ibid., p. 4.

46. This is Poem 260 in R.W. Franklins compilation of Emily's poems. Dickinson's choice to embrace being "Nobody" suggests a preference for the inner life and points toward transcending ego-driven desires for recognition, status, and power. During her lifetime, Emily was indeed a 'nobody' and could not even get one poem published without (male) editors changing her words, eliminating her dashes, adding their own punctuation, and then completing the poem by providing what they thought was a really good title. Only the "somebody" part of us cares about popularity, fame, validation, or power.

47. This is on pp. 137-138 (xvii: 3) of the Thomas Merton translation of Chuang Tzu called **The Way of Chuang Tzu.**

48. This is the beginning of Stanza 52 of "Adonais", Shelley's elegy

to his dear friend John Keats.

49. **The Life & Sayings of a Rare-born Mystic**, p. 120.

50. Hopkins' mountain with its "cliffs of fall" evokes an image of a sudden precipitous drop into despair. The phrase "no-man-fathomed" underscores the notion that these internal mindscapes are beyond rational or mental comprehension.

51. Goethe presents this dialogue shortly after Mephistopheles makes his initial appearance to Faust in the first third of Part One.

Mephistopheles is the Devil himself and he is suggesting that evil is a force that plays a role in the greater scheme of good.

52. This poem has been named "Odi et amo", meaning "Hate and love". Peter Green's translation of *excrucior* as 'tormented' captures the pain of the poet in observing his inner turmoil—other translations for this Latin word are 'tortured' and 'crucified'.

Stephen Mitchell in his recent book translating the poems of Catullus gives this rendering:

"I hate and I love. Perhaps you are wondering how this can be.
I don't know, but I feel it and I am in torment."

53. When one stays with Bidart's image of a fish wanting the fly, the question arises why would any creature hold on to what has neither nutrients nor nourishment and will surely lead to their own destruction?

54. Ginsberg's 112 paragraph-like lines of **Howl** were so controversial when it first appeared that both the publisher and the bookstore's manager were arrested for disseminating obscene literature.

55. **The Footnote to Howl** expresses the poet's capability to find holiness in the seemingly unholy. Ginsberg is suggesting that if everything and everyone is viewed as 'holy', then there must be a sacredness in the struggles and suffering of human beings.

56. Jack Kerouac addressed this letter that is dated January 10th, 1957 to Neal Cassady. Later that same year he published **On the Road** where the main character in the book named Dean Moriarty is essentially a literary incarnation of Neal Cassady. Kerouac's idea of "the vast awakenerhood" is about waking up to the profound interconnectedness of all things, embracing the moment with full awareness, and living with a sense of deep authenticity and infinite acceptance.

57. This saying is part of the collection of *logia*, or sayings, that are attributed to Jesus in the **Gospel of Thomas**. The text is part of the Nag Hammadi library, a collection of Gnostic texts discovered in Egypt in 1945. **The Gospel of Thomas** consists of 114 sayings of Jesus, and it presents a perspective on his teachings that differs in many respects from the canonical Gospels that are found in the New Testament. The emphasis is on an inner path to God, suggesting that the Kingdom of God is within you and all around you, but not recognized by most. The main suggestion is that ignorance is the true source of human suffering, and knowledge (*gnosis*) of the divine is the path toward liberation. This particular saying emphasizes the importance of self-expression and the dangers of not embracing the shadow sides of the personality that may be lying dormant in the unconscious.

58. These are the last two stanzas of Iris Dement's song *"Let the Mystery Be"*. The song was released in 1992 on her first album called **Infamous Angel**.

59. These lines come from the last of his four quartets called "Little Giddings", Part V, lines 26-29.

60. These lines from Blake's poem "The Marriage of Heaven and Hell" were written in 1793. Although Blake himself never used mind-altering substances, it is fascinating that this notion of cleansing "the doors of perception" has become a popular meme

for the proponents of using psychedelics to raise consciousness. Aldous Huxley's book **The Doors of Perception** (written in 1954) is a detailed account of his experiences after taking mescaline, a psychedelic drug derived from the peyote cactus. And Jim Morrison who for a got the name of his rock group The Doors from this same William Blake quotation.

61. Dickinson's use of the phrase "a sudden Guest" relates to the infinite as it manifests in two seemingly contradictory ways: it is at once a stranger and paradoxically also an intimate part of our existence. Dickinson often explores the conflict between the desire to comprehend what is mysterious and another wish to "just let the mystery be".

62. Although most writers on the internet credit these words to the Dalai Lama, he never did say this.

63. Bob Dylan's "*Gates of Eden*" can be read as a poetic and surreal attempt to transcend ego consciousness—a movement away from the illusions and constructs of the individual self toward a broader ineffable reality. The song's cryptic imagery and detached tone suggest a journey beyond the ordinary rational mind into a realm where the boundaries of ego dissolve.

Dylan's Eden isn't the Biblical lost garden of bliss from which the innocents were ejected. It's more like a state of consciousness where all our earthly concerns, social roles, and identities fall away. With no "kings", "sins", or "truths", there is the potential to discover innocence.

Dylan seems to be suggesting that the very act of "seeking" a clear path to Eden can reinforce the ego's sense of separation; to "seek" Eden with effort is as self-defeating as trying to become spontaneous.

In each verse, Dylan describes scenes—some surreal, some grotesque—from the human worlds of war and peace, possessions and politics, dreams and love. It's as if he's saying: "All these human efforts to control, to define, to strive—they're meaningless beyond a certain threshold; at the 'gates', they dissolve."

And the notion of there being "gates" to Eden is itself ironic. Maybe the gate is not real. It's only the seeker—the one who imagines "the gates" to be real—who creates the gate with their own mind. From this perspective, the entrance to Eden might be similar to the gateway to enlightenment—totally an inside job.

If this interpretation is correct, Dylan is suggesting that "innocence" or "original mind" is not something to be attained; rather it is what remains when conceptualization, striving, and clinging fall away.

64. **Spiritual Enlightenment: The Damnedest Thing**, p. 214. For more about Jed McKenna, see endnote #75.

65. Je Tsongkhapa was known as *"The Great Je"* and was born , in 1357 in Amdo, Tibet. He founded the Gelugpa lineage early in the 15th century and starting with the 1st Dalai Lama who was his direct disciple, all the other 13 Dalai Lamas have been part of his Gelugpa lineage.

66. *The Matrix* is a science fiction action film written and directed by the Wachowski brothers (Larry and Andy) who later went on to become the Wachowski sisters (Lana and Lilly). The film contains one of the most fascinating coincidences in the history of film related to the expiry date of Neo's driver's license. When the film was made in 1999, it shows the license as expiring on 9/11/2001. What expired on that fateful day was much more than Neo's license.

67 Thomas Metzinger PhD, a philosopher at the Johannes Gutenberg University in Mainz German, calls our experience of the self and the world a 'naive realism' because it is made of a virtual reality rather than what is actually real.

68. Years after my moment of clarity on Mount Shasta, I discovered that Yoko Ono was on that same day of the same year inaugurating the *Imagine Peace Tower* on a small island off the coast of Iceland. October 9th of 2007 would have been John Lennon's 67th birthday. Yoko on that day first turned on a tall tower of light that projected upwards for **4000 meters** from a white stone monument that had the words *"Imagine Peace"* carved in 24 languages. Because of the abundance of geothermal energy in Iceland, the light does not use energy from oil or gas. I see the fact that this was happening on the same day that I was looking toward a peak of a mountain that was also **4000 meters** as an example of a synchronicity. Carl Jung, who invented this concept, defined synchronicity as a meaningful coincidence, suggesting that it is an acausal connection to which an individual can assign meaning. I would suggest that a coincidence is God's way of remaining anonymous.

69. In **The Life Divine**, Aurobindo proposes that just as life evolved from matter, and mind from life, there's a next stage in this evolutionary process: the emergence of a higher, spiritual consciousness. In such an evolution, mind moves into higher mind and then to illumined mind and then to intuitive mind and then to overmind and then, lastly, to *supermind*. In the supramental consciousness of the *supermind*, the dichotomies of knower, knowing, and known are transcended. When there is no longer a separation between subject and object, because the concepts of time and space always pertain to a subject perceiving an object, there is neither time nor space.

70. From *Dialogue 48* of **I Am That** entitled *"Awareness is Free"*. Because there are different editions of this book each with different page numbers, this reference is to the number of the *Dialogue* rather than to the page.

71. From *Dialogue 51* of **I Am That** entitled *"Be Indifferent to Pain and Pleasure"*.

72. From *Dialogue 57* of **I Am That** entitled *"Beyond Mind, There is No Suffering"*. These three sentences appear together as part of a much longer answer by Nisargadatta where he is explaining to a questioner that he is neither the object nor the subject of his experience:

> Look—my thumb touches my forefinger. Both touch and are touched. When my attention is on the thumb, the thumb is the feeler and the forefinger—the self. Shift the focus of attention and the relationship is reversed. I find that somehow, by shifting the focus of attention, I become the very thing I look at and experience the kind of consciousness it has; I become the inner witness of the thing. I call this capacity of entering other focal points of consciousness, love; you may give it any name you like. **Love says: "I am everything". Wisdom says: "I am nothing". Between the two, my life flows.** Since at any point of time and space I can be both the subject and the object of experience, I express it by saying that I am both, and neither, and beyond both.

73. Here the Edwin Arnold translation is written not as Śunyata would recite it, but is exactly duplicated as Arnold himself wrote it:

End and Beginning are dreams!

In Sunyata's way of saying this, as recorded at the beginning of Chapter 7, Sunyata would add an "s" to both the "End" and the "Beginning":

Ends and Beginnings are dreams!

And when Sunyata wrote out this quotation, he would change the small "s" in "spirit" in the original Arnold translation to his own capital "S" ("Spirit").

74. This is only the second song written by Ringo Starr and it

appeared in The Beatles 1969 album called **Abbey Road.**

75. Jed McKenna's categories of *human adulthood* and *truth-realization* correspond exactly to Steve Forrest's categories of the *clean-up* and the *wake-up*. Jed McKenna is the pseudonymous author and narrator of a fictional story in **Spiritual Enlightenment: The Damnedest Thing.** He presents himself as a no-nonsense, brutally honest, and deeply unconventional teacher of spiritual enlightenment. He advocates for a stark, uncompromising pursuit of truth and goes about dismantling traditional spiritual concepts, practices, and teachings. He characterizes enlightenment as a process of *losing everything* rather than *gaining anything*, requiring the destruction of all attachments and false identities.

Jed views *human adulthood* as requiring taking full responsibility for one's life, shedding illusions, and living authentically—and he makes clear that this is still not an enlightenment. With the same orientation as Steve Forrest, Jed views the *truth-realization* of enlightenment as requiring the recognition that the personal self is an illusion.

Jed points out that most seekers do not achieve *human adulthood* as they want to skip the hard, messy, human work of growing up in favor of the shiny mirage of enlightenment; instead of maturing, they stay stuck in a spiritual adolescence, mistaking what are the high peaks of a genuine enlightenment for what he sees as the low valleys of stagnation and confusion. What Steve Forrest calls the *clean-up* is the process of moving into a mature *human adulthood*.

Jed McKenna himself—whoever he may be—still remains hidden behind his pseudonym. When his first book appeared in 2002, he introduces himself (on page 16) as a real enlightened teacher living in a "house in east central Iowa, about twenty miles from Iowa City, and half an hour from the Mississippi River". I had a good friend living in Iowa City and she assured me that she knew the spiritual scene of Iowa and that there never had been any such teacher remotely like Jed McKenna anywhere near her. Even if Jed McKenna does not exist, these works of fiction contain many great pointers for anyone who wants to pursue a spiritual path.

76. *Four Quartets*, "East Coker", III, lines 33-46. According to his biographer, T.S. Eliot was familiar with the writings of St. John of the Cross. This is the advice given by St. John of the Cross:

> In order to arrive at pleasure in everything,
>   desire to have pleasure in nothing.
> In order to arrive at possessing everything,
>   desire to possess nothing.
> In order to arrive at being everything,
>   desire to be nothing.
> In order to arrive at knowing everything,
>   desire to know nothing.

> *Ascent of Mount Carmel*
> Book I, Chapter XIII, Paragraph 11

Both the T.S. Eliot quotation and this one from St. John of the Cross emphasize that in order to arrive at the truth, it is necessary for an individual to let go of what they think that they might know.

Just before the quotation that is referred to in this endnote, T.S. Eliot wrote in *East Coker*, III, lines 23-26:

> I said to my soul, be still, and wait without hope
> For hope would be hope for the wrong thing; wait without love
> For love would be love of the wrong thing; there is yet faith
> But the faith and the love and the hope are all in the waiting.

The reason that hope would be for "the wrong thing" is that what might be hoped for would already be known in his mind and what he is really hoping for is to embrace that which he does not yet know.

77. This point of view is expressed and discussed in Chögyam Trungpa's book **The Myth of Freedom** (on p. 6):

"The attainment of enlightenment from ego's point of view is extreme death, the death of self, the death of me and mine, the death of the watcher. It is the ultimate and final disappointment."

What is being said here is that the pursuit of enlightenment from a place of ego never leads to an awakening because enlightenment involves transcending the very ego that is seeking enlightenment. The ego is associated with a sense of self, attachment to identity, and the drives for achievement, control, and self-preservation; it's the part of us that wants to feel important, validated, and secure. Enlightenment, by contrast, includes the insight that the ego's attachments, desires, and separateness are illusions.

From the ego's perspective, enlightenment is not what is expected. It's not about becoming a better version of oneself or gaining something extraordinary—it's about letting go entirely. The ego's disappointment stems from realizing its own impermanence and irrelevance.

The ego often views spiritual goals as another form of attainment with enlightenment as the ultimate prize since it is hypothesized as a state of permanent bliss. But the realization of enlightenment reveals that there is no 'self' to attain or achieve anything. The constructs of 'me' and 'mine' dissolve, leaving the ego with nothing to hold onto or glorify. In this sense, enlightenment is the ego's undoing, its ultimate 'failure'. The ego, clinging to its old paradigms, experiences this transition as a loss—the ego itself can never grok the truth that its own Death may be the beginning of a forever Life.

78. William Somerset Maugham put this translation of the **Katha**

Upanishad quotation used here as the epigraph of his novel (published in 1944) called **The Razor's Edge**. While this verse acknowledges the difficulty of the path, it also implies that with the skillful navigating upon a razor's edge, success is attainable. In the **Katha Upanishad**, the verse (1.3.14) about the razor's edge has been labelled "A Wake-Up Call From the Wise". A more exact (but longer) translation might be:

> *"Awake!*
> *Seek the wise and realize that the path to the Self is difficult to cross, similar to the knife-like sharpened edge of the razor, so say the wise."*

Maugham had a personal meeting with Ramana Maharshi during his visit to India in 1938. Maugham's experience at this ashram, coupled with his broader travels in India, allowed him a glimpse into Eastern philosophies and spiritual practices, which deeply resonated with him and was central in this novel.

Maugham's novel **The Razor's Edge** centers around Larry Darrell, a young American pilot deeply traumatized by his experiences in World War I. Unlike his peers, who resume their lives in pursuit of wealth and social status in the Roaring Twenties, Larry embarks on a quest for Self-knowledge. As he seeks to find a path free from suffering, his journey takes him from the coal mines of France to the ashrams of India. Larry's deeply spiritual questioning is juxtaposed with the lives of his friends and loved ones who fervently and unquestioningly pursue ego gratification. Larry walks the razor's edge in trying to keep focused on his spiritual quest.

Anne Baxter won the Academy Award for Best Supporting Actress (in 1946) for her performance in "The Razor's Edge" (the movie dramatizing the Maugham novel) by playing Sophie, a beautiful young woman addicted to alcohol who falls off the wagon and eventually gets brutally murdered. In order to heighten the drama, the movie takes the liberty of adding the detail (that does not appear in the novel) that Sophie is murdered when her throat is slashed by a razor's edge.

79. This quotation appears in a letter that Bruno Schulz wrote to a friend Andrzej Plesniewicz on March 4th of 1936. I picked out the quotation here because it echoes my goal of "maturing into childhood".

Schulz is one of the most accomplished (almost unknown) writers of the 20th Century. He was both Polish and Jewish, and all of his writings were in Polish. Born in 1892 in the Austro-Hungarian Empire (now in Ukraine), Schulz led a life that seemed to oscillate between the worldly and the extraordinary. His legacy is to have created in his writings and drawings a universe so rich and surreal that he transcended the boundaries of the troubled world of his immediate environment. Like his contemporary fellow Jewish European writer Franz Kafka, he blends the mundane with the mystical, and the commonplace with fantasy. He was murdered by a Nazi officer in 1942.

80. Coleridge wrote "Kubla Khan" in 1797 after he took a high dose of a medicine called laudanum—essentially a tincture of opium—that works as both a pain-killer and a sedative. The poem arrived fully-formed during an opium-induced dream. When he woke up, he says he remembered not less than 200 to 300 lines, but had only managed to write down the first 54 lines when there came a-knockin' a person on business from Porlock. And by the time this person left, all the rest of the poem was gone. These 54 lines are among the richest invocation in vivid imagery of a magical world. The contrast between the ordered beauty of the stately pleasure-dome that has been decreed by Kubla Khan and the wild untamed forces of nature where this dome abides suggests a tension between the human desire for control and the sublime power of the natural world. The "person from Porlock" has become a symbol for an interruption that can derail a work of genius.

In the 16th line of the poem where a woman wails "for her demon-lover", many a critic has noted that the Greek notion of *daemon* (δαίμων in Greek) evolved to become what in Christianity was known as a *demon*. And in Coleridge's handwritten manuscript of the original poem, it is not clear if the word is '*demon*-lover' or it might possibly be '*daemon*-lover'. This longing for a 'daemon-lover' can be paralleled with the human yearning for connection with the divine or the transcendent, as symbolized by the *daemon* in Socratic philosophy. Thus the "demon-lover" could be seen not just as a source of sorrow or unfulfilled desire, but also as a metaphor for the creative impulse and the pursuit of inspiration that is both elusive and intoxicating. This interpretation aligns with Coleridge's fascination with the untameable forces of nature and the sublime, reflecting the broader Romantic theme of the artist's struggle to capture and convey what is mysterious, navigating the fine line between inspiration and madness, guided by a *daemon* that is both muse and demon.

81. Action arises spontaneously from the source when the ego surrenders its agency. In Zen, the way to this still mind is called the *gateless gate*. Wumen Huikai (1183–1260), who combined Taoism with Buddhism, wrote this description of the *gateless gate*:

"The Great Way has no gate. A thousand roads enter it. When one passes through this *gateless gate*, he or she freely walks the universe."

When a still mind arises, one does not impose their will on the world but instead becomes a mirror for the universe, allowing its truths to be revealed effortlessly. This surrender of the ego's grasp creates a receptive space where the interconnectedness of all things becomes apparent. In this state, the universe "surrenders" not in the sense of defeat but as a gift—revealing its deeper truths to the one who is awake and aware and present.